Becoming Friends

Living & learning with Quakers

Developed for Quaker Life and
Woodbrooke Quaker Study Centre
by Ginny Wall

Acknowledgements

Many people have contributed to the development of the *Becoming Friends* course. Special thanks to John Crompton , Annie Foster and Ruth Quinn who made much valued contributions to the writing of the learning materials; the many unnamed Friends who wrote reflective pieces especially for the course; Sarah Stokes and John Fitzgerald at Friends House for all their inspired work designing the materials; Peter Daniels for skilful copy-editing; the Friends from Disley, Hebden Bridge, Lancaster, Norwich and Watford Local Meetings and Sheffield Area Meeting who threw themselves wholeheartedly into trialling and evaluating every aspect of the course; Friends who generously gave their time to test the online course, including Annique Seddon, Eleanor Tew and Kathleen Wallace; Beth and Peter Allen, Joycelin Dawes, Zélie Gross, William Heath, Mary Meeks, Dorothy Millichamp, Ruth Quinn, Julia Ryberg, Marion Wells-Bruges and Alex Wildwood for invaluable contributions and expertise at project 'think tank' sessions; colleagues at Woodbrooke and Friends House, especially the project team and board members, Michael Booth, Paul Bowers Isaacson, Judith Roads, Lizz Roe, Helen Rowlands and Richard Summers and all the wonderful people in the admin and marketing offices at Woodbrooke for whom nothing was ever too much trouble. Finally I would like to thank my partner Simon Booth and my daughters Ella and Beth for their patience, encouragement and support throughout the writing and production of the *Becoming Friends* course. Any errors that remain are the responsibility of the author.

© The Yearly Meeting of the Religious Society of Friends (Quakers) in Britain 2010

Project Developer Ginny Wall

Published by Quaker Books, London

Designed by Quaker Communications Department, Friends House

Printed by Information Press Ltd

FSC
Mixed Sources
Product group from well-managed forests and other controlled sources
Cert no. SA-COC-002048
www.fsc.org
© 1996 Forest Stewardship Council

ISBN 978 1 907123 10 8

A free and continuing licence for the use of this copyright material is granted to Woodbrooke Quaker Study Centre

Britain Yearly Meeting of the Religious Society of Friends (Quakers) is a registered charity, number 1127633

Dear Friends

Welcome to *Becoming Friends: Living & learning with Quakers*, the learning project from Woodbrooke and Quaker Life for those who are new to Friends and their meetings.

Friends around Britain Yearly Meeting have asked us for help providing the next stage of learning and support for newcomers to Friends after outreach programmes like Quaker Quest and Quaker Week have finished. Friends have told us that they hope for new ways to help newcomers deepen their understanding of Quakerism and their feeling of 'belonging' in their meetings, whether or not they are currently considering applying for membership.

We have worked closely with individuals and groups of Friends to develop and trial a course that meets these objectives. The result is *Becoming Friends:* an exciting, interactive learning experience that offers newcomers flexible course materials, accessible in an online or paper format, combined with options for support from meetings, in particular from a *Becoming Friends* 'companion'.

The *Becoming Friends* course has been designed to be as flexible as possible, with participants working at their own pace and for as long as they wish. There are options for working alone and with others, using a variety of approaches, and there is a choice of learning units and activities to suit a wide range of interests and learning styles.

We hope that meetings will want to provide a *Becoming Friends* 'companion' to support newcomers working with the learning materials. The companion can help newcomers find out more about Quakerism by sharing their own knowledge and experience and by helping to arrange conversations and interactions with other Friends. There is guidance for meetings working with *Becoming Friends* at page 278. Courses for *Becoming Friends* companions are available through Woodbrooke and Quaker Life. See www.woodbrooke.org.uk/becomingfriends or ring 0121 472 5171 for more information.

Experienced Friends and newcomers who took part in trials of *Becoming Friends* reported that the regular conversations between newcomers, companions and other Friends were a highlight of the learning experience for all concerned. One newcomer said of the course, "It made me talk to loads of other Friends...it gave me a good excuse to do what I wanted to do anyway." Another trials participant said "both of us ...learned so much through the Becoming Friends project and felt the whole experience had been a blessing."

Whether you are a newcomer to Quakerism or an experienced Friend, we hope that you find the *Becoming Friends* learning experience both interesting and enjoyable.

A free demonstration of the online *Becoming Friends* course is available at http://moodle.woodbrooke.org.uk . To sign up for the online course go to www.woodbrooke.org.uk/becomingfriends

Helen Rowlands
Head of Education
Woodbrooke

Richard Summers
General Secretary
Quaker Life

Ginny Wall
Project Developer
Becoming Friends

Permissions

Permission was kindly given to use extracts from:

Barratt Brown, A. *Wayside Sacraments* (Yorkshire Friends' Service Committee. Friends' Literature Committee, Scarborough 1932)

Bennett, Denise *Quaker Meeting* poem (Quaker Monthly, London October 2008)

Britain Yearly Meeting *Quaker Faith & Practice* (The Yearly Meeting of the Religious Society of Friends (Quakers) in Britain, Fourth Edition 1995, 2005, 2009)

Britain Yearly Meeting *Quaker Identity and the Heart of Our Faith* Quaker Life Study Materials (Quaker Life 2008) and various Quaker Life and Quaker Peace & Social Witness publications

'Caban' *contribution to Britain Yearly Meeting discussion forum* (BYM forum, 14.12.08)

Courbon-Taylor, Amyon and Stuart, David *Quaker Meeting* poem (Quaker Monthly, London August 2008)

Durham, Geoffrey *The Heart of Quakerism* (presentation to London Quakers 2009)

Fischer, Kathleen *Women at the Well: feminist perspectives on spiritual direction* (SPCK, London 1989)

Gillman, Harvey *A Light That Is Shining: an introduction to the Quakers* (Quaker Books, London 2003)

Gillman, Harvey *Consider the Blackbird: Reflections on Spirituality and Language* (Quaker Books, London 2007)

Gillman, Harvey *Reflections on membership and belonging* (previously unpublished, 2008)

Gillman, Harvey and Heron, Alastair (eds.) *Searching the Depths: essays on being a Quaker today* (Quaker Books, London 1996)

Gorman, George *The Amazing Fact of Quaker Worship* (Quaker Books, London 1973 – Swarthmore Lecture 1973)

Hosking, Anne *extract from unpublished letter* (1986)

Kline, Florence Ruth and Grundy, Marty (eds.) *Companions Along The Way: spiritual formation within the Quaker tradition* (Philadelphia Yearly Meeting of the Religious Society of Friends, Philadelphia 2000)

Levin, Jennie *Hearts & Minds Prepared* study pack (Woodbrooke Quaker Study Centre 2003)

McNaughton, Marion & Roe, Lizz *Finding the Prophetic Voice for our time* (Woodbrooke Journal 21, 2007)

McNaughton, Marion *Presentation to QPSW Conference 2009*

Morley, Barry *Beyond Consensus: Salvaging Sense of the Meeting* (Pendle Hill Pamphlet 307, Pendle Hill Publications, Pennsylvania 1993)

Nhat Hanh, Thich *Peace is Every Step: The Path of Mindfulness in Everyday Life* (Rider, London 1995). Reprinted by permission of The Random House Group Ltd.

Norris, Gunilla *Being Home: discovering the spiritual in the everyday* (Paulist Press Inc., New York/Mahwah, NJ 1991, 2001). Reprinted by permission of Paulist Press Inc. www.paulistpress.com .

Punshon, John *Encounter with Silence: reflections from the Quaker tradition* (Quaker Home Service 1987)

Smith, Jaci *Peace is not a dirty word* (article on BYM website 03.11.09) This article was previously published in DEA (Development Education Association) Journal, October 2006.

extracts from Twelve Quakers and God (Quaker Quest, Hampstead Monthly Meeting, London 2004)

Wildwood, Alex *Tradition and Transition: opening to the Sacred yesterday and today* (Woodbrooke Journal 9, 2001)

Yamanouchi, Tayeko *Ways of Worship* (Friends World News 113, Friends World Council for Consultation 1979)

Contents

Course units listed alphabetically, except for Opening and Closing units

Welcome to Becoming Friends: Living & learning with Quakers

Before you begin...

- This course aims to be very flexible and to give you plenty of choice.

- There's a wide range of material and activities on offer, but you can choose to do as much or as little as you like, and tailor the course to your own interests.

- There's guidance and a simple framework for approaching the course in the Opening Unit, if you find this helpful....

- ...but please feel free to use the course materials as a resource, choosing activities that interest you and approaching them in whatever way feels right for you.

Opening Unit

Introducing the course, meeting your
Becoming Friends companion and
planning the path

Opening Unit aims

This opening unit aims to help you:

- Find out about the Becoming Friends course, its structure and approach

- Plan your learning path using the Becoming Friends learning units

- Reflect on your own spiritual journey as you begin the course

- Meet your Becoming Friends companion and agree how you will work together

Guidance for working through this opening unit

1. The introductory information (pages 8–12) and frequently asked questions about the course (pages 13–15) are a good place to start.

2. You might like to arrange a meeting with your Becoming Friends companion (if you'll be working with one) at an early stage so that you can begin getting to know each other and plan how you will work together. You could talk to your companion about which topic units to work with. There's guidance about this meeting on pages 16–18.

3. Choose one (or more if you like) of the Introductory activities on pages 19–21 to begin the process of finding out more about Quakerism and reflecting on your own spiritual journey with Friends.

4. There is an option to explore some of the topics covered in this unit further by following up reading and links in the Further exploration section on page 22.

5. The Closing activity on page 23 provides an opportunity for reflection at the end of the unit.

6. There's no time limit for working through this unit – you can take as long or as short a time as you like.

Introduction to the course

Becoming Friends aims to be an engaging, interactive and flexible course that provides an opportunity to find out more about Friends in a way that is true to the experiential nature of our Quaker faith. There are many wonderful books about Quakerism, and some will be referred to during the course, but Becoming Friends aims to avoid just taking a 'here's a good book to read' approach.

Activities on offer will include:

- reading
- watching video extracts
- listening to audio clips
- taking part in conversations with Friends in your local or area meeting
- exploring Quaker and other websites
- spiritual practices
- reflection through conversation, writing and creative media

Throughout the course, you will be able to choose the activities you prefer, so we hope that this will enable you to learn in a way and at a pace that suits you.

Opportunities for sharing and support

An important part of the course will be the opportunities provided to speak to Friends about spiritual questions or issues and to share something of one another's faith journeys. This could be:

- reflecting with a Becoming Friends companion
- talking to other Friends in the local area
- engaging with Quaker websites
- discussing issues in online forums
- meeting in a small learning group with other newcomers or local Friends

A reflective journey

You will also be invited at regular intervals through the course to reflect on what you are learning, both about Quakerism and your own spiritual journey. This 'reflective' approach fits well with the Quaker belief that experience is central to the spiritual life.

Reflecting on our learning is a key element of the Becoming Friends course; it places an open attentiveness at the heart of our spiritual journeying. For Quakers, experience and experimenting are central to our understanding of ourselves and our faith, so the course includes many opportunities for reflection both as you learn and afterwards.

During the course, you may find it helpful to practise becoming more aware of your learning experiences through means such as:

- private reflection

- writing in a journal or book of spiritual discipline (there's guidance for journalling in Appendix 2 – Guidance, on page 282)

- drawing or creating something

- conversation face to face or by phone with your Becoming Friends companion or another friend

- group sharing

- sharing in an online discussion forum

- using the reflective journal facility on Woodbrooke's Moodle site

- adding to an online blog (something you set up separate from the course)

Structure of Becoming Friends

Opening Unit

This unit is about introducing the course, meeting your Becoming Friends companion (if you will be working with one) and planning the path. It lays the foundations for the rest of the course, so everyone is encouraged to work through this introductory unit.

Eight topic-based units (choose any)

These units cover different aspects of Quaker faith and practice, ranging from beliefs about God to living faithfully in the world.

You can choose *as many or as few* of the units as you like, *in any order*. You can follow your interests or main questions about Quakerism. A good place to start could be the Silence and Waiting unit, which explores the Quaker experience of silence, worship and spoken ministry, or Experiencing Quaker Community, which introduces the ways that Quaker communities are organised, nurtured and led. Where there are links between learning in different units, these will be highlighted so that they are easy to follow up.

You might like to talk to your Becoming Friends companion about your choice of learning units, the order and timescale for working with them, or you might prefer to begin with one and see how you get on before making any further choices.

Closing Unit

When you have finished the topic based units you have chosen, there is a last unit to engage with, which offers opportunities to reflect on your learning throughout the Becoming Friends course, on the journey you have shared with your companion, on any steps you wish to take to further your learning and spiritual development from here, and to take time to say goodbye.

More about the topic based units

The topic based learning unit titles (choose **any** and follow them in **any order**) are:

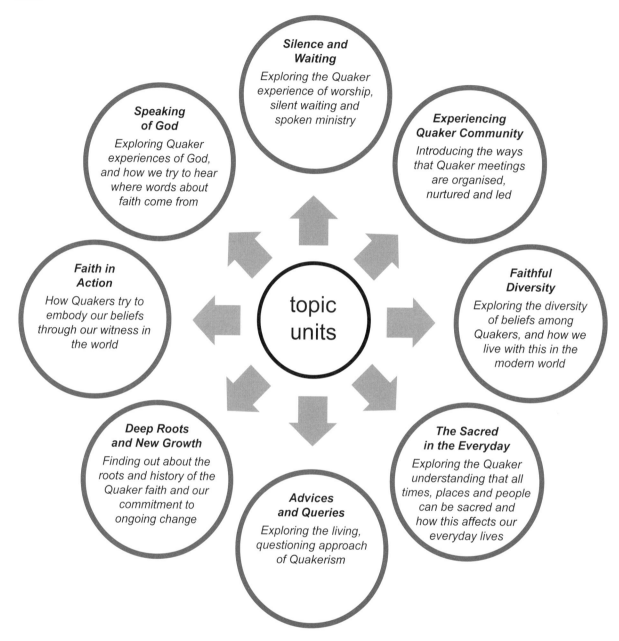

In each topic unit there will be three types of activities to choose from:

Distinctives: exploring the distinctive Quaker way in relation to that topic

Discovering: more about Quaker people and community, structures, resources and events

Deepening: opportunities for personal reflection and journalling, prayer or spiritual practice and spiritual friendship conversations

Each of these aspects of the learning process will feed into the others.

Some frequently asked questions about the course

Who is the course for?

This course has been designed to help those who are new to Quakers find out more about Quakerism, explore your own understanding of and connection with different aspects of our faith, and get to know Quakers better.

Do I need to be considering applying for membership?

The Becoming Friends course is not aimed at bringing participants into membership of the Religious Society of Friends. The course is for anyone who is interested in finding out more about Quakers, however recent their involvement with Quakerism.

If, however, you find that the process of taking part in the course does lead you to consider applying for membership, then please approach the overseers or elders in your local meeting and they will explain the membership procedure to you.

It may also be helpful to know that a number of Friends still draw on their experience of and participation in other faith traditions, finding that it enriches their experience of Quakerism. This may be the case for you.

What is a Becoming Friends companion?

An integral part of the Becoming Friends learning experience is the offer of support from a Becoming Friends companion while you work through the course. This experienced Friend will help you discover more about the Quaker way and provide you with a supportive, listening presence as you reflect on your learning. Usually your companion will be someone from your local area, but this may not always be possible, so some people may access an online Becoming Friends companion for this support.

You may feel that you would prefer to work through the course without a companion, in which case alternative ways of being supported include taking part in online discussions (there will be opportunities for these throughout the course), opting for activities that involve talking to Friends in your meeting, and making use of the existing support systems in your meeting, such as elders and overseers.

Please note that wherever course activities suggest working with a 'Becoming Friends companion', this can also be taken to include any experienced Friend you would like to work with on that activity, if you do not have a specific Becoming Friends companion.

Whether or not you work with a Becoming Friends companion, there will be opportunities to become part of the Becoming Friends online community throughout the course, and we hope this can become an enjoyable and supportive part of the learning experience for people who choose to work in this way.

Can I do the course online or on paper?

There are different ways of accessing the Becoming Friends course. Becoming Friends is available as an interactive online course using the Moodle learning platform, and as a paper based course.

Both versions offer a wide variety of opportunities to find out about Quakerism and explore your own relationship with the Quaker faith. If you're doing the course on paper, you can always go online to do some activities if you want to.

In some areas, Quaker meetings may offer group sessions using the Becoming Friends materials.

What kind of religious language will the course use?

Language used in the Becoming Friends course aims to be inclusive and to allow for a wide variety of approaches to the spiritual life. We hope to explore and celebrate the diverse nature of Quaker faith and the British Quaker community throughout the course. If there are times when you are not entirely comfortable with the language used, try to sense for the truth beyond the words, even if the words themselves may be strange or difficult. This effort is in itself a profound experience of the Quaker way.

How can I get hold of a copy of *Quaker faith & practice*?

You will find *Quaker faith & practice* in your local meeting house. It has a red cover and is usually on the table during meeting for worship. You may be able to borrow a copy during this course: ask your Becoming Friends companion for help with this.

You can also find it:

- online at: www.quakerweb.org.uk/qfp

- in the Quaker Centre bookshop, tel: 020 7663 1030
  email: quakercentre@quaker.org.uk or go to www.quaker.org.uk/bookshop

References in the Becoming Friends course are to the fourth edition published in 2009. You will find copies of previous editions in meeting houses, with slight variation in section numbering.

Meeting your Becoming Friends companion

You may have been told about this course by your local meeting, and have been offered a Becoming Friends companion who will work with you and support you while you participate in the course. If this has not yet happened, please speak to your local overseers to find out who coordinates the Becoming Friends companions in your area, so that you can be offered this support if it is available locally. If it is not available in your area, we may be able to offer the support of a Becoming Friends companion online.

Once you know who your Becoming Friends companion will be, you can arrange to meet so that you can get to know one another and plan how you would like to work together. Becoming Friends companions will have been prepared for this role, and will be familiar with the structure and approach of the course.

If, on the other hand, you would prefer to work through the course without a Becoming Friends companion (or none is available in your area), don't forget that alternative ways of getting support and hearing about different Quaker experiences include:

- being part of the Becoming Friends online community

- the Discovering activities in each unit that involve talking to local Friends about different aspects of their faith

- using the existing resources in your meeting, such as study groups, elders and overseers

Suggested elements for a first meeting with a Becoming Friends companion:

1. Worship and hellos

Taking time in silence together at the beginning will help to ground your conversation in worship.

2. Ground rules

It is helpful to consider ground rules for your work together, such as how you want the relationship to work, what kind of support you would like from your companion, whether you are going to take notes of sessions together, any particular issues regarding religious language or beliefs.

3. Confidentiality

Consider the confidential nature of your conversations together, and any limits which you want to place on confidentiality.

4. Getting to know each other

You might like to share with one another about one or more of the following 'getting to know you' questions:

- What first brought you to Quakers?

- What do you most value about Quakerism?

5. Sharing about the Opening Unit's 'Introductory activities'

You might take some time to share any reflections on the Introductory activity that you chose from the Opening Unit.

6. Looking at the Becoming Friends learning materials together

Have a look at the course materials together. If you have any questions about the course, raise these with your companion as s/he may be able to answer them, or can help you find the answers elsewhere.

7. Making choices about which learning units you wish to follow

Consider the topic based units together. Are there some that you feel drawn to working with? You don't have to make hard and fast decisions at this stage, but it may be helpful to consider the options together.

8. What's coming next?

Think about the next stages of your learning journey. Which unit are you going to work with next? Is there specific support or resources that you would like your companion to help you access at this stage?

9. Practicalities

Look at the activities in your chosen learning unit: you may wish to arrange conversations with Friends in your local or area meeting, a visit to another meeting or Quaker organisation, or perhaps do some searches online. Can your companion help you with any of this?

10. Meeting times and places

What times and places will suit you both for meeting up over the next few weeks or months as you work through the course? Are there any other practicalities to sort out?

11. Reviews and endings

Do you want to agree an overall timescale for your work together, perhaps including an interim point at which you will review progress and consider if both of you are happy to continue with your commitment?

12. Worship, and arranging next meeting

After all the conversation and practicalities are finished with, spending a few minutes in worship together can help bring you back to the spiritual ground for your work together. Don't forget to make arrangements for your next contact or meeting.

Introductory activities

Choose one (or more if you like) of the following five activities

Introductory Activity 1

Ask a Quaker a question

Is there a question about Quakers or the Quaker way that you would like to find the answer to? It might be something apparently trivial, or something very important to you. The Becoming Friends course is all about exploring your questions about Quakerism, so here is your opportunity to use it as an excuse to ask a Quaker a question. This could be your Becoming Friends companion, an elder, overseer or other experienced Friend at your meeting, or you could use the 'Ask a Quaker' facility on the Quaker Week website: www.quakerweek.org.uk

- You could record the results of this activity in a journal or blog

- You might like to share your question, and any answers you receive, with your Becoming Friends companion when you next meet

Introductory Activity 2

Find out how people came to Quakers

You could do this activity by:

- going to the Quaker Week website at: www.quakerweek.org.uk and exploring the information about Quakerism. You can watch some of the short 'talking heads' videos on the 'Introducing Quakers' page, where Friends talk about how they came to Quakerism. Do any of their experiences echo or contrast with your own?

- asking one or two local Friends to talk to you about how they came to Quakers (your Becoming Friends companion could help you arrange this).

Take some time to reflect on your own experience of coming to Friends. You might like to write about this in a journal or book of spiritual discipline, or use creative methods to respond, such as drawing, modelling, or music.

You could share some of your reflections with your Becoming Friends companion when you next meet.

Introductory Activity 3

Watch the video 'An introduction to Quakers'

Watch 'An introduction to Quakers' made by Friends at Watford Quaker Meeting. You can access the video in a number of different ways:

- online at
  - › www.watfordquakers.org.uk/videos.html
  - › www.quakerweek.org.uk/intro/quaker-worship
  - › www.youtube.com as 'Introduction to Quakers'

- on the DVD *An introduction to Watford Quakers*, available from the Quaker Centre bookshop (see Further exploration for contact details).

As you watch, you may like to note down any questions or issues that the video raises for you. You could share these questions with your Becoming Friends companion when you next meet, or simply come back to them at the end of the course and see if you have found answers or different understandings of any of the issues.

Introductory Activity 4

Questions for personal reflection

Take some time to reflect on one or more of the following questions:

- Where have you come from on your spiritual journey?

- What treasures do you bring with you?

- What do you want to give up or leave behind from previous faith experiences?

- What brings you to Quakers?

You could:

- respond to the questions in writing (you'll find guidance for journalling in Appendix 2 – Guidance on page 282)

- respond by drawing or using another creative method

- go online and blog about them

- discuss them on a Quaker discussion forum:
  - › the Britain Yearly Meeting forum at: www.quakerweb.org.uk/forum
  - › www.friendlink.org.uk (aimed mainly at young Quakers)
  - › the Opening Unit forum

- share some of your reflections with your Becoming Friends companion when you next meet

Introductory Activity 5

Introduce yourself on the Opening Unit discussion forum

Go to the Opening Unit forum in the Becoming Friends online course. Find the 'Introduce Yourself' discussion thread and make a posting which tells other course participants

- your name

- where you live and what local Quaker meeting you attend

- something that has made you smile in the last week

Try to add a comment to at least one other person's posting, so that you begin to get to know other people who are currently following the Becoming Friends course.

Further exploration

If you would like to explore some resources that give a more detailed introduction to Quakerism, here are some suggestions for reading, listening or viewing.

Celebrating the Quaker way, Pink Dandelion, Quaker Books, 2009

Coming home: an introduction to the Quakers, Gerald Priestland, Quaker Books, 2003

An introduction to Quakerism, Pink Dandelion, Cambridge University Press, 2007

An introduction to Watford Quakers (DVD), part 1 'An Introduction to Quakerism', Just Film, 2007. Also available at: www.watfordquakers.org.uk/videos.html or www.quakerweek.org.uk/intro (or on www.youtube.com as 'Introduction to Quakers').

A light that is shining: an introduction to the Quakers, Harvey Gillman, Quaker Books, 2003.

Meeting Quakers: a lively introduction to the Religious Society of Friends (Quakers) in Britain (DVD), Quaker Home Service Outreach Committee, Quaker Home Service, 2000, 2007.

New light: 12 Quaker voices, edited by Jennifer Kavanagh, O Books, 2008. Individual themes also available in the 'Twelve Quakers and...' series, Quaker Quest, 2004–2007.

Portrait in grey: a short history of the Quakers, John Punshon, Quaker Books, reprint 2006.

Quaker faith & practice: the book of Christian discipline of the Yearly Meeting of the Religious Society of Friends (Quakers) in Britain, 4th edition, Britain Yearly Meeting, 2009 (first published 1995).

Quaker speak, Alastair Heron, Quaker Outreach in Yorkshire, 2003.

Searching the depths: essays on being a Quaker today, edited by Harvey Gillman and Alastair Heron, Quaker Books, 1996

Many of these titles are available from the Quaker Centre bookshop:

Friends House
173 Euston Road
London NW1 2BJ

Tel: 020 7663 1030
Fax: 020 7663 1001

Website: www.quaker.org.uk/bookshop
Email: quakercentre@quaker.org.uk

Many of them will also be in your local meeting house library. You could ask your Becoming Friends companion to help you track down titles that interest you.

Closing activity

As you finish your exploration of this Opening Unit, you are invited to reflect on what you have gained from the unit, how your understanding of both yourself and Quakerism has changed, and what areas you would like to explore further.

This closing reflection can be a very good opportunity for sharing with your Becoming Friends companion, or you may prefer to write in a journal or book of spiritual discipline (there's guidance for journalling in Appendix 2 – Guidance on page 282), or to reflect using creative methods such as drawing, collage, model-making or working with materials such as textiles or wood.

You might use one or more of the following questions as a focus for your reflection:

- What have you gained from your work on this unit, whether as a result of positive or more challenging experiences?

- In what ways has your understanding changed as a result of your work on this unit?

- Are there areas that you would like to explore further – either as part of your own spiritual journey or relating to Quakerism?

- Has anything arisen that you would find it helpful to reflect on with your Becoming Friends companion?

Guidance for working through a topic unit

1. Each unit includes several activities in each of the sections Quaker Distinctives, Discovering and Deepening. You might like to choose one or more activities from each section (but *one* is enough – you don't have to do them all!). This selection from the three 'D's will help you achieve a balance between finding out about the Quaker faith, engaging with local Friends or practical activities, and spending time in reflection. Work through the activities in the order that feels right to you.

2. When considering which activities to choose, don't forget to consider options that take you out of your comfort zone, or away from your usual preference for learning style or content. We sometimes learn more through experiences that do not appeal to us at all at first.

3. You can take as long or as short a time as you like on each unit, from a week to several months. It may be a good idea to think about which activities you are going to work on at an early stage, so that you can arrange any contacts with other Friends suggested in the Discovering section – it could be useful to meet up with your Becoming Friends companion for help with this.

4. You will be invited to take time to reflect on your learning, especially through the Deepening activities and Closing activity in each unit. If you have a Becoming Friends companion, you may choose to meet regularly, but in any case, it could be helpful to arrange a meeting with them, perhaps towards the end of the unit, so that you can reflect on your learning together.

Advices and Queries

Exploring the living, questioning approach of Quakerism

In this unit we invite you to explore the advices and queries, a collection of questions and statements reflecting the experiential, questioning and experimental nature of Quaker faith. They are designed to provoke deep reflection and invite us to explore our relationship with God and the world at a deeper level, both as individuals and as a community.

 ## Advices and Queries unit aims

This unit aims to help you:

- become more familiar with the advices and queries, and the living, questioning faith that underlies them

- find out about their significance in the lives of Quakers

- reflect on your own understanding of and relationship to some of these guiding principles

Overview

The advices and queries are

> intended for use in our meetings, for private devotion and reflection, as
> a challenge and inspiration to us as Friends in our personal lives and
> in our life as a religious community, and as a concise expression of our
> faith and practice readily available to enquirers and to the wider world.
>
> *Quaker faith & practice* 1.05

This short collection of gentle but searching questions and challenging statements is a very good introduction to the Quaker faith, and to the current concerns and lives of members of the Religious Society of Friends. While Quakerism is a non-credal religion, the small book *Advices & queries* (also incorporated into *Quaker faith & practice* in chapter 1) gives a good indication of how Friends relate to God, to one another, and to the world as a whole.

In the Quaker tradition of speaking the unadorned truth, the questions are very direct, without asking how we 'think' or 'feel' about each issue, but simply how we live out these truths in our own lives. This is no catechism which instructs the faithful in what to believe, but rather a series of prompts that invite Friends to live faithfully, to reflect on their experience of the Divine and to pay attention to the things that really matter in life. A fundamental Quaker insight expressed in the advices and queries is that our living faith involves being willing to change, to live adventurously and to consider it possible that we may be mistaken.

A much loved quotation from an epistle to 'the brethren in the north', issued by a meeting of Quaker elders at Balby in 1656, sums up the spirit of the advices and queries:

> Dearly beloved Friends, these things we do not lay upon you as a rule
> or form to walk by, but that all, with the measure of light which is pure
> and holy, may be guided; and so in the light walking and abiding, these
> may be fulfilled in the Spirit, not from the letter, for the letter killeth,
> but the Spirit giveth life.
>
> *Quaker faith & practice* 1.01

You are invited to explore this tool for the spiritual journey through engaging with the activities in the 'D' sections of this unit, and to listen to your own responses as you go. It is not so important to understand all of the advices and queries immediately (this may be a life's work!), but to begin to let them challenge and inspire you as you embark on the next part of your journey...

Quaker distinctives

You will find *Advices & queries*:

- in your local meeting house, both in a little red book and in the first chapter of the larger red book *Quaker faith & practice*

- included in an 'Enquirer's Pack' from Friends House: ring freephone 0808 109 1651 or email outreach@quaker.org.uk to request one

- online at: www.quakerweb.org.uk/qfp/qfpchapter1.html

They are often referred to as 'the advices'. Some contain more of a 'query' for the reader than others.

Distinctives 1

Reading sections of *Advices & queries*

You could read one section of *Advices & queries* and take time with the questions and statements, so as to reach your own understanding of them. The sections are as follows:

- *A&q* 1–7: the inner life

- *A&q* 8–13: meeting for worship, and *A&q* 14–16: meeting for worship for business

- *A&q* 17–20: moving from worship to community

- *A&q* 21–30: living as a Quaker

- *A&q* 31–42: testimonies and faith in action

You may like to take one section at a time over several days or weeks.

Distinctives 2

Listening to *Advices & queries*

You may prefer to listen. There are mp3 audio files of *Advices & queries* available in this unit of the online Becoming Friends course. Why not download the audio files and listen on your computer or mp3 player whenever it suits you?

Distinctives 3

How young Friends made their own advices and queries

You can read the engaging story of how young Friends at an American Quaker summer camp came to appreciate the strength of working with advices and queries, rather than a set of imposed rules.

Turn to page 38 to read the story.

You will also find it on pages 7–11 of *Beyond Consensus* by Barry Morley (see Further exploration for details).

Distinctives 4

Watch the video 'Are Quakers Woolly Minded Liberals?'

This video was made by Friends at Watford Quaker Meeting. It includes reflections on how Quakers approach Truth, and the difficulty of being prescriptive and clear when trying to remain open to the movements of the Spirit. You can access the video in a number of different ways:

- online at
  - › www.watfordquakers.org.uk/videos.html
  - › www.youtube.com as 'Are Quakers Woolly Minded Liberals?'
- on the DVD *An Introduction to Watford Quakers* available from the Quaker Centre bookshop (see Further exploration for contact details).

Distinctives 5

The history of the advices and queries

You might like to read about how the advices and queries came to be a central part of Quaker faith.

You will find this in section 1.04 of *Quaker faith & practice*.

See also Discovery 4 if you're interested in the history of the advices and queries.

Discovery

Discovery 1

Discussion about the advices and queries

Introductory comment:

I don't think that there can be a 'Quaker way', the *Advices and queries* are not rules but starting points for questioning and thought. We go to meeting to wait upon the spirit, that spirit which is within and which will lead us. It is a sacrificial situation in which we offer ourselves and wait for guidance. Once it appears that we are being led we have the meeting as a fire in which we can test our leadings and which can offer support.

Caban Dec 14 2008 post to BYM Quaker discussion forum

You can consider the introductory comment, then go to the Advices and Queries unit forum and post your own thoughts on the issues raised. You might like to comment on other posts on this forum too.

Alternatively, you could discuss this introductory comment with your Becoming Friends companion, or others in your meeting, perhaps informally over coffee, or you might ask your companion to help you set up a group session.

Discovery 2

Comparing the advices and queries with the Ten Commandments or other church teachings

You could read the Ten Commandments by looking them up in a Bible at Exodus 20: 2–17, or look at part of another church's official teachings, for example:

- the Catholic Church's catechism – also available online at: www.catholicchurch.org.uk/ccb/catholic_church/what_does_the_catholic_church_teach/catechism or www.vatican.va/archive/catechism/ccc_toc.htm

- the Anglican Communion's 'Thirty-Nine Articles of Faith' in the Book of Common Prayer – also available online at: www.anglicancommunion.org/resources/acis/docs/thirty_nine_articles.cfm

Read sections alongside the advices and queries. How do they compare? What differences do you notice in the content, in the language?

How do they speak to you?

Discovery 3

What's your favourite of the advices and queries?

Ask one or two Friends in your meeting what is their favourite, or one that they feel is especially important. Ask them to explain the reasons for their choice.

- You could do this during the coffee time after meeting for worship, or

- You might like to ask your Becoming Friends companion to help you set up an informal meeting with other Friends in your meeting to talk about this question

Discovery 4

Advices and queries from former times

These can provide a fascinating insight into the development of the Quaker way.

- Look at the Queries of Philadelphia Yearly Meeting from 1806 on pages 42–43, or online at: www.qhpress.org/texts/obod/queries.html .

- Look in your meeting house for old versions of *Advices & queries* – they were included in a book called *Church Government* before the single volume *Quaker faith & practice* was brought out

- If this catches your interest, you could go to the library at Friends House or Woodbrooke Quaker Study Centre, and ask staff to help you find even older copies (there are some dating back to the 17th century)

Read sections and compare them with the current version of *Advices & queries*. What do you notice? What has changed in the content, and in the language used?

Do you feel drawn to any of the older advices and queries? You might copy out any that speak to you, and use them for your own guidance.

Discovery 5

Reflecting on the advices and queries with a group

Your Becoming Friends companion or an elder in your meeting could help you set up a small group session to explore the advices and queries. You might use the *Advices & queries* cards on pages 44–50 as a prompt for discussion.

1. Spread out the cards on a large table, or on the floor and spend a few minutes looking at them until you feel drawn to one, then pick it up.

2. In pairs, reflect on what this advice means to you, how it inspires or challenges you. How would you rewrite it to make it even more relevant to you? Spend five minutes, in turns, sharing your thoughts with your partner.

3. Come back together as a whole group and spend some time in worship sharing mode, where Friends have an opportunity to share at depth with one another any insights, experiences or challenges they have found during part 2 of the exercise.

Guidance for worship sharing is found in Appendix 2 – Guidance on pages 283–284.

Discovery 6

Reading *Advices & queries* in meeting for worship

Sections 1.05 1.06 and 1.07 of *Quaker faith & practice* cover arrangements for the reading of *Advices & queries* in meetings for worship and business. Depending on local procedures, you might ask to join the rota of those reading *Advices & queries* in meeting for worship. You could ask your Becoming Friends companion to help you with this.

- Be aware of how you go about choosing which advice to read, and of any ministry you or others feel led to give in connection with it

- Be aware of the working of the Spirit in this process

Deepening

Deepening 1

Taking one of the advices and queries deeper

You could write out, type or record one of the advices and queries. You might like to choose which one very carefully, or prefer to take a 'random' selection and see how it speaks to you.

- Carry this with you, or stick it up somewhere you will see it, for several days or longer, and read it at odd moments during your day

- Does it speak differently to you at different times, or when you are in different moods? What can you learn from this?

You could reflect on this experience with your Becoming Friends companion when you next meet.

Deepening 2

Taking an advice apart

You might like to choose one of the advices and queries and copy it onto a large piece of paper or card: you can write it out, or take the text from the online *Advices & queries* and copy and paste, or use one of the *Advices & queries* cards (pages 44–50) and enlarge to print it out.

- Cut up the text so that it is in simple phrases, or parts of sentences. Try moving the phrases around on a table or the floor, rearranging them in different orders and patterns.

- Pay attention to your responses to any of the words or phrases: do some seem to 'sparkle' or attract you, while others may cause you discomfort or difficulty? You may like to stay with one of these 'sparkling' or 'difficult' phrases and use it as a starting point for meditation, prayer or writing.

This is a form of 'sacred reading' or lectio divina, which was an essential part of the monastic tradition's approach to reading scriptures. It is used by many Quakers today as a spiritual practice. See page 270 in Appendix 1 – Spiritual Practices for further guidance.

You could reflect on this experience with your Becoming Friends companion when you next meet.

Deepening 3

Writing an advice and query

What issues regarding the spiritual life are important for you at the moment? You might spend a short while in silent reflection, then choose one of these areas to work with for this activity.

Write an advice and query that speaks to you at the moment about your chosen issue. Consider what language you feel comfortable using, but that would also be helpful to other Friends.

Consider your own response to the advice and query that you have written – you may like to spend some time reflecting, meditating or praying with it as your focus. Allow it to speak deeply to you.

You could reflect on this experience with your Becoming Friends companion when you next meet.

Deepening 4

A personal book of discipline

This could be made up of three or four advices and queries that you have chosen to work with, possibly including your own from Deepening 3, or some from former times that you have found through Discovery 4.

- You may like to choose ones that you feel especially drawn to at this time, or you may prefer to make a random selection and follow the 'winds of the Spirit'.

- Write or record them in your own personal book of spiritual discipline, which might be your journal, your online reflective diary, or a piece of paper you will keep in a chosen place.

- Discuss with your Becoming Friends companion or another Friend why you have chosen these particular advices and queries, and any hopes or resolutions that you wish to make in order to live by their wisdom.

You could reflect on how you have got on with this exercise at a future meeting with your Becoming Friends companion.

Deepening 5

Reflecting with your Becoming Friends companion

You might like simply to spend time with your Becoming Friends companion reflecting on the place of the advices and queries in their life, and in your own.

- You could ask your companion which advices and queries have been important to them at any particular times in their life.

- Are there any advices and queries which your companion has found especially challenging or difficult?

- Does this reflect your own experience?

- Are there ways in which either of you would like to work with the advices and queries in future?

Further exploration

If you would like to explore the subject of advices and queries further, here are some suggestions for reading, listening or viewing.

Beyond consensus: salvaging sense of the meeting, Barry Morley, Pendle Hill Pamphlets 307. May also be found in the *Hearts and minds prepared* pack.

An Introduction to Watford Quakers (DVD), 'Are Quakers Woolly Minded Liberals?', Just Film, 2007. Also available at: www.watfordquakers.org.uk/videos.html (or on www.youtube.com as 'Introduction to Quakers').

A light that is shining: an introduction to the Quakers, chapter 1 and 2, Harvey Gillman, Quaker Books, 2003.

Listening spirituality 2: corporate spiritual practice among Friends, Patricia Loring, Openings Press, 1997.

'Our queries and our conduct: past, present and future', David Maxwell, *Woodbrooke Journal*, Summer 2001, No 8.

Quaker faith & practice 11.42 (conclusion to chapter 11).

Many of these titles are available from the Quaker Centre bookshop:

Friends House
173 Euston Road
London NW1 2BJ

Tel: 020 7663 1030
Fax: 020 7663 1001

Website: www.quaker.org.uk/bookshop
Email: quakercentre@quaker.org.uk

Many of them will also be in your local meeting house library. You could ask your Becoming Friends companion to help you track down titles that interest you.

Closing activity

As you finish your exploration of the advices and queries, you are invited to reflect on what you have gained from the unit, how your understanding of both yourself and Quakerism has changed, and what areas you would like to explore further.

This closing reflection can be a very good opportunity for sharing with your Becoming Friends companion, or you may prefer to write in a journal or book of spiritual discipline (there's guidance for journalling in Appendix 2 – Guidance on page 282), or to reflect using creative methods such as drawing, collage, model-making or working with materials such as textiles or wood.

You might use one or more of the following questions as a focus for your reflection:

- What have you gained from your work on this unit, whether as a result of positive or more challenging experiences?

- In what ways has your understanding changed as a result of your work on this unit?

- Are there areas that you would like to explore further – either as part of your own spiritual journey or relating to Quakerism?

- Has anything arisen that you would find it helpful to reflect on with your Becoming Friends companion?

Extract for Distinctives 3:
How young Friends made their own advices and queries

From *Beyond consensus* by Barry Morley

This pamphlet is about the problem of distinguishing between 'consensus' and the Quaker 'sense of the meeting'.

I can illustrate the problem by drawing from my own experience as director of Catoctin Quaker Camp. I drove back to camp late one evening. As I came up the mountain road, my headlights fell on eight counselors who had gathered on a bridge just beyond camp property. Three of them were smoking cigarettes. The others were socializing. It is policy that no one smoke at camp. By smoking beyond the camp's boundary line, off-duty counselors maintained the letter of the policy. That was their intent. But I didn't want smoking outside the camp's property to become a significant social occasion which attracted smokers and non-smokers alike.

At the next staff meeting I expressed my concern. 'If you must smoke,' I said, 'I'd appreciate your going off to do it alone. I don't think it should be part of the fabric of the camp's social life.'

A long, heated discussion followed. (I've learned that addressing people's addictions always leads to long, heated discussions.) It became clear that the counselors really did enjoy one another's company and that going off with the smokers *was* an important part of the camp's social fabric. 'After all, we work hard and don't get to spend much time together.'

I pressed my points forcefully, twisting a few arms in the process. Because of my position as director my concerns carried weight. Still, I was unwilling to impose authority. I wanted agreement. So we all compromised, and after more than an hour of wrangling, achieved consensus. We allowed ourselves to settle for the arrangement that a smoker might go off to smoke with one or two other people.

But I knew that we had not reached a sense of the meeting. For years we had nurtured sense of the meeting among us. We knew what it felt like. Clearly, this wasn't it. I watched, sociologist-like, to see where this journey into forging a consensus would take us. Within a few weeks it took us back to the bridge just outside camp where groups of counselors hung around while some of them smoked. I learned what I had already suspected. I had gotten agreement without commitment. If I wanted commitment it would have to come through the sense of the meeting. Little did I suspect that an explosive issue lurking in the background would provide that opportunity.

Late in the winter a long article appeared in a Sunday edition of *The Washington Post* which described the struggles of a young man to recover from his involvement with drugs. The young man had been a counselor at Catoctin Quaker Camp. Though his performance had never given indication of a drug problem, one sentence in the article said that he had, on one occasion, brought drugs into the camp.

Reaction was swift. A meeting was called. Frightened parents demanded assurances that drugs would never be available to children at camp. Given the climate at the time, I knew that I could not make that guarantee. Arguments triggered by understandable fear and frustration grew heated. Acrimony was hurled and thrown back. Deep wounds were inflicted.

When counsellors and staff arrived the following summer for their week of pre-camp, I opened the first business meeting by saying, 'Let me tell you about my winter.' To virtually the same set of counsellors who had reached the smoking consensus, I laid out all sides of the drug issue as objectively as I could. I concluded by saying, 'In a few weeks I have to go to yearly meeting. They'll want to know what we've done about this. I think the best way to begin is to let you ask me questions for the purpose of clarification or information gathering.' The questions went on for an hour, most arising from disbelief over implicit lack of trust in their work. The intensity of the reaction seemed to them disproportionate.

Finally I said, 'I think we should set this aside for now. Take time to talk about it among yourselves. We can discuss it again at tomorrow night's business meeting. I also suggest that I not be there. You might talk more freely without me.' All of this was approved.

At the next night's business meeting we dealt with a few agenda items. Then I excused myself and retreated to my cabin. The meeting went on for two hours. Another closed meeting was asked for and scheduled. I had decided I would not inquire about those meetings; rather, I would wait until someone approached me. No one did.

If anything, the work of opening the camp went more smoothly than usual. Spirits and enthusiasm were high. Whatever process counselors and staff were working their way through seemed to spark their sense of purpose. Assigned jobs were completed. Unassigned jobs were undertaken. The 'things done' list grew. The 'things needing attention' list shrank. Paddles and life jackets were hung in rows. Canoes were washed and racked. Kitchen equipment was scrubbed. Climbing ropes and gear were checked and double checked. Overnight tarps were grommetted and roped. Pack-out food was procured, organized and stored. Shelters were cleaned and repaired. Overnight camping gear was distributed by unit. The rope swing and volleyball net were up. In business meetings, sense of the meeting came easily. But I remained ignorant of the direction of people's 'drug policy' thoughts.

Campers arrived and camp began. It ran like a finely tuned engine. The first week's overnight trips went out and returned. Around the campfire, hero stories abounded. But I continued to wonder about drugs and *The Washington Post*.

One morning a counselor came to me and said, 'We need to have another meeting and you need to be there.'

'When?' I asked.

'Tonight would be good,' she said.

After we had gathered, we took an extended moment of silence. With high hopes I asked, 'So where are we with this?'

A young woman answered. 'We can't seem to get anywhere. We've started to go around and around.'

'People are uncomfortable about making rules other people have to obey,' said another young woman.

A spasm of mini-panic displaced my hopes.

Then Ethan said, 'All we can do is ask each other questions.'

'Like what?' I asked.

'Like, 'Am I being true to myself?''

A ray of hope replaced my mini-panic. 'Like what else?' I asked.

'Like 'Am I being true to the spirit of Camp Catoctin?....''

'Do you people know what queries are?' I asked.

I was surprised that no one did. 'Queries are questions you ask yourselves. They keep you focused on whatever you want to focus on. When Ethan said, 'Am I being true to myself? Am I being true to the spirit of Camp Catoctin?' he was asking queries.'

'I don't see how that helps us,' said another young man.

'Well,' I said, 'if you wrote a set of queries, we could ask one at each business meeting. Then you could meditate on it for a minute. This would help you keep it in mind; or at least close to mind.'

'We could do that,' someone said.

In time honored Quaker fashion I suggested that a committee be appointed to develop a set of queries. When I asked who would like to be on it, everyone's hand went up. With some difficulty, we whittled the committee down to eight. I asked Ethan if he would be convenor. He said he would.

'When would you like to meet?' I asked.

'As soon as this is over,' he replied.

I explained that Quaker committee meetings are open and that people not specifically appointed to the committee might participate. We concluded with a moment of silence after which I left. Everyone else stayed.

The second week's overnight trips went out and returned. Around the campfire, hero stories abounded. Surely, camp had never run so well.

Then Ethan came to me and said, 'We need another meeting and you need to be there.'

Copies of the queries were handed out. We began the painful and time consuming process of arranging language and clarifying meaning. I was not yet completely satisfied when Charlie said, 'We don't need to nit-pick words any more. We know what our values are.'

The meeting fell silent. We had found the sense of the meeting, that place where silence acknowledges God's presence among us. The silence went on and on. It seemed a shame to end it.

When I went to yearly meeting I was asked what my response had been to the *Washington Post* article. I passed out copies of the queries. 'These are wonderful,' someone said. Yearly Meeting also fell silent.

That sense of meeting held for six years. At Catoctin Quaker Camp six years constitutes a generation of counselors. When a similar issue arose, it involved alcohol. This time, when the sense of the meeting was reached, it came in the form of a minute: 'We encourage each other to refrain from the use of substances which might harm our performance or the camp's reputation.' This, too, held.

from *Beyond consensus: salvaging sense of the meeting* by
Barry Morley, Pendle Hill Pamphlets 307

Extract for Discovery 4:
Advices and queries from former times

Rules of Discipline of the Yearly Meeting of Friends Held in Philadelphia 1806

Queries

First Query. Are all our religious meetings for worship and discipline duly attended; is the hour observed; and are friends clear of sleeping, and of all other unbecoming behaviour therein?

Second Query. Is love and unity maintained amongst you. Are tale-bearing and detraction discouraged. And where any differences arise, are endeavours used speedily to end them?

Third Query. Are Friends careful to bring up those under their direction, in plainness of speech, behaviour, and apparel; in frequent reading the holy scriptures; and to restrain them from reading pernicious books and from the corrupt conversation of the world?

Fourth Query. Are Friends careful to discourage the unnecessary distillation or use of spirituous liquors, frequenting taverns and places of diversion; and to keep in true moderation and temperance on the account of marriages, burials and other occasions?

Fifth Query. Are poor Friends necessities duly inspected, and they relieved or assisted in such business as they are capable of. Do their children freely partake of learning to fit them for business: And are they and other Friends children placed among Friends?

Sixth Query. Do you maintain a faithful testimony against oaths; an hireling ministry; bearing arms, training, and other military services; being concerned in any fraudulent or clandestine trade; buying or vending goods so imported, or prize goods; and against encouraging lotteries of any kind?

Seventh Query. Are Friends careful to live within the bounds of their circumstances, and to keep to moderation in their trade or business: Are they punctual to their promises, and just in the payment of their debts; and are such as give reasonable grounds for fear on these accounts timely laboured with for their preservation or recovery?

Eighth Query. Do you take due care regularly to deal with all offenders in the spirit of meekness, without partiality or unnecessary delay, in order for their help; and where such labour is ineffectual, to place judgment upon them in the authority of truth?

Ninth Query. Is due care taken to keep a regular record of births and burials?

And in the preparative and monthly meetings, when all the foregoing queries are read and answered, the following advices are to be read with a suitable pause between them:

That no young or single persons make or encourage proposals of marriage with each other without consent of parents or guardians, or keep company with those who are not of our religious society, upon that account; and if parents give their consent to, or connive at their children's thus keeping company, or marrying, that they be dealt with according to our discipline: And if any of our members have been present at marriages accomplished contrary to the rules of our discipline, that they also be dealt with.

That all public gifts and legacies be strictly applied to the uses intended by the donors; or, if any unforeseen occurrence should render such compliance difficult or impracticable, that an early application be made to the meeting for sufferings for its advice or assistance; and that timely care be taken for the renewal of trusts.

That Friends intending removal be careful to apply for certificates; and that the cases of such who remove without certificates, or of sojourners coming from other places and appearing as Friends, without producing certificates, be properly attended to.

That Friends carefully inspect the state of their affairs once in the year; and make their wills and settle their outward estates whilst in health.

And it is further recommended that in conducting the affairs of our meetings, Friends endeavour to manage them in the peaceable spirit and wisdom of Jesus, with decency, forbearance and love of each other.

1. Take heed, dear Friends, to the promptings of love and truth in your hearts. Trust them as the leadings of God whose Light shows us our darkness and brings us to new life.

2. Bring the whole of your life under the ordering of the spirit of Christ. Are you open to the healing power of God's love? Cherish that of God within you, so that this love may grow in you and guide you. Let your worship and your daily life enrich each other. Treasure your experience of God, however it comes to you. Remember that Christianity is not a notion but a way.

3. Do you try to set aside times of quiet for openness to the Holy Spirit? All of us need to find a way into silence which allows us to deepen our awareness of the divine and to find the inward source of our strength. Seek to know an inward stillness, even amid the activities of daily life. Do you encourage in yourself and in others a habit of dependence on God's guidance for each day? Hold yourself and others in the Light, knowing that all are cherished by God.

4. The Religious Society of Friends is rooted in Christianity and has always found inspiration in the life and teachings of Jesus. How do you interpret your faith in the light of this heritage? How does Jesus speak to you today? Are you following Jesus' example of love in action? Are you learning from his life the reality and cost of obedience to God? How does his relationship with God challenge and inspire you?

5. Take time to learn about other people's experiences of the Light. Remember the importance of the Bible, the writings of Friends and all writings which reveal the ways of God. As you learn from others, can you in turn give freely from what you have gained? While respecting the experiences and opinions of others, do not be afraid to say what you have found and what you value. Appreciate that doubt and questioning can also lead to spiritual growth and to a greater awareness of the Light that is in us all.

6. Do you work gladly with other religious groups in the pursuit of common goals? While remaining faithful to Quaker insights, try to enter imaginatively into the life and witness of other communities of faith, creating together the bonds of friendship.

7. Be aware of the spirit of God at work in the ordinary activities and experience of your daily life. Spiritual learning continues throughout life, and often in unexpected ways. There is inspiration to be found all around us, in the natural world, in the sciences and arts, in our work and friendships, in our sorrows as well as in our joys. Are you open to new light, from whatever source it may come? Do you approach new ideas with discernment?

8. Worship is our response to an awareness of God. We can worship alone, but when we join with others in expectant waiting we may discover a deeper sense of God's presence. We seek a gathered stillness in our meetings for worship so that all may feel the power of God's love drawing us together and leading us.

9. In worship we enter with reverence into communion with God and respond to the promptings of the Holy Spirit. Come to meeting for worship with heart and mind prepared. Yield yourself and all your outward concerns to God's guidance so that you may find 'the evil weakening in you and the good raised up'.

10. Come regularly to meeting for worship even when you are angry, depressed, tired or spiritually cold. In the silence ask for and accept the prayerful support of others joined with you in worship. Try to find a spiritual wholeness which encompasses suffering as well as thankfulness and joy. Prayer, springing from a deep place in the heart, may bring healing and unity as nothing else can. Let meeting for worship nourish your whole life.

11. Be honest with yourself. What unpalatable truths might you be evading? When you recognise your shortcomings, do not let that discourage you. In worship together we can find the assurance of God's love and the strength to go on with renewed courage.

12. When you are preoccupied and distracted in meeting let wayward and disturbing thoughts give way quietly to your awareness of God's presence among us and in the world. Receive the vocal ministry of others in a tender and creative spirit. Reach for the meaning deep within it, recognising that even if it is not God's word for you, it may be so for others. Remember that we all share responsibility for the meeting for worship whether our ministry is in silence or through the spoken word.

13. Do not assume that vocal ministry is never to be your part. Faithfulness and sincerity in speaking, even very briefly, may open the way to fuller ministry from others. When prompted to speak, wait patiently to know that the leading and the time are right, but do not let a sense of your own unworthiness hold you back. Pray that your ministry may arise from deep experience, and trust that words will be given to you. Try to speak audibly and distinctly, and with sensitivity to the needs of others. Beware of speaking predictably or too often, and of making additions towards the end of a meeting when it was well left before.

14. Are your meetings for church affairs held in a spirit of worship and in dependence on the guidance of God? Remember that we do not seek a majority decision nor even consensus. As we wait patiently for divine guidance our experience is that the right way will open and we shall be led into unity.

15. Do you take part as often as you can in meetings for church affairs? Are you familiar enough with our church government to contribute to its disciplined processes? Do you consider difficult questions with an informed mind as well as a generous and loving spirit? Are you prepared to let your insights and personal wishes take their place alongside those of others or be set aside as the meeting seeks the right way forward? If you cannot attend, uphold the meeting prayerfully.

16. Do you welcome the diversity of culture, language and expressions of faith in our yearly meeting and in the world community of Friends? Seek to increase your understanding and to gain from this rich heritage and wide range of spiritual insights. Uphold your own and other yearly meetings in your prayers.

17. Do you respect that of God in everyone though it may be expressed in unfamiliar ways or be difficult to discern? Each of us has a particular experience of God and each must find the way to be true to it. When words are strange or disturbing to you, try to sense where they come from and what has nourished the lives of others. Listen patiently and seek the truth which other people's opinions may contain for you. Avoid hurtful criticism and provocative language. Do not allow the strength of your convictions to betray you into making statements or allegations that are unfair or untrue. Think it possible that you may be mistaken.

18. How can we make the meeting a community in which each person is accepted and nurtured, and strangers are welcome? Seek to know one another in the things which are eternal, bear the burden of each other's failings and pray for one another. As we enter with tender sympathy into the joys and sorrows of each other's lives, ready to give help and to receive it, our meeting can be a channel for God's love and forgiveness.

19. Rejoice in the presence of children and young people in your meeting and recognise the gifts they bring. Remember that the meeting as a whole shares a responsibility for every child in its care. Seek for them as for yourself a full development of God's gifts and the abundant life Jesus tells us can be ours. How do you share your deepest beliefs with them, while leaving them free to develop as the spirit of God may lead them? Do you invite them to share their insights with you? Are you ready both to learn from them and to accept your responsibilities towards them?

20. Do you give sufficient time to sharing with others in the meeting, both newcomers and long-time members, your understanding of worship, of service, and of commitment to the Society's witness? Do you give a right proportion of your money to support Quaker work?

21. Do you cherish your friendships, so that they grow in depth and understanding and mutual respect? In close relationships we may risk pain as well as finding joy. When experiencing great happiness or great hurt we may be more open to the working of the Spirit.

22. Respect the wide diversity among us in our lives and relationships. Refrain from making prejudiced judgments about the life journeys of others. Do you foster the spirit of mutual understanding and forgiveness which our discipleship asks of us? Remember that each one of us is unique, precious, a child of God.

23. Marriage has always been regarded by Friends as a religious commitment rather than a merely civil contract. Both partners should offer with God's help an intention to cherish one another for life. Remember that happiness depends on an understanding and steadfast love on both sides. In times of difficulty remind yourself of the value of prayer, of perseverance and of a sense of humour.

24. Children and young people need love and stability. Are we doing all we can to uphold and sustain parents and others who carry the responsibility for providing this care?

25. A long-term relationship brings tensions as well as fulfilment. If your relationship with your partner is under strain, seek help in understanding the other's point of view and in exploring your own feelings, which may be powerful and destructive. Consider the wishes and feelings of any children involved, and remember their enduring need for love and security. Seek God's guidance. If you undergo the distress of separation or divorce, try to maintain some compassionate communication so that arrangements can be made with the minimum of bitterness.

26. Do you recognise the needs and gifts of each member of your family and household, not forgetting your own? Try to make your home a place of loving friendship and enjoyment, where all who live or visit may find the peace and refreshment of God's presence.

27. Live adventurously. When choices arise, do you take the way that offers the fullest opportunity for the use of your gifts in the service of God and the community? Let your life speak. When decisions have to be made, are you ready to join with others in seeking clearness, asking for God's guidance and offering counsel to one another?

28. Every stage of our lives offers fresh opportunities. Responding to divine guidance, try to discern the right time to undertake or relinquish responsibilities without undue pride or guilt. Attend to what love requires of you, which may not be great busyness.

29. Approach old age with courage and hope. As far as possible, make arrangements for your care in good time, so that an undue burden does not fall on others. Although old age may bring increasing disability and loneliness, it can also bring serenity, detachment and wisdom. Pray that in your final years you may be enabled to find new ways of receiving and reflecting God's love.

30. Are you able to contemplate your death and the death of those closest to you? Accepting the fact of death, we are freed to live more fully. In bereavement, give yourself time to grieve. When others mourn, let your love embrace them.

31. We are called to live 'in the virtue of that life and power that takes away the occasion of all wars'. Do you faithfully maintain our testimony that war and the preparation for war are inconsistent with the spirit of Christ? Search out whatever in your own way of life may contain the seeds of war. Stand firm in our testimony, even when others commit or prepare to commit acts of violence, yet always remember that they too are children of God.

32. Bring into God's light those emotions, attitudes and prejudices in yourself which lie at the root of destructive conflict, acknowledging your need for forgiveness and grace. In what ways are you involved in the work of reconciliation between individuals, groups and nations?

33. Are you alert to practices here and throughout the world which discriminate against people on the basis of who or what they are or because of their beliefs? Bear witness to the humanity of all people, including those who break society's conventions or its laws. Try to discern new growing points in social and economic life. Seek to understand the causes of injustice, social unrest and fear. Are you working to bring about a just and compassionate society which allows everyone to develop their capacities and fosters the desire to serve?

34. Remember your responsibilities as a citizen for the conduct of local, national, and international affairs. Do not shrink from the time and effort your involvement may demand.

35. Respect the laws of the state but let your first loyalty be to God's purposes. If you feel impelled by strong conviction to break the law, search your conscience deeply. Ask your meeting for the prayerful support which will give you strength as a right way becomes clear.

36. Do you uphold those who are acting under concern, even if their way is not yours? Can you lay aside your own wishes and prejudices while seeking with others to find God's will for them?

37. Are you honest and truthful in all you say and do? Do you maintain strict integrity in business transactions and in your dealings with individuals and organisations? Do you use money and information entrusted to you with discretion and responsibility? Taking oaths implies a double standard of truth; in choosing to affirm instead, be aware of the claim to integrity that you are making.

38. If pressure is brought upon you to lower your standard of integrity, are you prepared to resist it? Our responsibilities to God and our neighbour may involve us in taking unpopular stands. Do not let the desire to be sociable, or the fear of seeming peculiar, determine your decisions.

39. Consider which of the ways to happiness offered by society are truly fulfilling and which are potentially corrupting and destructive. Be discriminating when choosing means of entertainment and information. Resist the desire to acquire possessions or income through unethical investment, speculation or games of chance.

40. In view of the harm done by the use of alcohol, tobacco and other habit-forming drugs, consider whether you should limit your use of them or refrain from using them altogether. Remember that any use of alcohol or drugs may impair judgment and put both the user and others in danger.

41. Try to live simply. A simple lifestyle freely chosen is a source of strength. Do not be persuaded into buying what you do not need or cannot afford. Do you keep yourself informed about the effects your style of living is having on the global economy and environment?

42. We do not own the world, and its riches are not ours to dispose of at will. Show a loving consideration for all creatures, and seek to maintain the beauty and variety of the world. Work to ensure that our increasing power over nature is used responsibly, with reverence for life. Rejoice in the splendour of God's continuing creation.

Deep Roots and New Growth

Finding out about the roots and history of the Quaker faith and our commitment to ongoing change

This unit invites you to explore the historic beginnings of Quakerism in 17th-century Britain, and how it developed from there to the present day. The Quaker commitment to being open to new inspiration and possibilities means that the Quaker faith has grown and changed over the last 350 years; but the heart of our faith – our belief in 'that of God' in all people and our experience of the power of silent worship to transform our lives – remains unchanged. So the deep roots of Quakerism still nourish our lives today.

Deep Roots unit aims

This unit aims to help you:

- find out about the roots and history of the Quaker faith

- understand how the deep roots of Quakerism still nourish Friends today, enabling us to continue to grow

- explore your own response to the roots of the Quaker faith

Overview

At a time of political and religious turmoil, early Friends as a people felt themselves to be gathered, guided and ordered by God. From their experience of the immediacy of the presence of Christ sprang the form of worship and the way of life which became the distinctive testimonies of Friends, and which were upheld with courage in the face of great persecution.

From the beginning, Quakerism has grown and developed in response to social and religious change and through a commitment to being 'open to new light' (*Advices & queries* 7 in *Quaker faith & practice* 1.02), wherever it may come from. Like a well-rooted tree, the Quaker faith has accepted new directions of growth and weathered many storms.

Deep roots

George Fox, widely regarded as the founder of the Quaker movement, was a very serious-minded young man disillusioned by what he saw as the failure of those who professed themselves to be Christians to live up to their Christian standards. In 1643 he left his home seeking a new way.

Fox came to believe that God could speak directly to each person without the need for priests or churches, and he set out to spread his message, hoping to bring believers back to an original and pure form of Christianity.

George Fox's preaching rapidly recruited others seeking a faith which gave coherence and purpose to their lives. This faith is rooted in Christianity, but it was radical, and has remained so, because the early Friends found the basis of their faith was the individual relationship with and experience of God.

Early Friends believed that the Second Coming of Christ was actually happening within their own hearts, minds and spirits: they felt themselves to be in communion with the spirit of Christ and as a result completely transformed. Many felt called to follow Fox's example and began preaching this new way of seeking the presence of God always present within the human heart.

For the first Quakers, this conviction that there is 'that of God' in everyone led them to a radical understanding that all persons are equal before God and that the old social distinctions, reflected in language, conduct and dress, were wrong: this is the source of the Quaker Testimony to Equality. So all titles and forms of deference, such as removing your hat in the presence of social 'superiors', were to be abandoned, and women's participation in Quaker life was accepted alongside that of men. Their commitment to Truth demanded honest, simple speech, and a refusal to acknowledge double standards by taking oaths. For early Friends, it was also clearly wrong to pay tithes (church taxes) to support clergy, buildings and practices which were distortions of the original message of Christ. Such flouting of the laws and conventions of the day brought heavy punishments upon the first Quakers. George Fox himself spent many years in prison, and Friends had their possessions removed and suffered violence and persecution.

The first Quakers had a vision of the world transformed by Christ, who lives in the hearts of all: they sought to make the vision real by putting emphasis on Christian practice rather than primarily on dogma or beliefs. They recognised the realities of evil and conflict, but found it contrary to the spirit of Christ to use war and violence as means to deal with them. This led to the development of the Quaker 'Peace Testimony' which remains fundamental for Quakers today.

New growth

By the 18th century, when it became clear that the whole world would not follow the Quaker way, Friends withdrew into their own communities. But their faith and practice continued and were expressed in new developments such as schools in which girls' intellectual development was valued and the curriculum was closely related to everyday life and work.

The religious upheavals of the late 18th and early 19th centuries led to further changes in the Religious Society of Friends. The prison visiting of Elizabeth Fry and the involvement of Quakers in the abolition of the slave trade were obvious results of a fresh engagement with the world outside their own communities. At the same time, barred from English universities and the professions, Quakers entered into business and were pioneers in banking, science and industry. Their known honesty helped them to flourish in commerce.

Long term change-making in the world

From these early times, Quakers have taken a long-term, patient approach to living out our faith in the world, sticking with our testimonies whether it makes us unpopular or leads to a Nobel Prize. The Quaker approach is often to work for long-term goals or sustainable change that is well rooted in local communities: this means being prepared to stick at action for as long as it takes, or to work quietly away from the limelight. The ways that the testimonies are expressed has changed over time, but the fundamental commitment to equality, simplicity, peace and truth remains at the root of Quaker witness in the world.

A prophetic community

The wide spectrum of belief and witness among present day Quakers is not incompatible with the faith of the early Friends: direct spiritual experience remains the core of Quaker faith, whether this is understood as experience of God or of a spirituality inherent within humanity itself. Being deeply rooted but open to new growth enables Quakers to respond with careful discernment to the needs of the time, both spiritual and practical, as a prophetic community that continues to speak Truth to the world:

> The Truth is one and the same always, and though ages and generations pass away, and one generation goes and another comes, yet the word and power and spirit of the living God endures for ever, and is the same and never changes.
>
> Margaret Fell
> *Quaker faith & practice* 19.61

Quaker distinctives

Distinctives 1

An overview of Quaker history

There is a brief but detailed overview of Quaker history you might read, in an extract from *A light that is shining* by Harvey Gillman. This extract can be found on pages 70–74.

You could also look at a Quaker timeline, which charts significant events in Quaker history alongside major events in British and world history. The timeline can be found on pages 75–79.

For more detail about early Quaker insights and experiences, you can read chapter 19 of *Quaker faith & practice* or one of the books referred to in Further exploration.

Distinctives 2

Meeting early Quakers

Some of the lives or insights of early Quakers are described in the following extracts from *Quaker faith & practice*:

- George Fox (1624–1691): *Qf&p* 19.01–19.04
- Margaret Fell (1614–1702): *Qf&p* 19.07
- James Nayler (1617?–1660): *Qf&p* 19.09
- Isaac Penington (1616–1679): *Qf&p* 19.14
- William Dewsbury (1621–1688): *Qf&p* 19.05
- Mary Fisher (1623–1698): *Qf&p* 19.27
- Mary Dyer (d.1660): *Qf&p* 19.18
- Thomas Ellwood (1639–1713): *Qf&p* 19.16
- William Penn (1644–1718): *Qf&p* 19.28 and 19.47

You can also find more detailed accounts of some early Quakers' lives:

- in Wikipedia by clicking on their name in the list given at http://en.wikipedia.org/wiki/Category:English_Quakers

- by asking your meeting librarian for books on Quaker lives

You might also like to read extracts from:

- the Journal of George Fox at: www.strecorsoc.org/gfox/title.html

- the Journal of 18th-century Friend John Woolman at:
  www.strecorsoc.org/jwoolman/title.html

These journals are also available in most meeting house libraries (or to buy from the Quaker Centre bookshop – see Further exploration for contact details).

Distinctives 3

Listen to talks about Quaker history

You might like to listen to two talks about Quaker history given by Ben Pink Dandelion, Woodbrooke Quaker Study Centre's Tutor in Postgraduate Quaker Studies, called 'Who are the Quakers?' and 'The history of Quakerism'.

These talks can be downloaded from the Woodbrooke website at: www.woodbrooke.org.uk/news.php/6/a-very-short-introduction-to-quakerism

Distinctives 4

Quakers as a prophetic community

Early Friends felt inspired to speak prophetically (with an understanding transformed by God) to the world of their day; this is still part of the Quaker way. In the following two extracts the speakers urge Quakers to act as a prophetic community. They are separated by 350 years, so the language they use is different, but both are rooted in the same Quaker experience:

- George Fox (1656): *Qf&p* 19.32

- Marion McNaughton (2007): this extract by Marion McNaughton can be found on pages 80–83

Quakers discovered at an early stage that a prophetic community must also be a disciplined community, or it can lead to excessive individualism or impulsive action. So Friends have a long tradition of 'taking the community with you' when being open to new growth; this usually involves a process of waiting and discerning the way forward until the community is ready to act.

- The 'Nayler incident' in 1656 was a key stage in developing this discipline: *Qf&p* 19.11 and 19.12

- for a fuller account see also: http://en.wikipedia.org/wiki/James_Nayler

- A modern Quaker speaks of being 'centred, rooted, practised in waiting on God' when working with conflict, a modern prophetic role: *Qf&p* 20.71

Distinctives 5

The history of Quaker structures

You may be interested to read about how Yearly Meeting and Meeting for Sufferings came into being and how they evolved from the early days of Quakerism to the present day:

- Yearly Meeting: *Qf&p* 6.01

- Meeting for Sufferings: *Qf&p* 7.01

For a history of the advices and queries: *Qf&p* 1.04. See also Advices and Queries unit: Discovery 4 for an activity exploring old versions of *Advices & queries*

Distinctives 6

Quaker faith in action – in it for the long run

The following extracts bear witness to the steady, rooted Quaker approach to putting faith into action:

- 'slow but sure' change making in the world: *Qf&p* 23.13

- the long term work of the Quaker United Nations Office in building the institutions of peace and social justice: *Qf&p* 9.03 and 24.49

- see also: www.quno.org

- Education for Peace article at: www.quaker.org.uk/education-peace and pages 84–85

You can find out about Quaker actions in the past, where work still continues today on the modern equivalent of the same causes:

Abolition of slavery

- *Qf&p* 23.24–23.29

- online Quaker exhibition at www.quaker.org.uk/quakers-and-abolition-slave-trade

- information on the BBC website at: www.bbc.co.uk/history/british/abolition/abolitionists_gallery_03.shtml

Conscientious objection to war

- *Qf&p* 24.14–24.16 and 24.27

Keeping children safe from war

Kindertransport during World War II:

- read about Quaker work on the Kindertransport in *Quaker News* Winter 2008 edition – find a copy of this edition in your meeting house library, or download it from: www.quaker.org.uk/qn

- see an online Quaker exhibition of memories and tributes to Kindertransportees at: www.quaker.org.uk/kinder

Recent work with child soldiers in Uganda:

- read about Quaker work with child soldiers on pages 86–87 and at: www.quaker.org.uk/uganda

Prison reform & criminal justice

- *Qf&p* 23.94–23.100, and info on the Britain Yearly Meeting website at: www.quaker.org.uk/justice

Discovery

Discovery 1

What do our Quaker roots mean to us?

A modern Quaker, Deborah Rowlands, explains what her Quaker roots mean to her in an extract from *Quaker identity and the heart of our faith*.

You'll find this extract on pages 88–89.

If you would like to read the full text of *Quaker identity and the heart of our faith*, see Further exploration for details.

You could also ask your Becoming Friends companion, or another Friend in your meeting who has been a Quaker for a long time, about what their Quaker roots mean to them.

Discovery 2

Quaker history through the Quaker Tapestry

You might like to look at panels from the Quaker Tapestry that deal with events and people from Quaker history, and follow up any that interest you by discussing them with your Becoming Friends companion, or others in your meeting, or by finding books and information about them in your meeting house library or online.

You could:

- visit the Quaker Tapestry exhibition at Kendal, or contact them for more details:
  Tel: 01539 722975
  Email: info@quaker-tapestry.co.uk
  Website: www.quaker-tapestry.co.uk

- find out if there's a book with pictures from the tapestry in your meeting house library, or you could order a book or postcards from the exhibition

Quaker Tapestry panels about Quaker history include:

- A1 George Fox's convincement

- A2 James Nayler

- A3 James Parnell; Meeting for Sufferings

- A5 The voyage of the Woodhouse

- A6 John Woolman

- A8 Manchester Conference 1895

- B1 Firbank Fell: George Fox preaching

- B2 Mary Fisher

- B3 John Bright

- C1 Swarthmoor Hall

- C2 Margaret Fell

- D1 George Fox; Lichfield, Pendle Hill

- E1 George Fox at Ulverston: healing

- E5–6 Elizabeth Fry

Discovery 3

Exploring the Quaker timeline

Why not find an event or person that interests you or that you know nothing about on the Quaker Timeline (see Distinctives 1), and find out more? You'll find the timeline on pages 75–79.

You could:

- ask your Becoming Friends companion or an experienced Friend what they know

- see what it says in *Quaker faith & practice*

- look online at: www.wikipedia.org
  for example, see their article on the Valiant Sixty at:
  http://en.wikipedia.org/wiki/Valiant_60

- see if there's a relevant book in your local meeting library

- ask what anyone knows on a Quaker discussion forum:
  - ➤ the Britain Yearly Meeting forum at: www.quakerweb.org.uk/forum
  - ➤ www.friendlink.org.uk (aimed mainly at young Quakers)
  - ➤ the Deep Roots unit forum

Discovery 4

Talking about Quaker stories from the past

You might like to explore some Quaker stories from the past. Look through the Distinctives activities for examples, or you could read about:

- William Penn and his sword: *Qf&p* 19.47

- John Woolman writing a will: *Qf&p* 20.46

- Mary Hughes 'radiant with love': *Qf&p* 18.13

How about asking one or two Friends in your meeting to share with you Quaker stories that speak to them? The introductory questions below may be helpful. You could do this during the coffee time after meeting for worship, or your Becoming Friends companion might help you set up an informal meeting with other Friends.

Or you could consider the introductory questions, then go to the Deep Roots unit forum and post your own thoughts in response. You might like to comment on other posts on this forum too.

Introductory questions:

1. Are there any particular stories from Quaker history that speak to you?

2. In what way do they enrich your life as a Quaker now?

Discovery 5

Take a tour of or a course on Quaker history

Swarthmoor Hall is sometimes called the historic 'birthplace' of Quakerism. For more information you can contact them:

Tel: 01229 583204
Email: info@swarthmoorhall.co.uk
Website: www.swarthmoorhall.co.uk

- You can take a mini virtual tour of Swarthmoor Hall at: www.swarthmoorhall.co.uk/360_view.htm

- or read about the history of the hall and early Quakers at: www.swarthmoorhall.co.uk/history.htm

You can also take a virtual tour of '1652 country' – the places where George Fox and early Quakers met & worshipped – at: www.strecorsoc.org/qkrcntry/qc01.html (click on the photos at the bottom of the page).

Tours of the actual places in the '1652 country' and courses on Quaker history are run by Swarthmoor Hall and Woodbrooke Quaker Study Centre. For details of tours or courses coming up, contact:

- Swarthmoor Hall – contact details as above

- Woodbrooke Quaker Study Centre
  Tel: 0121 472 5171
  Email: enquiries@woodbrooke.org.uk
  Website: www.woodbrooke.org.uk

Deepening

Deepening 1

How do Quaker stories speak to you?

You might like to reflect on a person or incident from Quaker history that interests or appeals to you in some way. You can find examples in the Distinctives and Discovery sections of this unit, and there are Quaker stories in the *Journeys in the Spirit* series, available from Quaker Life or at: www.quaker.org.uk/journeyschild (issues 27–43). Reflect on why or how this Quaker person or story speaks to you.

You could talk to your Becoming Friends companion, or write in a journal or book of spiritual discipline, perhaps using these questions as a focus:

- Does this person or story resonate with something in your own life?

- How does this person or story show the 'breaking in' of new light, or the importance of rootedness in the spiritual life?

- How do your roots, spiritual or personal, nourish you?

- In what ways are you being invited to undergo change or growth now?

Deepening 2

A prayer reflecting on our Quaker roots, and seeking openness to new growth

Margaret Benefiel, a contemporary American Quaker, has written a prayer which reflects on the depth of the Quaker tradition and our meaningful encounter with it today.

You can find the prayer on page 90–92.

You might like to take some time to reflect deeply on your own response to the prayer; you could write or respond creatively.

You could also reflect on this with your Becoming Friends companion when you next meet.

Deepening 3

An image for your own rootedness

Consider the image of Quakerism as a well rooted tree, able to grow and even accept grafts, because of its rootedness. What image works for you to express your own rootedness, spiritually or personally?

You could express or reflect on this image of your own rootedness:

- by drawing, painting, or using another creative method

- in music, song or movement

- in writing

- by going online and blogging about the image

- by discussing the image on a Quaker discussion forum:
    - the Britain Yearly Meeting forum at: www.quakerweb.org.uk/forum
    - www.friendlink.org.uk (aimed mainly at young Quakers)
    - the Deep Roots unit forum

- by sharing with your Becoming Friends companion when you next meet.

Deepening 4

Reflecting with Quaker mystics

The writings of Quaker mystics from the past continue to inspire and challenge us on our spiritual journeys. The following extracts from *Quaker faith & practice* are by Quaker mystics:

- Isaac Penington: *Qf&p* 26.70 'give over thine own willing'; *Qf&p* 10.01: 'our life is love'

- George Fox: *Qf&p* 2.18 'be still and cool'; *Qf&p* 26.03 'all things were new'

- Margaret Fell: *Qf&p* 19.61 'the Truth is one'

- Francis Howgill: *Qf&p* 26.71 'return home to within'

- James Nayler: *Qf&p* 19.12 'a spirit ... that delights to do no evil'

- John Woolman: *Qf&p* 20.10 'a precious habitation'; *Qf&p* 26.61 'a principle which is pure'

- Thomas Kelly: *Qf&p* 2.22 'an inner, secret turning'; *Qf&p* 26.62 'shining into the darkness'

- Rufus Jones: *Qf&p* 26.32 'beauty breaks through'

Is there one extract, phrase or word that speaks to you in particular? You could incorporate it into your spiritual practice over the next few days or weeks, reading it or repeating it in the way of 'sacred reading' (see page 270 in Appendix 1 – Spiritual Practices for guidance about 'sacred reading'). You could print it or write it out and keep it somewhere that you will be able to see it.

You could also share some of your reflections with your Becoming Friends companion when you next meet.

Deepening 5

Engaging with the Quaker discipline of waiting for the right time for action or change

Advices & queries 28 (in section 1.02 of *Quaker faith & practice*) advises that 'every stage of our lives offers fresh opportunities', inviting us to 'discern the right time to undertake or relinquish responsibilities' and to 'attend to what love requires' of us.

This is a way for an individual to follow the Quaker community discipline of waiting and discerning the right time to act or make changes (see Distinctives 4). You could reflect on your own process of being open to 'fresh opportunities', and how you know it's the right time for change. You could write or respond creatively to the following questions:

- Have there been times in your life when waiting for the right time for action or change has proved fruitful?

- How did you know when it was the right time?

- If you have acted too quickly or without the discipline of waiting, what effect has this had on the change or action you took?

- Would it help to use the question 'what does love require of me?' in your discernment?

You could also share some of your reflections with your Becoming Friends companion when you next meet.

Further exploration

If you would like to explore the subject of Quaker history and roots further, here are some suggestions for reading, listening or viewing.

A faith to call our own. Quaker tradition in the light of contemporary movements of the Spirit, Alex Wildwood, Quaker Home Service, 1999 (Swarthmore Lecture).

'Finding the prophetic voice for our time', Marion McNaughton and Lizz Roe, *Woodbrooke Journal*, Autumn 2007, No 21.

'James Nayler: a pearl of faith', Stephen Sayers, *Woodbrooke Journal*, Autumn 2006, No 19.

A light that is shining: an introduction to the Quakers, Harvey Gillman, Quaker Books, 2003.

Living the way: Quaker spirituality and community, Ursula Jane O'Shea, Quaker Books, 2003 (first published by Australia Yearly Meeting, 1993). This is in the *Hearts and minds prepared* pack.

Minding the future, Christine A. M. Davis, Quaker Books, 2008 (Swarthmore Lecture).

Pictorial guide to the Quaker Tapestry, The Quaker Tapestry at Kendal, 1998.

Portrait in grey: a short history of the Quakers, John Punshon, Quaker Home Service, 1984.

Previous convictions and end of the millennium Quakerism, Christine Trevett, Quaker Home Service, 1997 (Swarthmore Lecture).

Quaker faith & practice, chapter 18, 'Faithful Lives'.

Quaker faith & practice, chapter 19, 'Openings'.

Quaker identity and the heart of our faith, Quaker Life Study Materials, Quaker Life, 2008, including Deborah Rowlands on 'Roots' and Rex Ambler on 'The prophetic message of early Friends'. Available online at: www.quaker.org.uk/sites/default/files/Faith-and-practice-proceeding.pdf or in hard copy by contacting Quaker Life on 020 7663 1140 or email: ql@quaker.org.uk

Quakerism: a theology for our time, Patricia Williams, Sessions, 2007.

Quaker Peace & Social Witness pages on the Britain Yearly Meeting website: www.quaker.org.uk/qpsw

Quaker Tapestry website: www.quaker-tapestry.co.uk

The Quakers: a very short introduction, Pink Dandelion, Oxford University Press, 2008.

Quakers in Britain: a century of change 1895–1995, Alastair Heron, Curlew Graphics, 1995.

Rooted in Christianity, open to new light: Quaker spiritual diversity, Timothy Ashworth and Alex Wildwood, Pronoun Press & Woodbrooke, 2009.

Searching the depths: essays on being a Quaker today, edited by Harvey Gillman and Alastair Heron, Quaker Books, 1996. 'Building on our Traditions' chapter by Rosalind Priestman.

Street Corner Society website pages: www.strecorsoc.org/docs_qq.html and www.strecorsoc.org/quaker.html with links to a wide selection of online historical Quaker texts including George Fox's and John Woolman's journals.

Swarthmoor Hall's website: www.swarthmoorhall.co.uk

Testimony and tradition, John Punshon, Quaker Home Service, 1990 (Swarthmore Lecture).

'Tradition and transition: opening to the sacred yesterday and today', Alex Wildwood, *Woodbrooke Journal*, Winter 2001, No 9. This is in the *Hearts and minds prepared* pack.

Woodbrooke's website or brochure for details of courses about Quaker history: www.woodbrooke.org.uk

Many of these titles are available from the Quaker Centre bookshop:

Friends House
173 Euston Road
London NW1 2BJ

Tel: 020 7663 1030
Fax: 020 7663 1001

Website: www.quaker.org.uk/bookshop
Email: quakercentre@quaker.org.uk

Many of them will also be in your local meeting house library. You could ask your Becoming Friends companion to help you track down titles that interest you.

Closing activity

As you finish your exploration of Quaker history and roots, you are invited to reflect on what you have gained through this unit, how your understanding of both yourself and Quakerism has changed, and what areas you would like to explore further.

This closing reflection can be a very good opportunity for sharing with your Becoming Friends companion, or you may prefer to write in a journal or book of spiritual discipline (there's guidance for journalling in Appendix 2 – Guidance on page 282), or to reflect using creative methods such as drawing, collage, model-making or working with materials such as textiles or wood.

You might use one or more of the following questions as a focus for your reflection:

- What have you gained from your work on this unit, whether as a result of positive or more challenging experiences?

- In what ways has your understanding changed as a result of your work on this unit?

- Are there areas that you would like to explore further – either as part of your own spiritual journey or relating to Quakerism?

- Has anything arisen that you would find it helpful to reflect on, with your Becoming Friends companion?

Extract for Distinctives 1:
An overview of Quaker history

'Origins and development: the growth of the Quaker outlook' from *A light that is shining* by Harvey Gillman

What we at this period of our history find striking about early Quakers in the 1640s and 1650s is their emergence at a time of revolutionary change which was breaking down old ideas of a strictly defined social order. The Roman Catholic Church had long ceased to have any power in Britain, although it was still feared by the political establishment. There was conflict in the Church of England between its Puritan and Catholic wings. There were questions about the role of the bishops; about the role of women (in the Baptist, Quaker and other Separatist communities women had an increasingly important place but it was among Quakers alone that women were fully accepted as having equal status in the worshipping group) and so on. Faction begat faction, as each group tried to establish its own particular truth.

As well as being overtly theological in nature, these conflicts were political and social in the widest sense. The whole question of how society could best be governed for the benefit of everyone was being raised and many of the answers given were radical. As George Fox (1624–1691) travelled up and down the country, he met with others who also had spent time seeking for a more intimate relationship with God. This search was taking them away from the mainstream churches, and was eventually to lead to the founding of what is now known as the Religious Society of Friends.

These men and women who later became Friends brought with them ideas they had found in the varying factions they had come from, and for a period the Quaker movement was a much less coherent movement than it later became. In today's world of rapid change with fewer than one quarter of the members of the Society born of Quaker parents, we can see a parallel. The challenge to modern Quakerism is a similar one: how today to fuse ex-Baptists, ex-Anglicans, ex-atheists, ex-Buddhists, ex-practising Jews, ex-so many things, into a united society (though not a uniform one).

The seventeenth century

In the seventeenth century it was George Fox who put his stamp on this emerging group. It would be a mistake however to equate a movement with one man, charismatic though he may have been. Throughout the north Midlands and the North West, groups had already set themselves apart from the mainstream churches. Many of them met in silence without priest or pastor. Many of them

had already rejected outward sacraments and were waiting for a new spirituality.
[...]

It was Fox with his administrative ability and Margaret Fell (1614–1702) who
later became his wife, who were able to fuse these groups into a society which
has survived, while most other religious groups originating at this time have died
away. Yet the Quaker movement was not to be united easily. There were clashes of
personality as well as of principles. James Nayler (1617–1660), whose enthusiasm
and charisma sometimes led his followers to excess, clashed with Fox on a
number of occasions. In the 1660s John Perrott, an Irish Friend from Waterford,
protested against the increasing centralising of decision-making among Quakers
and condemned the custom of removing hats when a Friend prayed aloud
in meeting, and of shaking hands at the end of meetings. This almost led to a
schism, but in spite of these differences Quakers spread and grew and met greater
persecution. Between 1650 and 1687, it has been estimated that 13,000 Friends
were imprisoned, 198 were transported and 338 died in penal institutions or of
wounds inflicted upon them while they were attending meeting.

Persecution did not cool the ardour of the men and women who left family and
home to become 'publishers of Truth'. It is from this period that the Quaker
custom of 'speaking truth to power' arises. In 1657 Mary Fisher (1623–1698), who
had sailed to Massachusetts to witness for the truth, travelled to Constantinople
to try to convince the Sultan. Others sought audience with the Pope and met with
imprisonment or death at the hands of the Inquisition. Mary Dyer was hanged for
her beliefs in 1660 on Boston Common by the very Puritans who had left England
to find liberty of worship. But it was this revolutionary desire to publish the truth
that God was immediately accessible to all human beings that eventually led to
the founding in the seventeenth and eighteenth centuries of Quaker groups in
centres throughout Europe, North America and the Caribbean.

The eighteenth century

Like most fervent movements, the Quaker movement began to lose something
of its impetus as its founding members died. From being a movement to preach
a new or regained truth, it took on the characteristics of an inward-looking sect,
handing down traditions and regulating the activities of its partisans. From being
a revival of the true universal church, Friends now saw themselves as a remnant
keeping precious their past insights. In the eighteenth and early nineteenth
centuries they became a 'peculiar' people, suspicious of the outside world, wearing
distinctive clothes, speaking a language full of distinctive jargon, addressing each
other as 'thee' and 'thou', and although they still held public meetings now and
again, very few newcomers were attracted to them.

But this introspection was not total and Friends were still concerned about
conditions in the world around them. John Bellers (1654–1725), for instance,
forms a link between the early persecutions and the subsequent period of
retrenchment, yet he carried on the social witness of the first generation of
Quakers with his schemes for the welfare of destitute children and in his writings
he speaks of the 'labour of the poor being the mines of the rich'. His theories

influenced later radicals such as Robert Owen and Karl Marx. Similarly John Woolman (1720–1772) was one of the first of the Society to condemn slavery, urge economic boycotts and care about conditions aboard ships. He also prompted Friends to see the connection between the way they lived, the possessions they owned and the violence and oppression which were part of the economic and political institutions of their day.

The interest some Friends showed in the social conditions of their day was matched by the fascination of other Friends for the natural world. If helping other people was a sign of the Christian life, the exploration of nature was a sign of human appreciation of a divinely inspired universe and the Quaker contribution was considerable. John Fothergill (1712–1780) played a notable role in the medical world; as did Peter Collinson (1694–1768) in botany. Towards the end of the period, John Dalton (1766–1844) and William Allen (1770–1843) made great contributions to chemistry. One of the most important discoveries of the eighteenth century, the smelting of iron by using coke rather than charcoal, was made by Abraham Darby (1678–1717) at Coalbrookdale in Shropshire. This and other inventions at Coalbrookdale had great bearing on the growth of the Industrial Revolution.

The nineteenth century

Gradually as the nineteenth century advanced Quakers began to look outwards from the small world of their own denomination as they were more and more open to religious and social insights from other traditions. The outside world had already witnessed the Methodist movement of which Quakers at first were very suspicious and yet this movement went on to influence most of the churches in one way or another. Some Quakers by the end of the eighteenth century believed that their Society had become too complacent, too introspective, and like many in other churches felt the need for greater personal commitment. During this period, often described as the 'quietist' period of Quaker history, the Bible had been read in the home, but there was fear in the Society that too much reliance on it at worship would interfere with the still small voice in the heart. Under the impact of the evangelical movement and the teaching of the Quaker evangelical Joseph John Gurney (1788–1847) these dissatisfied Quakers turned again to the Bible. They felt that without Biblical and doctrinal authority they were powerless to overcome the world of sin and separation and came eventually to place a greater emphasis than did their immediate forebears on personal salvation and the doctrine of atonement.

In this they realised that they were close to Christians of other persuasions and this led them to cross the barriers of distrust and to work with others to improve the society around them. Again William Allen was typical of this movement. His work with the Anti-Slavery Society and with the London poor reveals how Quakers were taking their religious convictions into the public arena and were beginning to co-operate with other churches. Similarly Joseph Lancaster (1778–1838), one of the first advocates of popular education on a national scale, drew other nonconformists into a society that later became the British and Foreign

Schools Society. One of the best known of all Quakers, Elizabeth Fry (1780–1845), belonged to an old Quaker family, the Gurneys. She seems first to have worn her membership of the Society quite lightly, but she was converted to a more evangelical faith and the fervour of this faith led her to prison visiting and then to prison reform.

There was however a backlash in more conservative Quaker circles who were afraid that such worldly activity and evangelical theology would dilute Quakerism. Eventually these conflicts led Quakers in North America to split up into different factions. Some of these divisions still remain, although gatherings are held to broaden mutual understanding of the different Quaker traditions. Even today the conferences are not always easy affairs when theology is discussed, yet there is much greater co-operation than previously.

There has always been a tension among Quakers between, on the one hand, the idea that the leadings of the light within were sufficient for spiritual fulfilment and, on the other hand, a reliance on the Bible and the atonement for sins through the crucifixion of Jesus of Nazareth. This tension was brought to the surface by the evangelical emphasis on scriptural authority and the perceived need for salvation, a position held by many prominent Quakers towards the middle of the nineteenth century. Later in the nineteenth century, the tension grew into conflict as among some Friends the growing belief in the scientific method was leading to a reassessment of the nature of authority and historical accuracy. Texts were being studied and questioned, and Biblical infallibility, a belief close to the hearts of many an evangelical according to which the Bible was literally true, was no longer being taken for granted. This led to three distinct trends among Quakers: the traditionalists or conservatives, who quietly relied upon the Light of Christ within; the evangelicals for whom the Bible was growing in importance as a source of authority; and the new modernists or liberals whose theology was suspect to both the others as it questioned both the distinctiveness of some of the old customs and the literalness of the Bible. Under the impact of the new Biblical criticism and the work of Charles Darwin, the modernists were questioning their faith and were trying to see how the new knowledge fitted in with the old certainties. Whereas in the United States these trends resulted in splits, in Britain there has been no comparable division.

The twentieth century

There was no doubt that for many (often contradictory) reasons, groups of Quakers were confused about the direction their Society was taking. This search for a new direction and revival came to a head in a national conference held in Manchester in 1895. Under the leading of John Wilhelm Rowntree (1868–1905), Quakers saw the need for a greater commitment to an understanding of the origins of their Society, to a new teaching ministry (which eventually led to the creation of Woodbrooke College, the Quaker study centre in Birmingham), and to a new vision of the role of Quakers in the twentieth century.

This was on the whole a triumph for a more liberal, outward-going emphasis but if it was a form of religious liberalism it was a liberalism enhanced by a mystical awareness of the presence of God. The notable exponent of this stream of Quakerism was the American, Rufus M. Jones (1863–1948). For him the personal experience of God is a mystical experience. In his *The Flowering of Mysticism*, he describes it thus: 'Mysticism is an immediate, intuitive, experimental knowledge of God, or one might say it is consciousness of a Beyond or of Transcendent Reality or of Divine Presence.' The emphasis in this book is on the light within; less is placed on historical crucifixion.

The last quarter of the twentieth century and the beginnings of the twenty-first century have brought about the transformations in the Society which I shall consider in chapter Six. What is important about these different historical emphases in Quakerism is that to a varying extent they are still alive in the Religious Society of Friends. There are still enthusiasts who wish to carry the message of George Fox into the market place; quietists who feel that too much outward activity gets in the way of the Spirit; evangelicals who witness to the effect in their lives of Jesus Christ, their saviour and redeemer; liberals whose gospel is a social one and whose emphasis is on religious humanism; mystics who speak of the Spirit in all things; radicals who try to deconstruct the nature of religious experience, and others who would simply call themselves Christians, for whom no other title quite fits their understanding of religion. Indeed, it is one of the joys, though not unmixed sometimes with anxiety, to have all these Quakers sitting down together in worship. For it is worship which brings Quakers together. And it is out of worship that arises the Quaker idea of service in the world.

from *A light that is shining: an introduction to the Quakers*,
Harvey Gillman, Quaker Books, 2003

for Distinctives 1:
Quaker timeline

1509–1547 Henry VIII

1547– 53 Edward VI

1553–1558 Mary I

1558–1603
Elizabeth I

1559 Act of
Uniformity

1599–1658
Oliver
Cromwell

1559 John Knox founded
Church of Scotland

1534 Henry
VIII Defender
of Faith.

1549 Book of
Common Prayer

1538 Bible in
every church

| 1500 | 1510 | 1520 | 1530 | 1540 | 1550 | 1560 | 1570 | 1580 | 1590 |

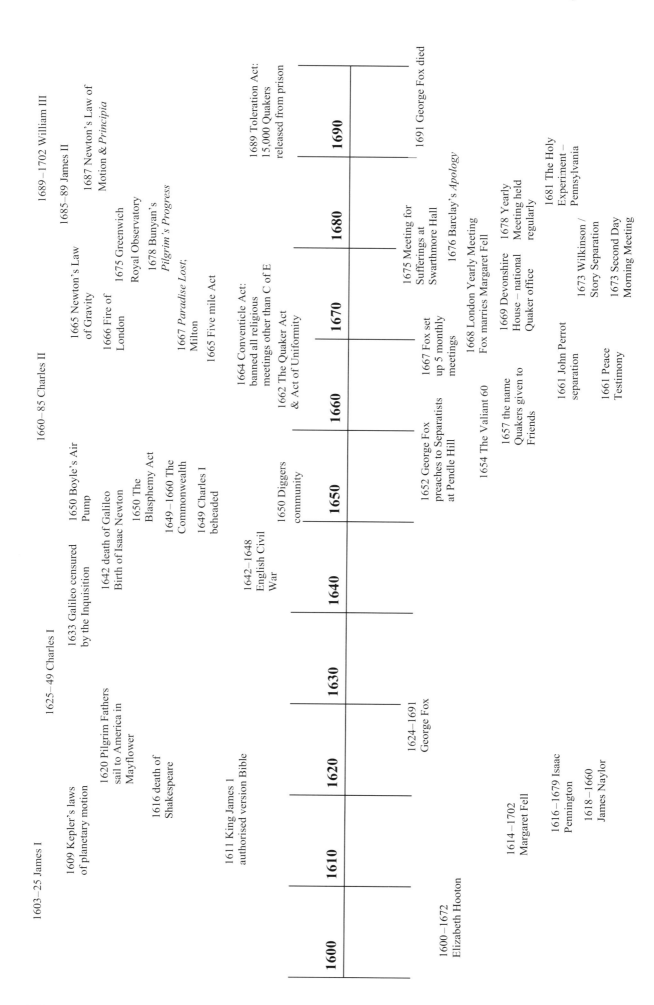

1603–25 James I

1625–49 Charles I

1660–85 Charles II

1685–89 James II

1689–1702 William III

1687 Newton's Law of Motion & *Principia*

1689 Toleration Act: 15,000 Quakers released from prison

1691 George Fox died

1609 Kepler's laws of planetary motion

1633 Galileo censured by the Inquisition

1650 Boyle's Air Pump

1665 Newton's Law of Gravity

1666 Fire of London

1675 Greenwich Royal Observatory

1678 Bunyan's *Pilgrim's Progress*

1620 Pilgrim Fathers sail to America in Mayflower

1642 death of Galileo Birth of Isaac Newton

1650 The Blasphemy Act

1667 *Paradise Lost;* Milton

1616 death of Shakespeare

1649–1660 The Commonwealth

1665 Five mile Act

1649 Charles I beheaded

1611 King James 1 authorised version Bible

1642–1648 English Civil War

1664 Conventicle Act: banned all religious meetings other than C of E

1662 The Quaker Act & Act of Uniformity

1650 Diggers community

1600	**1610**	**1620**	**1630**	**1640**	**1650**	**1660**	**1670**	**1680**	**1690**

1624–1691 George Fox

1652 George Fox preaches to Separatists at Pendle Hill

1675 Meeting for Sufferings at Swarthmore Hall

1676 Barclay's *Apology*

1667 Fox set up 5 monthly meetings

1668 London Yearly Meeting Fox marries Margaret Fell

1669 Devonshire House – national Quaker office

1678 Yearly Meeting held regularly

1681 The Holy Experiment – Pennsylvania

1654 The Valiant 60

1657 the name Quakers given to Friends

1661 John Perrot separation

1673 Wilkinson / Story Separation

1661 Peace Testimony

1673 Second Day Morning Meeting

1600–1672 Elizabeth Hooton

1614–1702 Margaret Fell

1616–1679 Isaac Pennington

1618–1660 James Naylor

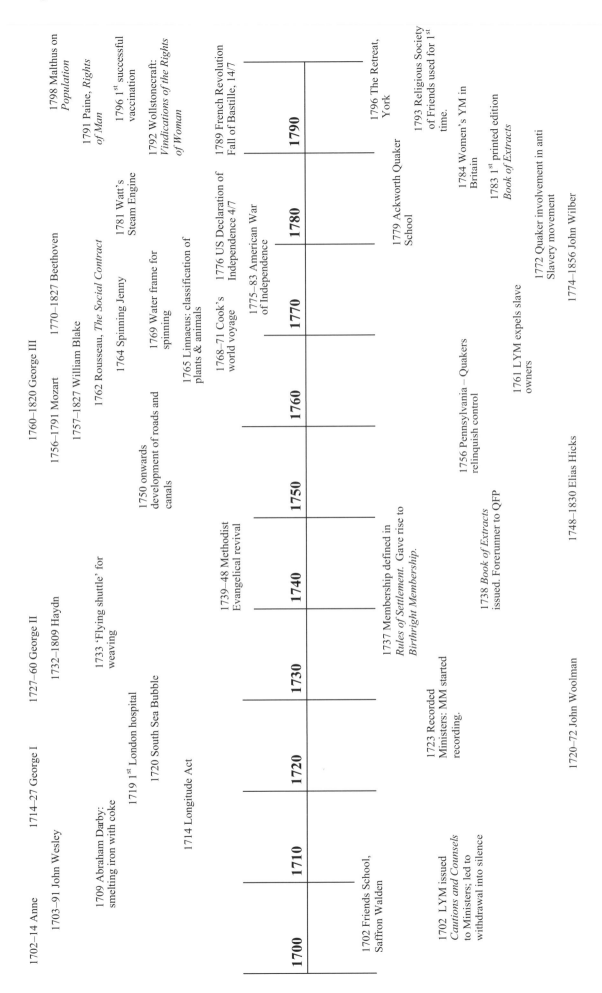

1702–14 Anne

1703–91 John Wesley

1714–27 George I

1727–60 George II

1732–1809 Haydn

1756–1791 Mozart

1757–1827 William Blake

1760–1820 George III

1770–1827 Beethoven

1709 Abraham Darby: smelting iron with coke

1719 1st London hospital

1720 South Sea Bubble

1714 Longitude Act

1733 'Flying shuttle' for weaving

1762 Rousseau, *The Social Contract*

1764 Spinning Jenny

1750 onwards development of roads and canals

1769 Water frame for spinning

1781 Watt's Steam Engine

1765 Linnaeus: classification of plants & animals

1768–71 Cook's world voyage

1776 US Declaration of Independence 4/7

1775–83 American War of Independence

1789 French Revolution Fall of Bastille, 14/7

1791 Paine, *Rights of Man*

1792 Wollstonecraft: *Vindications of the Rights of Woman*

1796 1st successful vaccination

1798 Malthus on *Population*

1739–48 Methodist Evangelical revival

1700 **1710** **1720** **1730** **1740** **1750** **1760** **1770** **1780** **1790**

1702 Friends School, Saffron Walden

1702 LYM issued *Cautions and Counsels* to Ministers; led to withdrawal into silence

1723 Recorded Ministers: MM started recording.

1737 Membership defined in *Rules of Settlement*. Gave rise to *Birthright Membership*.

1738 *Book of Extracts* issued. Forerunner to QFP

1756 Pennsylvania – Quakers relinquish control

1761 LYM expels slave owners

1720–72 John Woolman

1748–1830 Elias Hicks

1772 Quaker involvement in anti Slavery movement

1774–1856 John Wilber

1783 1st printed edition *Book of Extracts*

1784 Women's YM in Britain

1779 Ackworth Quaker School

1793 Religious Society of Friends used for 1st time.

1796 The Retreat, York

Timeline 1800–1890

1800 1810 1820 1830 1840 1850 1860 1870 1880 1890

1820–30 George IV

1830–37 William IV

1837–1902 Victoria

1895 Marconi, wireless and telegraph

1879–1955 Einstein

1865 Lister, antiseptics in surgery

1876 Bell, telephone

1885 electric lighting

1885 Pasteur, inoculation

1890 1st London tube

1897 Freud begins analysis

1884 Fabian Society

1885 Women's Co-operative Guild

1892 Kier Hardie MP

1813 Davey's safety lamp

1846 Lister, 1st use of anaesthetic

1869 JS Mill *The Subjection of Women*

1866 Mendel, *Laws of Hereditary*

1871 *Descent of Man*, Darwin

1829 Stephenson's Rocket

1825 Darlington Stockton Railway

1840 Voyage of Beagle, Darwin

1859 *Origin of the Species*, Darwin

1861–65 American Civil War

1875 Booth and Salvation Army

1882 Married women's property Act

1831 Faraday, electricity

1833 Factory Act

1848 *Communist Manifesto*

1878 Women admitted to London university

1811–16 Luddite Riots

1819 Atlantic crossing steam ship

1833 Abolition of Slavery Act

1854–56 Crimean War

1866 Non conformists admitted to Oxford and Cambridge

1824 Trade Unions recognised

1807 Anti Slave Trade Act

1859 marriage to non members without penalty

1887 Richmond Declaration (US) Gurneyite.

1886 *The Gospel of Divine Help* Edward Wordsell

1895 Manchester Conference

1897 Scarborough Summer School

1896 YM open to women

1884 *A Reasonable Faith* critical of dogmatic evangelicalism

1868 Friends Foreign Mission Association founded

1869 Fritchley schism

1861 Revision of *Book of Discipline*

1852 Friends Temperance Union

1859 *Quakerism Past & Present*, JS Rowntree

1857 YM open to all Friends

1860 Peculiarities of dress and speech optional

1845 Wilbur/Gurney split

1845 Adult School Movement

1808 Sidcot School

1842 Sibford School

1823 Bootham School

1831 The Mount School

1813 Elizabeth Fry at Newgate Prison

1824 *Advices & Queries* LYM in present form

1827 Hicksite Separation US

1833 Friends admitted to Parliament. Joseph Pease 1st Quaker elected 1833–41

1836–1925 Joseph Rowntree

1839–1922 George Cadbury

1811–89 John Bright, Quaker Cabinet Minister

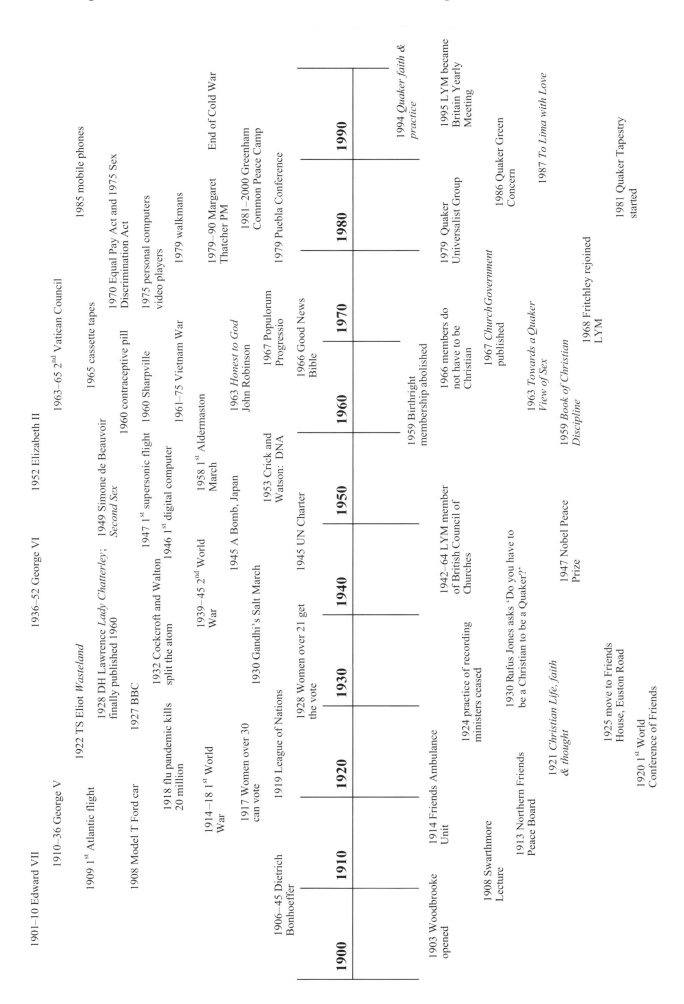

from 'An orientation to prophecy' by Marion McNaughton

Quakers as a prophetic community

As Quakers today we have inherited, from Judaism and then Christianity, a long prophetic tradition of richness and complexity and it is ours to use. So how are we choosing to respond to it? Today in the Quaker family we interpret prophecy in different ways, yet I believe there is an underlying unity in our practice, and if we understand our tradition as a whole, we can make this diversity a gift not a stumbling block. Here are some key elements:

- Quaker prophecy is the experience of the word of God, alive among us, directly felt and recognised. It can come out of silence, speech, scripture, song, however we worship, however we minister.

- There is always a message of some kind: enlightening, clarifying, demanding.

- The message is intended for us and for others. Who they are can be familiar, those in our meetings, or still unknown, those we reach out to. These are the tasks of teaching and mission.

- There can be both individual Quaker prophets and also prophetic Quaker communities. Both have their strengths and their limitations. Both can exist together.

- George Fox never felt he needed to verify his leadings, but noted that whenever he consulted scripture, he found them confirmed. After the fall of James Nayler, Friends came to understand that prophecy must be tested, and we do this today. Some of us confirm leadings by reference to scripture, others by reference to the collective discernment of the gathered meeting. But the leading from God always remains primary.

- Quaker prophecy today, as in the Hebrew tradition, has the same dual purpose, the same triangular relationship with God. To enlighten, nurture and extend the spiritual community. And also to speak truth to those in power, to take prophetic action, to press for change in the world.

- We can do both! We must do both! Both are holy. Abraham Heschel, a Jew, marched from Selma to Montgomery with Martin Luther King in 1965. It was a bloody, confrontational event, but it was for him a deeply spiritual occasion. When he returned, he told his daughter, 'I felt as if my legs were praying'.

There is a whole spectrum of prophetic possibility open to us, calling for our attention. Do we practise it all? Or do we settle for just a part, just one place on the spectrum? What does the Lord require of us? I see our diversity as an uncomfortable challenge that we hold out to each other, for all of us to be more than we are being at present. Some of us concentrate on silent waiting, some on proclamation, some on mission, some on social action. All of these things are part of the prophetic tradition, and none of us fulfils them all. So we serve as uncomfortable reminders and loving prompts to each other – Friend, is there something you are neglecting?

What kind of voice?

So what kind of Quaker prophetic voice is needed today? What will enable people to hear the voice of God? What will bring the changes we long to see?

Let us go back to Jeremiah* for a moment, prophesying for twenty three years without anyone listening to him. His name has been immortalised for this. The dictionary says:

> Jeremiah: someone who is pessimistic about the present and foresees a calamitous future; a person given to woeful lamentation and complaining.

Well, I don't know about you, but I find it incredibly hard to listen to someone filled with woeful lamentations and complaining, for twenty three minutes, let alone twenty three years. The Hebrew prophets were always ready to blame the people for refusing to hear the word of God. But I have to wonder, could it have been something to do with the way the word of God was being preached? Did the prophets fall into the trap of expressing their own frustration and anger? Did their own despairing voices sometimes speak louder than God's?

I was recently at a conference when a Friend who was deeply concerned about a matter of great spiritual importance, stood up and lectured us for a long time about how urgent this was, how we must all stop what we were doing and turn our energies to this one problem. We listened with sinking hearts. When he finished and sat down, the person next to me leaned across and whispered, 'This nagging has to stop!' This was not the response he had been hoping for.

How can we help each other from falling into this trap? Let us think for a moment of those self-appointed prophets we all turn away from. They are well-intentioned. But they drown us in their urgency and their fear. They make us feel guilty and inadequate. They blame us. They depress and immobilise us. They are doing their best but they are having no effect. This nagging has to stop.

If we want to bring the Kingdom of Heaven we must have insight, skills, compassion, abounding love, and methods that work. We must be people that

---

* Jeremiah 25:3 'For twenty three years...the word of the Lord has come to me, and I have spoken persistently to you, but you have not listened.'

fill other people with hope, not despair. It is no good being right for twenty three years if no-one is listening to us.

Effective prophecy energises and encourages people. It acknowledges their failures and inadequacies, but it doesn't blame – it comforts and consoles. It believes in people. It is an invitation to return to God. And because it is deeply rooted in God, it can bring others to God;s presence. Open Isaiah at chapter 40 and hear the unknown prophet we call Second Isaiah pour out love and consolation:

> Comfort ye, comfort ye my people, says your God. Speak tenderly to Jerusalem, and cry unto her that her warfare is accomplished, that her iniquity is pardoned.

This is a prophetic voice we can respond to. It lifts our hearts, it renews our strength, we can 'mount up with wings like eagles'.

So what do we need in prophecy that will enable people to hear the voice of God? It is very simple. Jean Leclerq, a Benedictine, has said:

> We must love the age we live in. From the point of view of faith, the best age for each of us is the one God has placed us in, the one he has given us, and which we must give back to him.

We must love the age we live in.

Sometimes this is very hard to do, but it is our task.

> If I speak in the tongues of mortals and of angels, but do not have love, I am a noisy gong or a clanging cymbal. And if I have prophetic powers, and understand all mysteries and all knowledge, and if I have all faith, so as to remove mountains, but do not have love, I am nothing.
>
> 1 Corinthians 13

Effective prophets work from a place of love. They nurture us, they inspire us to engage with our faith in deeper and deeper ways. We are inspired, we lead committed lives which return us always to our spiritual core. It is circular. Our outward lives are shaped from within, our actions bring us closer to God, and we live God's truth in the world.

Because whatever form it takes, prophecy is essentially mystical. God breaks through. The world is imperfect, but it is still wholly of God, wholly divine. The prophets are those who enable us to see that God is always available to us, the kingdom is always about us. Rosa Parks, one of my inspirations, one of the enablers of the American Civil Rights Movement, sat down in the middle of a bus and simply enacted the kingdom of heaven, a world of justice and equality. And God's voice was heard. One of the people sitting at the back, unable to move, said later, It was holy in that bus.

When we can prophesy with this kind of love, this kind of clarity, this kind of holiness, God's voice will be heard.

We have come a long way as a people of God. We have grown and changed. We have found new ways and held on to old ways. We are still gathered, waiting to hear God's voice, waiting for prophecy to flourish amongst us. We will hear God's voice again and again …saying familiar and comforting things, saying challenging and uncomfortable things. In love, let us listen with open hearts.

from 'Finding the prophetic voice for our time', Marion McNaughton and Lizz Roe, *The Woodbrooke Journal*, Autumn 2007, No 21

Extract for Distinctives 6:
Quaker faith in action – in it for the long run

Peace is not a dirty word

There has been a tendency for those of us in the peace education field to shy away from referring to it as such. In an effort to sell education for peace, we have packaged it to fit with the PSHE [Personal, Social and Health Education] and Citizenship agenda, calling it human rights, conflict resolution, anti-bullying... anything to make it less problematic for schools. Each of these is an element of educating children and young people to be peaceable, to appreciate the potential of conflict when handled creatively, and to celebrate difference. But, as we concluded at the last Peace Education Network (PEN) meeting, 'peace is not a dirty word'. I can't imagine that many would disagree with this. And yet, providing education for peace to schools can be so controversial.

Herein lies a quandary. Why is it that the concept of peace is so applauded, but working in a non-violent way to achieve it is suspect? Should we present our work in a way that will cause least offence and get us through the door of schools, or does this reinforce the reticence and infer that working for peace is somehow distasteful or, worse still, tantamount to indoctrination? Should we be upfront about our message even if this presents schools with a challenge and may reduce the direct work we are able to do?

I personally believe that education for peace is greater than the sum of its parts. It is not just about teaching children about their rights or putting on an Africa day where children learn that the continent exists and that they eat different food there. I believe that this pragmatic response to getting into schools actually compromises the tenets of what we are trying to achieve. I figure it's the approach taken that makes the difference between providing peace education and educating for peace.

I don't think it is possible to teach students that child-on-child bullying is wrong, without challenging bullying behaviour between teachers, parents and on the international stage. To try undermines our credibility and makes nonsense of what we are teaching. Equally, citizenship education must be about more than turning out young people who will vote every four years and won't speed or drop litter. It is about encouraging young people to look at the community and world they live in and question what they see.

I guess this is where the controversy comes in. But I work for the Religious Society of Friends, and Quakers generally don't have a problem with being viewed as controversial. Because of their involvement in, and position on, activities such as non-violent direct action, they have, collectively and individually, regularly been viewed as subversive over the years. *Quaker faith & practice* 24.11 advises, 'we should not automatically accept the categories, definitions and priorities of the world'.

Although not a Quaker myself, I chose to work for them because I am in sympathy with the beliefs and values they aspire to; values of truth, integrity and peace, which I believe are integral to education for peace. Quakers acknowledge the realities of conflict and of evil, but contend that war and violence are not effective means of dealing with them. Instead, they determine that we must 'wage peace', using tools which include 'speaking truth to power', and living and working as a 'witness' to these values. According to the Quaker way, how each individual undertakes this is for personal discernment.

So how do I relate all this to getting peace education into schools? To witness means not only telling, but demonstrating to children that truth and integrity are important in working for a more just society. And whilst 'speaking truth to power' usually refers to engaging with those who are central to political, economic and military decision-making to present an alternate worldview, I believe the concept can be similarly applied to the 'gatekeepers' in schools and LEAs.

The current fact-driven education system, with its emphasis on testing, creates an environment where structural violence is almost inevitable. This academic violence undermines our educational system and creates a generation of passive learners. Education should not inhibit children, it must teach them to think for themselves and empower them to learn for learning's sake, not simply to pass exams. Affecting the way in which children are educated is an integral part of educating for peace.

Education for peace is about identifying that young people have the power to change things they see as wrong in their community and more widely, as well as developing in them the imagination to find alternative responses to conflict. I believe that the means we employ to provide education for peace are indistinguishable from the content of the lessons. We must be uncompromising in presenting what we provide for school otherwise we compromise what we offer young people.

Jaci Smith,
Peace Education Advisor

This article was previously published in *DEA (Development Education Association) Journal*, October 2006.

Extract for Distinctives 6:
Quaker faith in action – in it for the long run

Uganda

Quaker Peace & Social Witness (QPSW) has been undertaking work and partnerships in Uganda since October 2000.

QPSW in Uganda

Based in Gulu District, the home of the Acholi people, QPSW's Uganda programme is committed to building a peace that will last.

Since 1986 the conflict between the Lord's Resistance Army and the Ugandan Government has continued to destroy the lives of the two million people living in the north of Uganda.

The majority of the population live in camps for displaced people, dependent on food aid and subject to the violent attacks of the LRA, including the regular abduction of children who are forced to join its ranks.

Peace but not peace

Since 2006 the Juba Peace talks have achieved an unprecedented series of agreements between the rebels and the Government of Uganda that set out steps for peace and development. While a 'final peace agreement' has not been achieved, the LRA is not currently active in Uganda and people are starting to move tentatively back to their village homes. The LRA remains unchecked, however, in the Democratic Republic of the Congo, where it continues to threaten the region's stability. Many abducted Ugandans remain within its ranks.

Our work

Coordinated from Friends House in London, a small team of QPSW staff supports local groups who are working towards a peaceful resolution of the brutal conflict. A current focus is the reintegration of the many formerly abducted children who have been able to escape from the LRA, and are returning to their communities. Part of this process involves seeking reconciliation between communities and those who have harmed them, in order that society might move into a well-founded future.

Empowering Hands

To contribute to this need, QPSW is working with Empowering Hands, a group of 30 girls who had been abducted or otherwise affected by the conflict, to help them explore their place in society, and encourage their peers through sharing their experiences on radio and through drama. EH's network of peer support groups is currently developing its work to reach those who are now moving away from the camps of displaced people. Their focus remains enabling those caught up in the conflict to develop trust in each other in a way that assists society to function better.

Justice and reconciliation project

In 2008 QPSW has published two pieces of research in partnership with the Justice and Reconciliation Projects, a local research-based group in Gulu. The findings of *With or Without Peace* and *Sharing the Burden* are helping to direct our own work and that of others in the field of re-integration.

Reflecting on peace

Working with the Mennonite Central Committee, QPSW is supporting a handful of key local peacebuilders to come together on a regular basis to reflect on their own approach to peace and its effectiveness. This group seeks to offer moral support at this difficult time in Uganda, as well as enabling new ideas and insights to be shared.

Civil society leaders

As a member of the Northern Uganda Advocacy Partnership for Peace (NUAPP) QPSW has supported a recent visit of civil society leaders from northern Uganda to the UK. The aim of the visit was to allow these local leaders to meet policy-makers and parliamentarians to bolster international support for the conflict's peaceful resolution. This visit included valuable time in Northern Ireland where the leaders met community representatives whose experience they see as comparable to their own.

Partnerships

Relationships are the bedrock of QPSW's approach in Uganda. Our work in northern Uganda is developed through ongoing communications with local groups and individuals seeking to build peace.

In the UK we are a member of NUAPP, a coalition of UK-based NGOs (NUAPP's current members are Christian Aid, Conciliation Resources, QPSW, Tearfund and World Vision). NUAPP exists to connect UK-based policy-makers with information and opinion from peacebuilders in northern Uganda in order to build UK and international support for a permanent peaceful resolution to the LRA conflict.

from Quaker Peace & Social Witness Uganda pages at:
www.quaker.org.uk

Extract for Discovery 1:
What do our Quaker roots mean to us?

'What does Quakerism mean to me?' by Deborah Rowlands

1. Roots

I was asked to take part in this presentation as 'a traditional Quaker'. I expect most of you know the quote from Samuel Bownas, a Quaker of the seventeenth century who was told:

> 'A traditional Quaker; thou comest to meeting as thou went from it, and goes from it as thou came to it but art no better for thy coming; what wilt thou do in the end?' I saw by experience wherein my shortness had been in being contented and easy with a form of truth and religion, which I had only by education ... but all this though very good in its place, did not make me a true Christian; I was but a traditional Quaker. (*Qf&p* 19.60, part)

Like Samuel, I got the Quaker habit early in life. Both my parents come from families whose Quaker roots go back to the seventeenth century – and then I married into the Rowlands family, which gave my children another different pile of Quaker antecedents to live down – or up – to.

My Quaker forbears didn't always have an easy time of it – more than one on both sides of the family were disowned for 'walking disorderly' in some way including fox hunting and teenage pregnancy. They were plain country Friends – grocers, weavers and manufacturers – not the great names of Quaker history. Doubtless, each in their turn struggled over their faith and how to live by it. This faithfulness, and the testing of it over the last three hundred and fifty years, is part of the experience the Society has to build on.

The picture is my grandmother, Laura Jane Moore – I think she has an even more worried look than me! She grew up in the 1880s when the Society was still strongly evangelical:

Heaven and Hell were ever present realities and entered into all the details of our lives. This made it extremely difficult for me, with my always thoughtful and logical mind. I might see a bird fly across the sky or a dog running along the road, and would wish I were that bird or dog so that I need not believe what seemed impossible.

Whilst still at school, she was reading *A reasonable faith*, one of the books that led up to the Manchester Conference of 1895, which is one of the turning points towards the liberal phase, which characterised the twentieth century.

The Quakerism that I grew up with saw itself as a natural part of the Christian Church. I have served Friends on national ecumenical bodies, but also, for the past ten years I have belonged to a local ecumenical fellowship that meets every month to read the Bible together, pray and share ideas about our faith. We have experienced times of deep sharing, despite very real differences of faith, and I have grown immeasurably through the gentle challenge of their strong convictions. It is natural for me to use the imagery and language of the Bible, and Quaker writing based on it, to express my understanding of the Spirit.

Like my grandmother, I have found Quakerism is a reasonable faith. I can bring into it my scientific and mathematical training, and my aesthetic, moral and emotional senses too; it accepts and uses all of me. Religion and Life are one, or neither is anything, said John Wilhelm Rowntree. The Spiritual Life is first of all a life, said Thomas Merton. Jesus calls us, not to a new religion but to Life, said Dietrich Bonhoeffer. Quakerism gives me a path for an integrated life, one that has wholeness; a spirituality that links inextricably the individual, how we are together as a Society, and what we do with our lives.

from *Quaker identity and the heart of our faith*, Quaker Life, 2008

Extract for Deepening 2:
A prayer reflecting on our Quaker roots and seeking
openness to new growth

Prayer by Margaret Benefiel

Oh God, we thank you for the great depth of the Quaker tradition.
...You have met us throughout our history, very deeply,
both as individuals and corporately.

As Sarah Jones admonished in 1650:
'Seek not the manifestations but that which manifests.'
We see how when we seek you, the source of the manifestations,
you meet us in a very deep place, and you transform us.
You transform us as individuals.
You transform our families.
You transform our meetings.

And God, as we allow you to do your transforming work in us,
and as we rely totally on you, not focusing on the manifestations,
you strip away what is not essential.
Sanctify us to be your vessels.
You also give us eyes to see through the manifestations
in the ocean of darkness
so that we can unmask the powers,
speak truth to power,
and allow you to do your powerful work in transforming society.

And God, as we seek to know what Quaker spirituality is,
we know that it is revealed in the lives of those who came before us,
and in our own lives.
We know that as we hear the stories of other Friends' walks with you,
as we let our stories be drawn out of us by Friends
who listen deeply to us
as we steep ourselves deeply in the stories,
we meet you.

And so, God, we give you thanks for people
like Sarah Jones, one of the earliest Quaker writers,
for George Fox,
for Margaret Fell,
for John Woolman,
for Catherine Phillips,
for John Wilbur,
for Lucretia Mott,

for Marjorie Sykes,
for Thomas Kelly,
for Simeon Shitemi,
for Elise Boulding,
for David Niyonzima,
all of whom at different times and places
have lived into what it means not to seek the manifestations,
but to seek that which manifests,
and to allow you to shape them and transform them
and work through them in the gathered community,
and in the world at large.

And God, when we ask the question,
'Is it important that there be a Quaker spirituality?'
we can only lay that one at your feet,
acknowledging that you have worked powerfully in the past,
you continue to work powerfully in the present,
and that if you want to continue to work through the Society of Friends,
you will show us that.
You will show us how.
You will keep us alive in the ways that you want us to be alive.

Please forgive us when we make idols of our forms,
when we make idols of our traditions.
Help us to continue to seek you anew,
each day,
in each time and place in which we find ourselves,
in each culture,
in each transformation which goes on in our society.
We know that Quaker spirituality is only worth something
when it is the continual new life breathed by your Spirit.
Help us let go of forms and structures that have served us well in
     the past
when they no longer serve us now,
when they no longer serve your purposes.

Help us come to you with that radical trust
that you will lead us into what we need
for our time,
for our place,
for the future.
We confess that we too often get into ruts
and we focus on the manifestations instead of that which manifests.
We think that the particular committee structure we have at our
     meeting,
the particular way that our worship flows,
is the only way
or the best way.

Soften our hearts to be aware of your nudges
as you breathe life into some of the forms that we have
and as you invite us to let go of
other forms we've been using
and move into something new.
God, as we seek to be faithful Quakers,
to learn from our own tradition
and to learn from other traditions,
we pray that you will help us to go deeply
into our own tradition
and to courageously encounter ourselves and one another at those
     deep places.

As we read journals and letters and epistles,
and listen for that place where words come from,
as we go deeply into our own tradition
and encounter other Friends' relationships with you;
The more deeply we go there,
the more deeply we will be able to receive
what other traditions have to offer us.
We will be able to connect with the deep stories of those traditions
     as well.

So give us the courage not to stay on the surface
and sample just a little bit of everything,
but to plunge into the depth of our particular path,
and then experience the deep connections
that will lead us to [friendship] with other traditions.

We know, God, that we're at a time in the history of our world
when the transformative power that early Friends experienced
and that Friends throughout the centuries have experienced,
is greatly needed.
And God, we offer ourselves to you,
to be available for you to work in us in those ways,
in those same ways that you have worked in Friends of old.

We want to be vessels
who are completely available to you.
So please give us the courage and openness
to give ourselves completely to you,
and to see what will happen when we let your power work through us.
Thank you, God.
Amen

Experiencing Quaker Community

Introducing the ways that Quaker meetings are organised, nurtured and led

This unit invites you to find out more about the Quaker experience of being a Spirit-led community. This distinctive understanding and approach to community is evident in our local and national structures, how we run and nurture our meetings, and the Quaker way of doing business and making decisions.

 Experiencing Quaker Community unit aims

This unit aims to help you:

- become more familiar with the ways that Quaker meetings are organised and led

- understand how we live out our commitment to one another and nurture our community as Quakers

- explore your own response to experiencing community with Quakers

Overview

The Quaker approach to community invites each of us to live up to our unique potential, while learning to go beyond the boundaries of our own small selves as part of our commitment to one another. This is a profoundly counter-cultural approach and it is at the heart of the Quaker way. Early Quaker Isaac Pennington described the experience of community among Quakers in this way:

> Our life is love, and peace, and tenderness; bearing one with another, and forgiving one another, and not laying accusations one against another; but praying for one another, and helping one another up with a tender hand.
>
> *Quaker faith & practice* 10.01

Of course, Quaker meetings are in no way perfect as communities. We often fail to live up to Isaac Pennington's description, and experience our human inadequacy and brokenness. As members of the Religious Society of Friends, however, we continually renew a commitment to trusting in something greater than us as individuals: our community embodies, however imperfectly, Divine love at work in the world. Quakers have developed traditions of spiritual hospitality and nurture to promote a healthy community and to deal with conflicts when they do arise. These include our system of pastoral care under the guidance of elders and overseers, and specific tools for addressing concerns such as meetings for clearness and threshing meetings (see Distinctives 1 for more on these).

Our way of making decisions reflects the Quaker understanding that the Spirit is at work in our community. Our business meetings are also meetings for worship based on silence, and they carry the same expectation that

> God's guidance can be discerned if we are truly listening together and to each other, and are not blinkered by preconceived opinions. It is this belief that God's will can be recognised through the discipline of silent waiting which distinguishes our decision-making from the secular idea of consensus.
>
> *Quaker faith & practice* 3.02

This process of waiting for the guidance of the Spirit involves learning to let go of our own personal agendas and allow decisions to be 'discerned' rather than voted on, argued about or pushed through. In the words of John Punshon, 'the meeting for business cannot be understood in isolation; it is part of a spiritual discipline.' (*Quaker faith & practice* 2.85).

Quakers do not have ordained ministers, so we all share responsibility for the wellbeing of our meetings. However, certain roles such as elders, overseers and clerks are filled by Friends for specific periods of time to ensure that our communities are effectively led, organised and nurtured. For Quakers,

> to be without an ordained clergy is not to be without either leadership or ministry. The gifts of the Spirit to us include both. For us, calls to particular ministries are usually for a limited period of time, and those gifts pertain to the task rather than the person. In one lifetime a person may be called to a number of ministries.
>
> *Quaker faith & practice* 12.02

'Ministry' may involve being asked to serve in a particular role such as elder, or it may be very different: we all have gifts and all minister to one another. For some Friends their ministry may involve working with children and young people, while for others it may be providing a warm welcome for visitors, working on the meeting house garden or introducing Quakerism to enquirers through outreach activities such as Quaker Quest or Quaker Week.

Quakers are part of a community that goes beyond the local meeting. Although the local meeting community is probably the first point of contact for most Friends and is where we attend meeting for worship, our membership is actually of our area meeting. The area meeting covers something like a county or city and is made up of several local meetings. In Britain, 'Britain Yearly Meeting' is the name of the national body to which all area meetings belong, and is the final constitutional authority of the Religious Society of Friends in England, Scotland, Wales, the Channel Islands and the Isle of Man. A yearly meeting is a forum for working out the ministry and witness of Quakers in the wider world; it is also an annual assembly of Quakers to which all are welcome, where worship, work and fellowship are shared by the national community of Friends.

Quaker distinctives

Distinctives 1

The healthy Quaker meeting

There is guidance about how Quakers try to nurture our communities in *Quaker faith & practice*: in *Advices & queries* 17–22, which is in section 1.02; in section 12.01; and in the introduction to chapter 12, 'Caring for one another', If you prefer listening to the *Advices & queries*, there are mp3 audio files of them available in this unit of the online Becoming Friends course.

You might also like to watch the video 'An Introduction to Quakers' in which Quakers discuss their experience of community, among other themes. You can access the video in a number of different ways:

- online at
  - › www.watfordquakers.org.uk/videos.html
  - › www.quakerweek.org.uk/intro/quaker-worship
  - › www.youtube.com as 'Introduction to Quakers'

- on the DVD *An introduction to Watford Quakers*, available from the Quaker Centre bookshop (see Further exploration for contact details).

To find out more about specific Quaker discernment and support methods, you could read the following sections of *Quaker faith & practice*:

- meetings for clearness: *Qf&p* 12.22–12.25

- threshing meetings: *Qf&p* 12.26

- support groups: *Qf&p* 12.27

- guidance if you have a particular concern: *Qf&p* 13.08
  - › for more about 'concerns', see the Faith in Action unit

Distinctives 2

Local, area and national Quaker structures

These structures fulfil different roles but are all interrelated. They changed in 2007, so copies of *Quaker faith & practice* earlier than the fourth edition will not reflect current arrangements.

You might like to look at two diagrams giving an overview of the relationships between the different Quaker structures. You'll find these diagrams on pages 108–109.

You could read the following sections of *Quaker faith & practice* online, or in the fourth edition book, for an introduction to the roles of different meetings:

- local meetings: *Qf&p* 4.33

- area meetings: *Qf&p* 4.01–4.02

- Yearly Meeting: *Qf&p* 6.04–6.05
  - ➤ Yearly Meeting history: *Qf&p* 6.01

- Junior Yearly Meeting: *Qf&p* 4.21

- Meeting for Sufferings: *Qf&p* 7.02

- centrally managed work: *Qf&p* 8.02
  - ➤ more about the four central committees: *Qf&p* 8.08–8.11

Distinctives 3

The Quaker business method and decision-making

The Quaker Life leaflet 'How Quaker meetings take decisions' gives a clear overview of this process. You'll find the text of this leaflet on pages 110–112.

You could also read the helpful introduction to Quaker decision-making on the Scottish Quaker website: www.quakerscotland.org/businessmeetings

You might like to watch the video 'Who's in charge and how are decisions made?' made by Friends at Watford Quaker Meeting about the Quaker approach to decision-making. You can access the video in a number of different ways:

- online at
  - ➤ www.watfordquakers.org.uk/videos.html
  - ➤ www.youtube.com as 'Who's in charge and how are decisions made?'

- on the DVD *An introduction to Watford Quakers*, available from the Quaker Centre bookshop (see Further exploration for contact details).

Distinctives 4

Elders, overseers and clerks

You could read the following sections of *Quaker faith & practice* to find out about the roles of elders, overseers and clerks in our meetings, and the nominations process by which they are appointed:

- elders and overseers: *Qf&p* 12.11
- elders: *Qf&p* 12.12
- overseers: *Qf&p* 12.13
- clerks: *Qf&p* 3.12
- nominations process: *Qf&p* 3.23

Distinctives 5

How do Quakers approach ministry?

Section 10.05 of *Quaker faith & practice* discusses the Quaker understanding of ministry (other than spoken ministry in meeting for worship – see Silence and Waiting unit for more on this).

You might also like to listen to or read about Quakers' experiences of ministry:

- there are audio clips about ministry on the Becoming Friends online course
- you'll find these extracts on pages 113–114

Distinctives 6

Children and young people in Quaker communities

Quakers seek to ensure that children and young people are welcome and integrated into Quaker meetings. The following sections of *Quaker faith & practice* talk about how Quakers try to do this:

- *Advices & queries* 19: Qf&p 1.02
- taking the nurture of children seriously: *Qf&p* 10.10
- a baby in meeting: *Qf&p* 2.50
- children as respected community members: *Qf&p* 2.75
- Junior Yearly Meeting as community: *Qf&p* 21.06

See also Discovery 5 for more about children and young people.

Discovery

Discovery 1

What's Yearly Meeting like?

To find out more about national Quaker gatherings and structures, you could ask your Becoming Friends companion to arrange for you to talk to a Friend with experience of any of these:

- Yearly Meeting

- Junior Yearly Meeting or other events for young people

- a national Quaker conference

- Quaker Life: Central Committee or Representative Council

- Summer Gathering

You might ask the Friend what the gathering was like – how was it organised and how was community nurtured? What did they find enjoyable or challenging about the experience?

You could also join in a discussion about experiences of national Quaker gatherings on a Quaker discussion forum:

- the Britain Yearly Meeting forum at: www.quakerweb.org.uk/forum

- www.friendlink.org.uk (aimed mainly at young Quakers)

- the Experiencing Quaker Community unit forum

Discovery 2

Exploring membership and belonging

How do we come to feel a sense of belonging, or come to consider applying for membership as Friends? Harvey Gillman considers these questions in 'Reflections on membership and belonging'. You'll find this article on pages 115–117.

You could also look at editions 25 and 26 of *Journeys in the Spirit* (a resource for Friends working with children and young people), which are about 'belonging and joining'. Read through the materials and try out any of the activities that interest you – sometimes activities aimed at young people work very well for adults too! *Journeys in the Spirit* is available

- in many meeting house libraries (ask your librarian)

- online at: www.quaker.org.uk/journeyschild

- from Quaker Life
  Email: ql@quaker.org.uk
  Tel: 020 7663 1013

Discovery 3

How have local Friends experienced their role as elder, overseer or clerk?

Ask your Becoming Friends companion, or another experienced Friend in your area, about their experience in the role of elder, overseer or clerk.

- What was this experience like?

- What were the main responsibilities of the role?

- Did they receive any training or support?

- Were there aspects of this service that were a particular challenge or joy?

Discovery 4

What are Quaker business meetings really like?

Why not arrange to attend a Quaker business meeting in your local area? Your Becoming Friends companion can help with this and explain local procedures. You could discuss your experience afterwards with your companion or other experienced Friends – use some of the questions below if they are helpful.

You might also ask your Becoming Friends companion to help you set up a small group session to explore local Friends' experience of Quaker decision-making and our business method: you could use the questions below as starting points for discussion.

- Do your business meetings seem to you like meeting for worship?

- Do you seek to discern the will of God for the meeting as a whole?

- Have you experienced occasions when a decision has been reached that really felt Spirit-led, or otherwise?

- Are you listening to the Spirit speaking through human beings and to the response of those who listen?

- When the meeting moves towards a decision with which you are not in sympathy, do you accept this with good grace?

Discovery 5

What's going on for children and young people locally and nationally?

You could ask to discuss this locally with an overseer or other person with responsibility for children and young people in your meeting (your Becoming Friends companion can help arrange this).

- What provision is made for children and young people in your meeting?

- How well are they integrated into the life of the meeting?

- Are their insights and energy welcomed in the meeting?

- In what ways do they challenge Friends locally to renew their commitment to worship and action?

To find out what is going on at a national level, you could explore:

- the pages about working with children and young people at: www.quaker.org.uk/cyp

- the Young Quaker Space website at: www.yqspace.org.uk

Discovery 6

How is my local meeting nurtured ?

Ask your Becoming Friends companion, or another experienced Friend, about spiritual hospitality and nurture in your local meeting, and how Friends promote the health of the meeting community. You could ask:

- What efforts does the meeting make to grow closer as a community?

- Are there ways for Friends locally to share their joys and concerns, and those things in their inner life which matter most to them?

- What activities has the meeting used for fostering friendship in the meeting?

- How does the meeting deal with difficulties or conflicts when they arise?

- How do Friends locally minister to one another outside meeting for worship?

Deepening

Deepening 1

Your own sense of ministry

What gifts do you have? Do you experience a sense of calling to any particular ministry? Section 2.66 of *Quaker faith & practice* speaks about ministry.

Perhaps you would like to spend time reflecting on the questions this raises for you.

- You might like to use the 'ministry cards' on pages 118–120 to reflect on your own sense of ministry. Cut the cards out and try moving them around on a table or the floor: are there any which speak to you, either in a positive or negative way?

- You could also reflect on ministry with your Becoming Friends companion when you next meet.

Deepening 2

Your own experience of community

A healthy community is a place of growth, through both the nurture and the challenge we experience within it. Section 10.19 of *Quaker faith & practice* speaks of the challenge of community.

- Does this reflect your own experience?

- How have you been shaped by your experience of community, either with Quakers or other people?

- What gifts or challenges do you bring to your local Quaker community?

You could also reflect on this with your Becoming Friends companion when you next meet.

Deepening 3

Responding creatively to the experience of community

The Quaker way of experiencing community includes the invitation to:

- let go of our own agendas and desired outcomes

- allow ourselves to be upheld, even prayed for, by others

- hear the truth, even when it is uncomfortable for us.

You might like to take some time to reflect deeply on your own response to these invitations. You could:

- respond by drawing, painting or using another creative method

- respond in music, song or movement

- respond in writing

- go online and blog about your response

- discuss your response on a Quaker discussion forum:
  - the Britain Yearly Meeting forum at: www.quakerweb.org.uk/forum
  - www.friendlink.org.uk (aimed mainly at young Quakers)
  - the Experiencing Quaker Community unit forum

- share some of your reflections with your Becoming Friends companion when you next meet.

Deepening 4

Learning to listen as spiritual friendship

Learning to listen to one another at a deep level is central to the experience of spiritual friendship and discernment at the heart of our Quaker community life. You could try an exercise in deep, prayerful listening with your Becoming Friends companion, or ask someone else you feel drawn to do this with.

You'll find the listening prayer practice on page 268.

You could use one of the example focus questions given in the exercise:

- 'In what ways have you experienced God in your life during the last week?

- 'What has been going on in your prayer life this month?'

or use one that asks about community, such as:

- 'Is there a time when you have felt truly upheld and cared for in a community or group situation?'

or use a question of your own.

You may wish to reflect on how you have got on with this exercise at a future meeting with your Becoming Friends companion.

Deepening 5

Reflecting on your local Quaker community

You might like to spend time on your own or with your Becoming Friends companion reflecting on your response to any of the following questions:

- How are you feeling upheld by your local Quaker meeting?

- Do you have an awareness of the other members of the local Quaker community?

- Do you have a growing awareness of the contribution you already make to sustaining the quality and depth of worship and community in your local meeting?

Further exploration

If you would like to explore the subject of Quaker community, decision-making and structures further, here are some suggestions for reading, listening or viewing.

Advices & queries 14–15 and 17–22, in *Quaker faith & practice* 1.02.

Beyond consensus: salvaging sense of the meeting, Barry Morley, Pendle Hill Pamphlets 307. This is included in the *Hearts and minds prepared* pack.

Beyond majority rule: voteless decisions in the Religious Society of Friends, Michael Sheeran, Philadelphia Yearly Meeting, 1983.

An introduction to Watford Quakers (DVD), part 1 'An Introduction to Quakerism', Just Film, 2007. Also available at: www.watfordquakers.org.uk/videos.html or www.quakerweek.org.uk/intro (or at: www.youtube.com as 'Introduction to Quakers').

A light that is shining: an introduction to the Quakers, Harvey Gillman, Quaker Books, 2003.

Listening spirituality 2: corporate spiritual practice among Friends, Patricia Loring, Openings Press, 1997.

Quaker faith & practice 2.88–2.91, spirit of worship in decision-making.

Quaker faith & practice, chapter 3, 'General counsel on church affairs', especially sections 3.02–3.07 – decision-making and 'sense of the meeting'.

Quaker faith & practice, chapter 10, 'Belonging to a Quaker meeting'.

Quaker faith & practice, chapter 12, 'Caring for one another'.

Quaker speak, Alastair Heron, Quaker Outreach in Yorkshire, 2003.

Quality and depth of worship and ministry, Committee on Eldership and Oversight, Quaker Books, 2001.

Scottish Quaker website: www.quakerscotland.org/businessmeetings

Woodbrooke's website or brochure for details of courses about nurturing our meetings and training for Quaker roles: www.woodbrooke.org.uk

Many of these titles are available from the Quaker Centre bookshop:

Friends House
173 Euston Road
London NW1 2BJ

Tel: 020 7663 1030
Fax: 020 7663 1001

Website: www.quaker.org.uk/bookshop
Email: quakercentre@quaker.org.uk

Many of them will also be in your local meeting house library. You could ask your Becoming Friends companion to help you track down titles that interest you.

Closing activity

As you finish your exploration of the Quaker experience of community, you are invited to reflect on what you have gained through this unit, how your understanding of both yourself and Quakerism has changed, and what areas you would like to explore further.

This closing reflection can be a very good opportunity for sharing with your Becoming Friends companion, or you may prefer to write in a journal or book of spiritual discipline (there's guidance for journalling in Appendix 2 – Guidance on page 282), or to reflect using creative methods such as drawing, collage, model-making or working with materials such as textiles or wood.

You might use one or more of the following questions as a focus for your reflection:

- What have you gained from your work on this unit, whether as a result of positive or more challenging experiences?

- In what ways has your understanding changed as a result of your work on this unit?

- Are there areas that you would like to explore further – either as part of your own spiritual journey or relating to Quakerism?

- Has anything arisen that you would find it helpful to reflect on with your Becoming Friends companion?

for Distinctives 2:
Local, area and national Quaker structures

local meetings (2–19 per area meeting)
the first place of belonging for most Quakers

area meetings (about 70 in BYM)
the focus for membership and primary
authority

**regional gatherings and general
meetings** (not in all areas)
support life and witness of Quakers in their
area

Britain Yearly Meeting
holds the ultimate authority for Quakers in
Britain

**Friends World Committee for
Consultation**
a channel of communication and support
between Quakers worldwide

for Distinctives 2:
Local, area and national Quaker structures

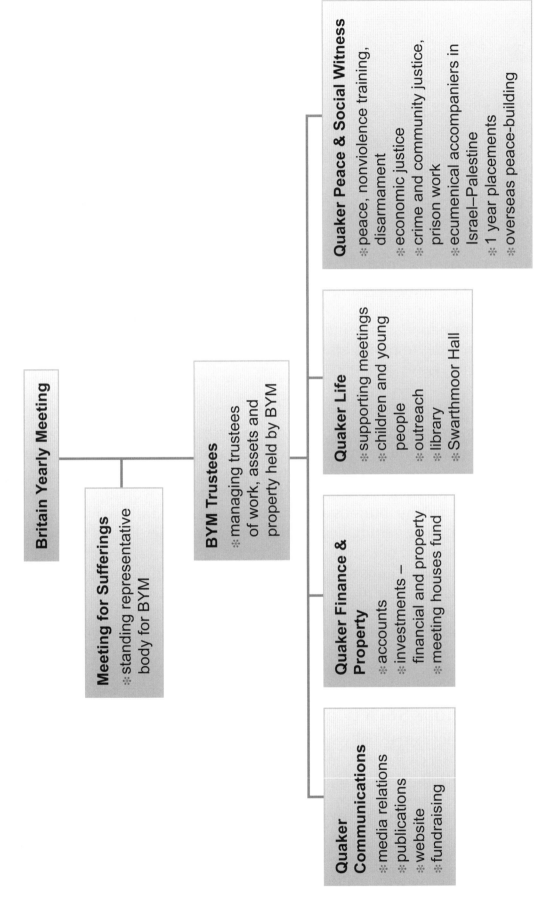

Britain Yearly Meeting

Meeting for Sufferings
* standing representative body for BYM

BYM Trustees
* managing trustees of work, assets and property held by BYM

Quaker Peace & Social Witness
* peace, nonviolence training, disarmament
* economic justice
* crime and community justice, prison work
* ecumenical accompaniers in Israel–Palestine
* 1 year placements
* overseas peace-building

Quaker Life
* supporting meetings
* children and young people
* outreach
* library
* Swarthmoor Hall

Quaker Finance & Property
* accounts
* investments – financial and property
* meeting houses fund

Quaker Communications
* media relations
* publications
* website
* fundraising

Extract for Distinctives 3:
The Quaker business method and decision-making

The following is the text of a leaflet published by Quaker Life.

How Quaker meetings take decisions

This is intended as both a guide for newcomers and a helpful reminder to more experienced Friends.

What's special about a Quaker business meeting?

A Quaker business meeting is essentially a meeting for worship, except that it has a pre-arranged agenda. Whether it be a working party, a committee, a local, regional or national meeting, the process is the same: Friends coming together in silence in order to draw closer to God and each other, and to seek the guidance of the Inward Light.

What's going on in the meeting?

A meeting starts with a period of quiet worship. The clerk then opens the business part of the meeting. As in a secular meeting, someone presents an item, and answers questions of clarification. But rather than debating the matter, the gathering then tries to discern, in an atmosphere of worship, what love requires of us. Spoken contributions are offered as ministry and are wrapped in silence. If things seem to be getting heated, the clerk or another Friend may ask for a period of silence. A touch of humour often helps the process. No vote is taken, as we are not trying to reach consensus or establish the will of the majority, but to work in harmony with the Spirit. This approach can be very liberating, because it ensures that minority views are not dismissed or suppressed. A minute is drafted by the clerk and presented to the meeting; it is for all those present to agree the record of their deliberations.

Can I come to a business meeting if I am not a member of the Religious Society of Friends?

Yes – attenders are usually welcome to attend open business meetings. You will need to let the clerk know in advance that you would like to come. You may be asked to withdraw for certain agenda items.

What is my role in the meeting?

As in any meeting for worship, your primary role is to listen respectfully to others and to 'the promptings of love and truth in your heart'. Even if you disagree strongly with another contribution, listen patiently to each to learn what you can, trusting that you will be heard in the same spirit. It is helpful if you prepare beforehand, read the papers and reflect prayerfully on the business, but remember that responsibility for the outcome belongs to the meeting as a whole, not to any individual. Come to the meeting with heart and mind prepared – not heart and mind made up.

What is the clerk doing?

The clerk is rather like a cross between a chair and a secretary. Clerks prepare the agenda, do the necessary administration and guide the meeting through the items of business. The clerk has to try and discern the outcome of each item (often called 'the sense of the meeting'), and to prepare a draft minute to lay before the gathering. Although it is the meeting that is really in charge, clerks carry a lot of responsibility. We need to support them and do all we can to avoid making their job more difficult by holding private conversations while a minute is being drafted, for instance, or by quibbling over a good-enough minute.

Who can speak, and how often?

Once an item on the agenda has been introduced to the meeting anyone may speak, but remember, this is a meeting for worship. If you feel led to minister, test your prompting first. Equally, don't let shyness or a sense of unworthiness hold you back – you have a responsibility to help the meeting by sharing any relevant insight or information you may have. In formal meetings it is the practice to stand and wait to be called by the clerk; if another Friend is called or the clerk stands, you should sit down again. There is no need to repeat a point which has already been made, or to speak twice to the same matter unless asked to do so. Try to resist the temptation to be argumentative. The point is not to win an argument but to uphold our community as we work together for a better world.

Are minor matters dealt with differently from main items?

Some matters may be complex or controversial, and a wide range of views will need to be expressed. It may take more than one meeting to find unity; a rushed decision driven by the clock may well turn out to be unsatisfactory. Other matters will be routine or minor or relatively straightforward, so that they can be swiftly dealt with. Though the process remains the same, it is not necessary to consider every item at great length or in deep solemnity. That said, a matter that looks routine beforehand sometimes turns out to raise unforeseen controversy!

What if I don't agree with the minute?

If you feel the minute doesn't reflect the sense of the meeting, or is badly worded, there will be an opportunity to comment after the draft minute is presented. If you don't agree with the decision reached, try to set aside your disappointment and accept that the decision has nevertheless been reached collectively through the discipline of waiting together in the Light, in a sincere search for love and truth. The right decision is important, but no more so than reaching it by the right process – a process in which you played your full part. Remember that unity is not the same as unanimity. You may need to continue reflecting on the matter and talking it over with other Friends. Sometimes, at a subsequent meeting, it becomes clear to the meeting that a new direction is needed.

Isn't all this asking too much of people?

The discipline we have laid upon ourselves is a demanding one. Quakers are human, not saints. A more experienced or self-confident Friend may drown out a quieter voice that the meeting needed to hear. Strong feelings on an issue may make some Friends intolerant or even aggressive. But it is worth struggling with the challenge, for when the process works the reward is a powerful sense of rightness and unity.

Further reading:

Quaker faith & practice, chapter 3

Barry Morley, *Beyond consensus: salvaging sense of the meeting*

Patricia Loring, *Listening spirituality*

Michael Sheeran, *Beyond majority rule*

Further copies of this leaflet and information about the Religious Society of Friends (Quakers) may be obtained from:

> Quaker Life
> Friends House
> 173 Euston Road
> London NW1 2BJ
>
> Email: ql@quaker.org.uk
> Tel: 020 7663 1140

It is also on the website:
www.quaker.org.uk/how-quaker-meetings-take-decisions

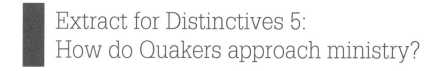

Extract for Distinctives 5:
How do Quakers approach ministry?

Ministry extracts

Friend 1

My ministry as a Quaker concerns how I live my life, sustain relationships and try to be open to the Light. In my local meeting it involves supporting the clerk, coming up with ideas and seeing them through if the meeting says that's what they'd like, and bringing some cheer in individual relationships as well as in business meeting. Currently skills I have which Friends are making use of include clerking a trustee body, line-managing a senior member of staff, and keeping the area meeting paperwork under control during a hiatus in finding clerks. I notice that some people in meeting really appreciate ordinary friendship: a postcard when I'm away, a phone call when I've missed seeing them. I also notice that this releases in them reciprocal signs of friendship which I find builds the feeling of Friends as a community. I feel very fortunate that retirement gives me availability for more actions which I regard as ministry. These actions are giving and receiving: the blessing of receiving ministry is as important to me as the giving of ministry.

Friend 2

I have come to experience all of my life as Quaker ministry, including the times that I do not live up to the Light, and maybe especially those times. The 'Equipping for Ministry' course has taught me that the most important thing is commitment to obeying the Light. I continue to feel called to be here in this city as manager of this meeting house but have begun to see that the task is to be myself in this place.

One of the other things that has become more important to me as a ministry is to uphold and love in prayer those Friends I have come to know in a deep spiritual way as kindred spirits. I have a sense that it is the manifestation of the Spirit within that person that I am called to help grow and that it will happen, perhaps in spite of me!

Silence, time alone and deep listening are increasingly important for my inner wellbeing. I have also begun to understand and experience decision-making in a different way. I need time now for decisions to be properly discerned otherwise they are likely to have consequences that I have not thought through and are wrong. It seems strange to talk about daily discernment as a ministry. But I come back to where I started: all of a committed life is ministry.

Friend 3

I wake up in the morning and consider the day ahead, the things I must do. Whether it is housework, or looking after guests, or visiting prison, or shopping for an elderly Friend, or spending leisure time with my husband, or talking to young offenders – whatever my activities, these I consider to be my ministry, the work God has given me to do that day, and I pray that I may do it well, with God's help. The 'Equipping for Ministry' course enabled me to form a daily spiritual practice which allows me to do this.

Friend 4

I think the only way I minister outside meeting for worship is the voluntary work I do at Claridge House* and the meeting for healing I have at my home once a month. My poor health makes it difficult for me to do much for other people on a more personal basis. However, the work that is being done at Claridge House is really important as it enables people to have time for rest and relaxation which gives them an opportunity to take stock of their lives. So, although it is only a small contribution I am able to give, it does help.

Friend 5

(who is based in Russia and travels among Friends as part of his ministry)

One of Friends House Moscow's roles is as a resource to the Russian-speaking world. Seekers come onto our website forum and ask deep, difficult questions! BYM's Quaker faith and practice is being translated into Russian and gets posted there as sections are completed and then the discussion takes place on finding the right words to capture the meaning and then discussion of the meaning itself! Of course you cannot beat face-to-face encounters and so sometimes we travel. The advantage of Russia being so big is that it takes time to get there, and this helps to have heart and mind prepared, especially if you are on a train for a couple of days.

Two particular delights stand out in my memory: a Quaker wedding in Kazan in the worst blizzard for years; and holding a membership interview in Siberia in springtime. And you can't rush these precious personal sharings. Sergei and I spent a long weekend in Altai province high up in the mountains near the Chinese border. He got married at Friday lunchtime and in the evening, with his bride, we caught a plane to go and see Vadim. Travelling in the ministry brings untold pleasures but none more so than the intimate sharing of spiritual journeys and rites of passage.

---

*   Claridge House is a Quaker centre for healing, rest and renewal, associated with the Friends Fellowship of Healing.

Extract for Discovery 2:
Exploring membership and belonging

Reflections on membership and belonging

As a spiritual nomad who has pitched his tent amongst Friends, I am fascinated by the issue of membership. To some this is a theological issue, to others a social one, to yet others, a psychological question. What am I joining (and why not); why, how; and what is the meaning of the step anyway? These are some of the questions attenders may ask themselves when membership is raised.

Recently, in a meeting for clearness for someone contemplating joining Friends, it came to me in the silence that there were at least four concerns that might beset anyone reflecting on this. I shall put them in terms of four polarities (or paradoxes): exploring/finding; inner/outer membership; acknowledging the real/aspiring to the ideal; and giving to/taking from the life of the meeting. A fifth paradox occurs to me as I write this: leaving behind/taking up. And there is something else which unites all these concerns.

Friends in Britain Yearly Meeting do not see membership in terms of salvation, although we might say that in a sense we are saved from isolation into community. We do not equate membership with having found the truth. We do not proclaim that here alone truth may be found. For me membership has been a matter of finding a milieu in which exploration is validated, where finding is rejoiced in, and where not finding is accepted as part of the journey – even losing is not seen as a disaster. We find because we have explored; we explore because we have found. What I have explored and found is relationship with fellow seekers and with that power to which, symbolically, I give the name God or Spirit. This is usually expressed as discipleship. We are learners, sometimes humble, in the school of Christ.

To be alive is to be on a spiritual journey as we seek for connection, meaning, and ways of being and acting in the world. Why then limit as it were this spirituality to membership of one group? If being alive and being self-aware were sufficient for deepening one's participation in the family of God, why then the need to make public something which is already present, why make outer what is already inner? And if one is already committed to the Quaker way, why the need to put a name on a list to prove it? Again to write personally, I have found in my own life that I cannot split the inner from the outer. Indeed the division seems to me to be an artefact of the mind. Where does the inner end and the outer begin? Membership among Friends seems to me to be more about making a public commitment. Just as in a relationship, we know that a public ceremony is a statement both of present joy and future commitment, with change as an inevitable part of human existence, so it seems to me that membership is an outer ratification of a state of being and of growing. However being committed to one person does not deny friendship to others. We belong to the universal by being part of the small local scene. It is hard to embrace the whole of creation if you have difficulty with the small patch of soil on which you are standing. For me, being a Friend is a way into being a mature human being. Being mature is something about acceptance of self and an awareness of the needs of self for interconnectedness.

This leads me to the real/ideal polarity. I once met someone who told me that he had no partner because no one was ever good enough. With that sort of desire for perfection, he probably never would. The contemporary flight from membership of all sorts is partly a result of our disenchantment with the religious and political ideals that have been held out before us and have led to the mass destruction and oppressions of the twentieth century. We do not want to be hurt again. But there is a time when we may realise that the neurotic pursuit of ideals is harmful, that elements of beauty and truth may still be found in the details of existence, that maturity is, in the lovely words of the American Quaker John Jungblut, a hallowing of our diminishments. Most of us have experienced the irritations of church politics even among Friends; we have heard and seen behaviour that is not Quakerly; we have most of us been disappointed to find bigotry and unkindness amongst those we worship with. For me my association with Friends has led me to expect less and hope for more. In spite of my vexations, I still want to remain part of the human race; in spite of what I find an intense self-introspection among Friends (of which no doubt I am a part), I still feel I want to proclaim my membership to this small band of travellers. And I cannot live out my life in reaction to the hurts of the past.

For some, membership of Friends is about 'having made it'. Indeed there is something in the history of Friends which suggests membership is a recognition of virtue: a church of the saved, not of the sinners. No wonder our perfectionism has led several people to talk about not being good enough. And then to realise that you do not have time to commit to this and that committee or group or go to this place or that meeting adds to the sense of guilt. I know people who have resigned from Friends because they have felt guilty about not having time for the organisation. There are times in our lives when we have time; there are times when we need to take and times when we can give. Such is the dilemma of being human. Membership is about aspiration and turning to the light; it is surely not about getting everything right.

The fifth of the dilemmas may be seen in terms of leaving behind/taking up. In the evangelical schema of salvation the wicked self is put aside in the new life in Christ. I would prefer to talk of the self being transcended, transformed, but not dismissed. We are all we have been; we are the result of all those we have met. Our path is made up of lots of side roads, diversions, ends which seemed to be dead but which have brought us to new life. There is much in my own life I am sorry for, ashamed of, but I am where I am because of having been there, and having become aware (more or less) of what I have done. I have to accept my past journey, even repent of parts of it, but not let the future be bound by it.

In conclusion it seems to me that membership is about grace and forgiveness; about hope and about accepting reality. About worshipping together and being vulnerable together. It is fraught with dangers, not least the one which makes people see you in a false light – no, I am not a bible-basher; a fundamentalist; a wearer of a broad brim hat; a virtuous paragon; an exemplar of minimalist frugality. I am a human being who reaches out to others and to the Spirit within. I have a holistic understanding of the spiritual life; I have joined these other human beings who are equally frail and sometimes misguided and who sometimes dream dreams (and have nightmares) and have visions of a divine commonwealth. They dare to think that everyday life is where this commonwealth is being established.

Harvey Gillman
2008

spoken ministry in meeting for worship	prayerfully supporting individuals in meeting
helping others feel closer to God	service on committees and other Quaker bodies
doing practical jobs around the meeting house	coming regularly to meeting for worship
reading from something brought to meeting	a call to political action or witness
listening to others	writing articles or stories for Quaker or other publications

spiritual friendship	going to Quaker business meetings
bringing flowers or food to meeting	encouraging others to develop their gifts
visiting sick or needy people or prisoners	participating in or leading study groups
joining in public vigils or local faith activities	working with other churches
letter writing	voluntary work

helping with tea and coffee after meeting for worship	helping with children's meeting
making time to attend Quaker social events	being a parent or carer
visiting other Quakers	telling Friends about good Quaker courses or events I've attended
calling in on or doing shopping for a neighbour, or member of my meeting	my job
campaign work	

Faithful Diversity

Exploring the diversity of beliefs among Quakers, and how we live with this in the modern world

This unit invites you to find out more about the diversity of beliefs among Quakers in Britain (and elsewhere in the world) and how we hope to find unity in that diversity by being open to different people's expressions of truth: Quakers try to connect with 'that of God' in everyone, by embracing a deliberate spiritual practice of openness and listening to those who are different from us.

 ## Faithful Diversity unit aims

This unit aims to help you:

- become aware of the diversity of faith perspectives among Quakers in Britain and beyond

- understand how Quakers try to respond to both the gift and challenge of being a diverse faith community

- reflect on your own experience of and response to diversity of belief

Overview

Quakers share a way of life rather than a set of beliefs. We seek to experience God directly, within ourselves and in our relationships with others and the world around us. Our unity is based on shared understanding and a shared practice of worship, not on our beliefs all being the same.

The Quaker way has its roots in Christianity and finds inspiration in the Bible and the life and teachings of Jesus. Quakers also find meaning and value in the teachings of other faiths; we acknowledge that ours is not the only way.

This Quaker openness to 'new light, from whatever source it may come' (*Advices & queries* 7, in *Quaker faith & practice* 1.02) has led to a growing diversity of faith among British Friends over the last century. Our community now includes Friends whose faith perspective is based in traditional biblical Christianity, alongside Friends who describe themselves as Buddhist Quakers, Jewish Quakers, non-theist Quakers, pagan Quakers and humanist Quakers.

This diversity of faith perspectives is experienced by Friends as both a challenge and a gift: it calls us to listen to one another with ever deepening awareness.

Beyond Britain Yearly Meeting, in the world family of Quakers, there is also a rich variety of experience, some of which is unfamiliar to Friends in Britain. Some Quakers make frequent and joyful use of song and Bible study, and may be led by a pastor; for others silent waiting on God is the basis of worship, from which spoken ministry develops. Many Friends from around the world have a vivid experience of personal salvation through the teaching, life, death and resurrection of Jesus Christ; many hesitate to express their deepest spiritual experiences in words. It is important for many British Friends that we see ourselves as part of the world family of Friends, learning about and connecting with Quakers in other traditions as well as our own.

George Fox advised early Friends to

> be patterns, be examples in all countries, places, islands, nations, wherever you come, that your carriage and life may preach among all sorts of people, and to them; then you will come to walk cheerfully over the world, answering that of God in everyone.
>
> *Quaker faith & practice* 19.32

The Quaker spiritual insight into the fundamental equality and worth of all people – seeing 'that of God' in all people – springs from deep experience and has been re-affirmed by successive generations of Quakers. We have a fundamental commitment to equality and inclusion in our own Quaker family and the wider community, affirming the love of God for all people, whatever their age, sexuality, race, religion, state of health, disability or gender. (You can explore the Quaker commitment to equality further in the Faith in Action unit).

Quakers try to connect with 'that of God' in everyone, by embracing a deliberate spiritual practice of openness and listening to those who are different from us. This affects how we relate to one another as Quakers, how we build relationships with other churches and faith communities, and how we relate to the people that we meet in our daily lives.

Quaker distinctives

Distinctives 1

Quaker faith & practice on diversity of belief

You could read any of chapter 27 'Unity and diversity' in *Quaker faith & practice*, or you may prefer to read some of the following sections for a quick overview:

- Quakers and other faiths: *Qf&p* 27.01 and 27.03
- Jesus: *Qf&p* 27.09–27.10
- Quakers and the Christian church: *Qf&p* 27.18
- creeds: *Qf&p* 27.25
- the Bible: *Qf&p* 27.34
- priesthood: *Qf&p* 27.35
- sacraments: *Qf&p* 27.38
- being a 'bridge people': *Qf&p* 27.44

Distinctives 2

A Quaker faith in transition?

In 'Tradition and transition: opening to the sacred yesterday and today' (see Further exploration for details), modern Friend Alex Wildwood writes about the Quaker faith in a time of transition. He discusses the pluralism of belief among British Friends, and how he sees this as an opportunity for spiritual growth.

You'll find an extract from 'Tradition and Transition' on pages 134–135.

Distinctives 3

Are Quakers Christian?

You might like to watch the video 'Are Quakers Christian?' made by Friends at Watford Quaker Meeting. It includes reflections on how different Friends relate to the Christian tradition and Quakerism's roots within it. You can access the video in a number of different ways:

- online at
  - www.watfordquakers.org.uk/videos.html
  - www.youtube.com as 'Are Quakers Christian?'

- on the DVD *An Introduction to Watford Quakers* available from the Quaker Centre bookshop (see Further exploration for contact details).

Distinctives 4

Quakers around the world

Robert Vogel, an American Friend, writes about 'Quakers around the world' in an extract from *Searching the depths: essays on being a Quaker today* (see Further exploration for details). You'll find this extract on pages 136–137.

If you are interested in finding out more about Quakers around the world, you could also:

- read sections 9.01–9.02 of *Quaker faith & practice*, which discuss the world family of Friends

- look at books of faith and practice from other Quaker Yearly Meetings around the world online at: www.quakerinfo.com/fandp.shtml

- check out the information about different kinds of Friends on the website of the Friends World Committee for Consultation at: fwccworld.org/kinds_of_friends/index.shtml

- view a graph showing numbers of Quakers worldwide in 1937 and 2007, also on the FWCC website, at: fwccworld.org/kinds_of_friends/index.shtml

Distinctives 5

How do Quakers relate to other faiths?

The video 'How do Quakers relate to other faiths?', made by Friends at Watford Quaker Meeting, includes reflections on the approach that Friends take to interfaith work and diversity within our own community. You can access the video in a number of different ways:

- online at
  - www.watfordquakers.org.uk/videos.html
  - www.youtube.com as 'How do Quakers relate to other faiths?'

- on the DVD *An Introduction to Watford Quakers* available from the Quaker Centre bookshop (see Further exploration for contact details).

Discovery

Discovery 1

How are Quakers approaching ecumenical and interfaith work?

The Quaker Committee for Christian & Interfaith Relations (QCCIR) works on ecumenical and interfaith work at a national level.

You could have a look at a recent issue of QCCIR's newsletter 'CIRcular' and discuss any issues raised by it with your Becoming Friends companion. You can download recent editions of CIRcular at: www.quaker.org.uk/newsletters or you could look in your local meeting library for recent copies.

You could also look at the inter-church and interfaith information at: www.quaker.org.uk/inter-church-and-interfaith or read any of the leaflets at: www.quaker.org.uk/inter-church-and-interfaith-leaflets

To find out more about ecumenical and interfaith work going on locally, talk to Friends in your local or area meeting who are currently serving on ecumenical or interfaith bodies about their work (you could ask your Becoming Friends companion to help arrange this).

Discovery 2

How diverse is belief in my local meeting?

You might like to ask your Becoming Friends companion or an elder to discuss with you the diversity of belief in your local meeting, and how this comes out in spoken ministry in meeting for worship. It is important to keep this conversation general, rather than naming names of individuals in meeting.

- How does this compare with what you and your companion know of the diversity of belief in Britain Yearly Meeting generally?

- Are there aspects of this diversity that you find challenging, or welcome?

Discovery 3

Reflecting on the grounds of our faith with a group or companion

You could ask your Becoming Friends companion or an elder in your meeting to help set up a small group session exploring the faith perspectives among local Friends, using the questions below as a focus (or you might prefer to simply discuss the questions with your Becoming Friends companion).

Share the following questions with the group as starting points for reflection, and perhaps ask your companion or an experienced Friend to lead this. It might be helpful to write or print out copies of the questions.

- Do you describe yourself as Christian?

- How do you relate to the Christian roots of Quakerism?

- What is the ground of your faith as a Friend?

After people have had a brief opportunity for personal reflection on the questions, spend some time in worship-sharing mode as a group, sharing with one another any responses, insights, experiences or challenges relating to the questions.

Guidance for worship sharing is found in Appendix 2 – Guidance on pages 283–284.

Discovery 4

Discussion about what diversity means to us

You could consider the introductory questions below, then go to the Faithful Diversity unit forum and post your own thoughts on the issues raised. You might like to comment on other posts on this forum too.

Alternatively, you could discuss the introductory questions with your Becoming Friends companion, or others in your meeting: you could do this informally over coffee or ask your companion to help you set up a group session.

Introductory questions:

- What does diversity of belief mean to you personally?

- What have you experienced as a blessing and a challenge of diversity?

Deepening

Deepening 1

Your own faith journey

You might like to consider the different approaches to faith among British Quakers that you have encountered during this unit, using these questions:

- Where would you place yourself in relation to Christianity and other approaches to faith found among British Friends?

- In what ways has your faith, or faith identity, changed during the course of your life?

- How is your relationship with Quakerism affected by your faith identity?

You could

- respond to the questions in writing

- respond by drawing or using another creative method

- go online and blog about them

- discuss them on a Quaker discussion forum:
    - the Britain Yearly Meeting forum at: www.quakerweb.org.uk/forum
    - www.friendlink.org.uk (aimed mainly at young Quakers)
    - the Faithful Diversity unit forum

- share some of your reflections with your Becoming Friends companion when you next meet.

Deepening 2

Reflect on *Advices & queries* 16 and 17

Advices & queries 16 and 17, found in section 1.02 of *Quaker faith & practice*, focus on diversity and answering 'that of God' in others. If you prefer to listen to *Advices & queries*, there are mp3 audio files available in this unit of the online Becoming Friends course.

- You could spend time reflecting on these advices and queries, allowing them to speak to you at a deep level.

- You may find it helpful to respond to the advices and queries in writing or using creative methods.

- You could also reflect on this experience with your Becoming Friends companion when you next meet.

Deepening 3

Your own response to diversity

What is your own response to diversity of belief among Quakers and in the wider community?

You can use the Diversity cards on pages 138–140 as a prompt for your reflection. Copy or print the cards and cut them up. Then spend some time ordering or sorting the cards to reflect which kinds of faith positions you are more comfortable with, and which you are more challenged by, or want to know more about.

- Reflect on what this sorting process reveals to you, both about yourself and your own response to diversity

- Do you feel led to respond in any way?

You might wish to reflect on how you have got on with this exercise at a future meeting with your Becoming Friends companion.

Deepening 4

Reflecting with your Becoming Friends companion

You might like to spend time with your Becoming Friends companion reflecting on how each of you responds to the challenge of diversity among Quakers.

- Are there aspects of being part of a diverse faith community which your companion has found especially challenging or welcome?

- Does this reflect your own experience?

Further exploration

If you would like to explore the subject of faithful diversity further, here are some suggestions for reading, listening or viewing.

CIRcular, Quaker Committee for Church & Interfaith Relations newsletter. Available in local meeting house libraries or to download at: www.quaker.org.uk/newsletters

A faith to call our own: Quaker tradition in the light of contemporary movements of the Spirit, Alex Wildwood, Quaker Home Service, 1999 (Swarthmore Lecture).

Friends World Committee for Consultation website: fwccworld.org/kinds_of_friends/index.shtml#

Interfaith pilgrims: living truths and truthful living, Eleanor Nesbitt, Quaker Books, 2003 (Swarthmore lecture).

An introduction to Watford Quakers DVD, Just Film, 2007. Also available at: www.watfordquakers.org.uk/videos.html includes: 'Are Quakers Christian?' and 'How do Quakers relate to other faiths?' (also on www.youtube.com as 'Are Quakers Christian?' and 'How do Quakers relate to other faiths?').

New Foundation Fellowship website :www.nffuk.org Quakers in the UK seeking fresh understanding of the radical Christian vision of George Fox.

Previous convictions and end of the millennium Quakerism, Christine Trevett, Quaker Home Service, 1997 (Swarthmore lecture).

Quaker faith & practice, chapter 9, 'Beyond Britain Yearly Meeting' including ecumenical and interfaith links.

Quaker faith & practice, chapter 26, 'Reflections'.

Quaker faith & practice, chapter 27, 'Unity and diversity'.

Quaker identity and the heart of our faith, Quaker Life Study Materials, Quaker Life, 2008. Includes sections about diversity of faith perspectives among British Friends. Available online at: www.quaker.org.uk/sites/default/files/Faith-and-practice-proceeding.pdf or in hard copy by contacting Quaker Life on 020 7663 1140 or email: ql@quaker.org.uk.

Quaker Universalist Group website: www.qug.org.uk Universalist Quakers in the UK.

Rooted in Christianity, open to new light: Quaker spiritual diversity, Timothy Ashworth and Alex Wildwood, Pronoun Press & Woodbrooke, 2009.

Searching the depths: essays on being a Quaker today, edited by Harvey Gillman and Alastair Heron, Quaker Home Service, 1996

To Lima with love: the response from the Religious Society of Friends in Great Britain to the World Council of Churches document Baptism, Eucharist and Ministry, Quaker Home Service, 1987

'Tradition and transition: opening to the sacred yesterday and today', Alex Wildwood, *Woodbrooke Journal*, Winter 2001, No 9. Also in *Hearts and minds prepared* pack.

What canst thou say? Towards a Quaker theology, Janet Scott, Quaker Home Service, 1980 (Swarthmore lecture).

Young Quaker Space website: www.yqspace.org.uk

Many of these titles are available from the Quaker Centre bookshop:

Friends House
173 Euston Road
London NW1 2BJ

Tel: 020 7663 1030
Fax: 020 7663 1001

Website: www.quaker.org.uk/bookshop
Email: quakercentre@quaker.org.uk

Many of them will also be in your local meeting house library. You could ask your Becoming Friends companion to help you track down titles that interest you.

Closing activity

As you finish your exploration of faithful diversity among Quakers, you are invited to reflect on what you have gained through this unit, how your understanding of both yourself and Quakerism has changed, and what areas you would like to explore further.

This closing reflection can be a very good opportunity for sharing with your Becoming Friends companion, or you may prefer to write in a journal or book of spiritual discipline (there's guidance for journalling in Appendix 2 – Guidance on page 282), or to reflect using creative methods such as drawing, collage, model-making or working with materials such as textiles or wood.

You might use one or more of the following questions as a focus for your reflection:

- What have you gained from your work on this unit, whether as a result of positive or more challenging experiences?

- In what ways has your understanding changed as a result of your work on this unit?

- Are there areas that you would like to explore further – either as part of your own spiritual journey or relating to Quakerism?

- Has anything arisen that you would find it helpful to reflect on with your Becoming Friends companion?

Extract for Distinctives 2:
A Quaker faith in transition?

Extracts from 'Tradition and transition: opening to the sacred yesterday and today' by Alex Wildwood

Throughout our history Quakers have been non-credal in the sense that belief in propositions is not what defines our faith. But today a growing number of British Friends make the unwarranted leap from this fact to the statement that belief is irrelevant or unimportant to Quakerism. I have heard it said that you can believe what you like as a Quaker, and I think that this is a serious misrepresentation of our faith and the real root of the 'problem' which some people see in our diversity today. Clearly any group needs to have some sense of a common practice and identity, a shared belief system. Even a group such as liberal Friends, with a strong emphasis on experience, must recognise that experience never exists in a vacuum. We are always trying, through dialogue with others, to make sense of our shared identity of being 'Quaker'. This is especially important in a time of transition such as our own.

Ben Pink Dandelion identifies three implicit 'articles of faith' in the theologically 'liberal' phase of Quakerism which became dominant by the early twentieth century and continue to be influential to this day:

- Faith is rooted in experience

- Faith has to be 'relevant' to the age

- We are open to new light (and revelation is progressive).

[...]

I see the growing awareness of the preciousness and fragility of our planetary home and a developing sense of the awesome mystery of the universe we inhabit as signs of ... emergent spiritual awareness. Today increasing numbers of people are seeking not dogmatic formulations of faith and morality or doctrine imposed from outside but an authentic way of life in which values and meaning arise from within. They are hungry for a living experience of Spirit, something which points them to the Reality beyond and all around themselves, our embeddedness in the greater-than-human world. Hence the growing interest in 'Green' Spirituality, in paganism and shamanic and other nature-based religious practices.

There is a growing realisation (or perhaps it is better described as a remembering, for it was there in the earth-centred cultures which our industrialised civilisation has all but eradicated) that the dualism inherent in much of Western religion – the separation of body–mind, flesh–spirit, male–female, heaven and earth, human–animal – is at the very root of our problem.

[...]

As we explore what has meaning for us today in the 'previous convictions' of earlier generations of Friends we will have to marry these with both our scientific understanding of our evolving universe and with our painful awareness of the very real threats to our world. In doing this it is helpful to see faith as a verb, to appreciate faithing as a process we engage in both individually and collectively. We are constantly 'faithing the future' in the light of greater knowledge and awareness.

Seen as a process, it is important to acknowledge that there are stages to faith development both for the individual and the collective. My sense is that we are today facing a collective rite of passage, a coming of age of truly global proportions, as humanity moves from its spiritual infancy to a growing realisation that we are, in Matthew Fox's phrase, 'co-creators' with the divine. We are moving, in other words, to that place predicted by early Friends 350 years ago – when religion would be something known 'experimentally' rather than as a dogmatic formulation of belief.

[...]

Traditionally the basis of our unity in meeting for worship and in our business meetings – and therefore of our discernment of call and our witness 'in the world' – has been the sense of Christ as 'the Presence in the midst', the Guide who led us in our 'seeking the will of God'. Yet today this fundamentally Christian basis of our unity as Friends can no longer be assumed. I believe what is most important is that we are conscious and explicit about this, that we name this as a transitional time.

I believe that we are now being invited to embrace both what Quakers have advocated as a relationship to Christ in our hearts, and an evolutionary sense of a new inclusive spirituality rooted in the earth, the body and the feminine – and that at the deepest levels of experience these two are not in contradiction. I also believe that Friends, unencumbered by dogmatic formulations of faith, have much to offer the many seekers of this age. Our Quaker meetings and experimental worship could indeed be laboratories for William Penn's 'experiment upon the human Soul'. I believe there is again 'a great people to be gathered' as we clarify and maintain our distinctive Quaker experience of the Christian revelation and combine this with a wider, more inclusive sense of Spirit.

[...]

A pluralist Quakerism only works if each of us feels free to speak at a deep level of our encounters with the Spirit – both within and beyond the traditional 'frame' of religious experience. If we lose either polarity of our Quaker heritage – our distinctive sense of being 'rooted in Christianity' or our sincere willingness to be 'open to new light' – then we will have lost what our evolving tradition has valued as the Truth.'

from 'Tradition and transition: opening to the sacred yesterday and today' by Alex Wildwood, *Woodbrooke Journal*, Winter 2001, No 9

Extract for Distinctives 4:
Quakers around the world

Extract from 'Quakers around the world' by Robert Vogel

In most countries there is only one expression (or mode of worship), with the notable exception of the USA. In Canada, the continent of Europe, the Middle East, Australia and New Zealand, Quakers worship in silence-based unprogrammed meetings. In most parts of Africa, Asia and Latin America where missions were established, Friends hold programmed worship services. Only in the United States does one find all expressions of Quakerism; from 'liberals' to 'conservatives' to 'orthodox' to 'evangelical'. [...]

One common element is that virtually all these groups claim George Fox as their founder. Reading his *Journal*, one can find statements that support different emphases. Fox's first deeply spiritual experience was that 'There is one, even Jesus Christ, that can speak to thy condition' (1647). Later in his ministry, Fox counselled: 'Be patterns, be examples in all countries, places, islands, nations, wherever you come, that your carriage and life may preach among all sorts of people, and to them; then you will come to walk cheerfully over the world answering that of God in every one' (1656).

Then in 1671, Fox wrote a letter to the Governor of Barbados which is essentially a near-repetition of the so-called 'Apostles Creed'.[...] Today Liberal (unprogrammed) Quakers emphasize the phrase 'that of God in every one', while Evangelical Friends find Fox's early experience and the Barbados letter important for them. [...]

It might help to remind ourselves that the first Quakers thought of their movement as a revival of primitive Christianity: today, the question of whether one is a Christian or not would not occur to the majority of Quakers, considered worldwide. During the 1991 World Conference of Friends, Duane Comfort of Evangelical Friends Mission said, 'We are Christians first and then add our Quaker distinctives.' Zablon Malenge, former General Secretary of the Africa Section of FWCC [Friends World Consultation Committee], put it this way: 'In Kenya, A Quaker is one who has graduated from a Christian level to something more than Christianity. Christianity then forms the basis of Quakerism.'

It is largely due to the missionary efforts of programmed and pastoral Friends that their message has spread to the Middle East, and parts of Asia, but especially to eastern Africa and to Latin America. This missionary work has brought into the Society a large number of people in the technologically 'less-developed' countries who are poor in this world's goods. FWCC estimates that there are

122,000 members in Africa, 51,000 in Latin America and about 4,000 in Asia. The numerical centre of the 'Quaker world' has shifted to the South Atlantic area, and this will surely affect the future of the family of Friends.'

from 'Quakers around the world' by Robert Vogel,
in *Searching the depths: essays on being a Quaker today*,
edited by Harvey Gillman and Alastair Heron, Quaker books, 1996

A traditional Christian who believes Jesus Christ died to save us from sin	A person who describes himself as a 'neo-classical Graeco-Romano pagan'
Someone with no particular set of beliefs but who finds meditation practices helpful	A Buddhist
A Muslim	A Buddhist who voices strong views about karma and reincarnation, such as 'suffering in this life is the result of bad karma from a previous life'
A non-theist (someone who does not believe there is a God)	A secular humanist who considers all religious belief to be superstition
An evangelical Christian with conservative moral views (eg about abortion and homosexuality)	A person for whom participating in sacraments is very important

A Baptist	Someone who describes herself as 'post-Christian'
An Anglican	A modern Pagan
A Roman Catholic	A Hindu
Someone who says the only religious label they want is 'Quaker'	A Christian priest or minister
A member of the reform tradition of Judaism	A Christian who questions the language and imagery of traditional Christianity

A person who is both a Quaker and a member of another faith community

A Pagan who worships the triple goddess and the horned god

Someone who describes herself as 'a spiritual seeker'

Someone who is opposed to the main elements of Christian belief

Someone who describes himself as a non-denominational Christian

Faith in Action

How Quakers try to embody our beliefs through our witness in the world.

This unit invites you to find out more about how Quakers try to put faith into practice. Experience in worship leads us to a shared commitment to equality, peace, simplicity and truth, which we try to live out and foster in the world. This is often referred to as Quaker testimony and underpins a lot of Quaker thinking and work.

Faith in Action unit aims

This unit aims to help you:

- understand how Quakers feel called to live out our beliefs through witness in the world

- find out about the Quaker commitment to equality, peace, simplicity and truth

- reflect on your own experience of being called to live out your beliefs

Overview

Quaker faith springs from a deeply held belief in living our lives according to our spiritual experience. Some of our spiritual insights, which we call our testimonies, spring from deep experience and have been a part of Quaker faith for many years. These Quaker testimonies arise out of an inner conviction and challenge our normal ways of living.

- They exist in spiritually-led actions rather than rigid written forms.

- They are governed by continuing spiritual experience and are not imposed in any way.

- They require us to search for ways in which the testimonies can become true for ourselves.

- They emerge and change over time.

> The word 'testimony' is used by Quakers to describe a witness to the living truth within the human heart as it is acted out in everyday life. It is not a form of words, but a mode of life based on the realisation that there is that of God in everybody, that all human beings are equal, that all life is interconnected. It is affirmative but may lead to action that runs counter to certain practices currently accepted in society at large... These testimonies reflect the corporate beliefs of the Society, however much individual Quakers may interpret them differently according to their own light. They are not optional extras, but fruits that grow from the very tree of faith.
>
> Harvey Gillman, *Quaker faith & practice* 23.12

Truth and integrity

Quakers try to live according to the deepest truth we know, which we believe comes from God. This means speaking the truth to all, including people in positions of power. Integrity is the guiding principle we set for ourselves and expect in public life.

Justice, equality and community

Quakers recognise the equal worth and unique nature of every person. This means working to change the systems that cause injustice and hinder true community. It also means working with people who are suffering from injustice, such as prisoners and asylum seekers.

Simplicity

Quakers are concerned about the excesses and unfairness of our consumer society, and the unsustainable use of natural resources. We try to live simply and to give space for the things that really matter: the people around us, the natural world, our experience of God.

Peace

Perhaps Quakers are best known for our peace testimony. This arises from our conviction that love is at the heart of existence and all human beings are equal in the eyes of God, and that we must live in a way that reflects this. It has led Quakers to refuse military service, and to become involved in a wide range of peace activities from practical work in areas affected by violent conflict to the development of alternatives to violence at all levels from personal to international.

Faithful living

Putting faith into action is not easy! But with loving advice and a supportive community, Quakers are encouraged to keep trying. A story about early Quaker William Penn shows that each of us has to find our own way, at our own pace, to living out our faith:

> When William Penn was convinced of the principles of Friends, and became a frequent attendant at their meetings, he did not immediately relinquish his gay apparel; it is even said that he wore a sword, as was then customary among men of rank and fashion. Being one day in company with George Fox, he asked his advice concerning it, saying that he might, perhaps, appear singular among Friends, but his sword had once been the means of saving his life without injuring his antagonist, and moreover, that Christ had said, 'He that hath no sword, let him sell his garment and buy one.' George Fox answered, 'I advise thee to wear it as long as thou canst.' Not long after this they met again, when William had no sword, and George said to him, 'William, where is thy sword?' 'Oh!' said he, 'I have taken thy advice; I wore it as long as I could.'
>
> *Quaker faith & practice* 19.47

Concerns

When individuals or groups of Quakers feel led to put our faith into action, we may call this 'acting under a concern'; this means more than the normal everyday sense of 'being concerned' about something, but refers to a powerful spiritual experience of being compelled to act in a certain way. To ensure that we are clear within ourselves and as a community about the rightness of such action, Quakers have developed a process of deep reflection for testing out 'concerns'. In this way we support and challenge one another to really live in accordance with the 'promptings of love and truth' in our hearts (*Advices & queries* 1, in *Quaker faith & practice* 1.02).

Testimonies about faithful lives

Another way in which Quakers use the word 'testimony' is when we celebrate the faithful lives of individual Friends: we write an account of a Friend's life called a 'testimony to the grace of God as shown in the life of...'. These accounts are published as a source of encouragement and inspiration to us in living our own call to faith in action.

Local and national Quaker work

Quakers try to put our faith into practice in many different ways, at local, national and international levels. In this unit you can find out about Quaker activities in your local community and about national Quaker work, including work organised through the Quaker Peace & Social Witness department of Britain Yearly Meeting.

Quaker distinctives

Distinctives 1

Faith into action in *Quaker faith & practice*

Advices & queries 31–42 (in section 1.02 of *Quaker faith & practice*) offer thought-provoking guidance about how we put our faith into action as Quakers. If you prefer to listen to *Advices & queries*, there are mp3 audio files available in this unit of the online Becoming Friends course.

To find out more about particular aspects of Quaker faith in action, you could also read any of the following sections of *Quaker faith & practice*:

- Simplicity: *Qf&p* 20.27 and 20.35

- Truth and integrity: *Qf&p* 20.45, 20.54 and 20.56

- Equality: *Qf&p* 23.32, 23.33 and 23.36

- Peace: *Qf&p* 20.68, chapter 24 introduction, 24.04, and 24.11

- Personal peace witness: *Qf&p* 24.27, 24.37 and 24.38

- Social responsibility: *Qf&p* 23.22, 23.23 and 23.94

- Environment: *Qf&p* 25.02, 25.10 and 25.14

Distinctives 2

Acting under a 'concern'

Quakers sometimes speak of a specific call to action or lived witness as acting under a 'concern'. It may take some time to find out or discern exactly what it is that we feel led to do, though, so Quakers have developed ways of working out what our 'concern' is and supporting one another in taking action.

You could read about discerning concerns in an extract from Marion McNaughton's presentation to the Quaker Peace & Social Witness conference 2009. You'll find this extract on pages 159–160.

You might also like to read the following sections of *Quaker faith & practice* for an overview of 'concerns' and Quaker approaches to discerning and supporting a 'concern':

- a special inward calling: *Qf&p* 13.02

- a sense of 'rightness': *Qf&p* 13.03

- discerning a concern: *Qf&p* 13.05

- support from your meeting: *Qf&p* 13.09

Distinctives 3

Quakers talk about the testimonies

You might like to watch the video 'The Quaker Testimonies' made by Friends at Watford Quaker Meeting about the Quaker approach to living our faith. You can access the video in a number of different ways:

- online at
  - › www.watfordquakers.org.uk/videos.html
  - › www.youtube.com as 'The Quaker Testimonies'

- on the DVD *An introduction to Watford Quakers*, available from the Quaker Centre bookshop (see Further exploration for contact details).

Distinctives 4

A Quaker view on ...

The Quaker Peace & Social Witness leaflet 'A Quaker view on...' gives a helpful overview of past and present Quaker approaches to:

- peace, conflict and violence

- human rights

- crime and punishment

- racial and religious prejudice

- the environment

You'll find the leaflet on pages 161–170 or you can access it online at: www.quaker.org.uk/education (click on the leaflet title in the left hand menu)

For more about the history of Quaker faith in action, see the Deep Roots unit.

Distinctives 5

Faithful lives

The Quaker custom of writing testimonies to the grace of God in the lives of Friends provides us with real examples of how individuals have lived out their faith: these testimonies can inspire us to action in our own lives.

There are testimonies to the grace of God in the lives of Friends in the following sections of *Quaker faith & practice*:

- Elizabeth Fry (1780–1845): *Qf&p* 18.08

- Katie Riley (20th century): *Qf&p* 18.19

- John Bright (1811–1889): *Qf&p* 23.07

- Stephen Henry Hobhouse (1881–1961): *Qf&p* 23.51

- Percy Cleave (1880–1958): *Qf&p* 23.59

- Joan Frances Layton (1908–1990): *Qf&p* 23.60

You could also read recent testimonies to the grace of God in the lives of Friends in local Quaker newsletters and documents for yearly meetings.

- You could ask your Becoming Friends companion to help you track down copies in your local meeting library

- You could look at the testimonies for Yearly Meeting 2008 at: www.quaker.org.uk/files/YM2008-Testimonies.pdf

- You can also see the current yearly meeting documents online by clicking the current year's page at: www.quaker.org.uk/ym

Discovery

Discovery 1

Quaker Peace & Social Witness work

QPSW publish factsheets about different aspects of their work, which give a good introduction to Quaker faith in action and offer ways of getting involved. You can look at an example of a QPSW factsheet by:

- turning to pages 171–172

- downloading one from www.quaker.org.uk/qpsw-factsheets

- requesting one from QPSW (email qpsw@quaker.org.uk or tel 020 7663 1000)

You could also go to www.quaker.org.uk/qpsw and select any subjects from the left hand menu that interest you, to find out more about Quaker work and resources in areas ranging from housing to disarmament.

You may be interested in the QPSW presentation 'Sustainable Security' at: www.quaker.org.uk/sustainable-security-display
To borrow this display for your meeting house, email: disarm@quaker.org.uk or ring 020 7663 1067.

Discovery 2

Exploring local Friends' experience of faith in action

If you would like to explore local Friends' experience of putting their faith into action, you could ask your Becoming Friends companion to help you set up a small group session. The questions below may be useful starting points for discussion, or you may prefer to discuss other questions with your Becoming Friends companion.

- How do you try to live out the Quaker testimony to equality, simplicity, peace or truth in your life?

- Have you ever done anything especially challenging or difficult in living out one of the testimonies?

- Are there elements of the Quaker testimonies that you do not agree with or find more challenging than others?

You could also join in a discussion about experiences of faith in action on a Quaker discussion forum:

- the Britain Yearly Meeting forum at: www.quakerweb.org.uk/forum
- www.friendlink.org.uk (aimed mainly at young Quakers)
- the Faith in Action unit forum

Discovery 3

Discussion about issues of concern

You could consider the introductory questions below, then go to the Faith in Action unit forum and post your own thoughts on the issues raised. You might like to comment on other posts on this forum too.

Alternatively, you could discuss the introductory questions with your Becoming Friends companion, or others in your meeting.

Introductory questions:

- What is an issue that currently concerns you or that you feel passionate about?
- Do you have a suggestion for action that Friends could take? This could be something quite small and possibly happening online.

Discovery 4

Find out about other Quaker faith in action

You might like to find out more about:

Any local Quaker action

Ask your Becoming Friends companion, or others in your meeting. Is there anything you feel led to get involved with?

Circles of Support & Accountability

This is a scheme that decreases the likelihood of sex offenders re-offending by using trained volunteers from the community: www.circles-uk.org.uk
Tel: 0118 950 0068
Email: info@circles-uk.org.uk

Disarm

QPSW disarmament programme: www.peaceexchange.org.uk
You can download *Disarm* newsletters from:
www.quaker.org.uk/online-resources
Tel: 020 7663 1067
Email: disarm@quaker.org.uk

Living Witness Project

Quakers for sustainability: www.livingwitness.org.uk
You can download *Earthquaker* newsletters from the website.
Tel: 01865 725 244
Email: laurie@livingwitness.org.uk

The Retreat

A not-for-profit specialist mental health provider founded and run by Quakers:
www.theretreatyork.org.uk
Tel: 01904 412551
Email: info@theretreatyork.org.uk

Turning the Tide

About non violent power for social change: www.turning-the-tide.org
Download *Making Waves* newsletters from
www.quaker.org.uk/online-resources
Tel: 020 7663 1064/1
Email: denised@quaker.org.uk or stevew@quaker.org.uk .

Discovery 5

Talk to a Friend about putting Quaker values into action

You might like to ask your Becoming Friends companion or another Friend in your meeting about how they put their Quaker values into action. You could ask them:

- Think of a time when you put your Quaker values into action.

- What did you do? Why was it important to you?

- Was it easy or difficult?

- Why did you do it? Did you want to do it?

- Did other people ask you about what you did? How did you explain it?

- How does being a Quaker generally affect your life and the choices you make?

Discovery 6

Quaker Tapestry on faith in action

Many of the panels from the Quaker Tapestry deal with faith in action. You might like to look at these and follow up panels that interest you by discussing them with your Becoming Friends companion, or others in your meeting, or by finding books and information about them in your meeting house library or online.

You could:

- visit the Quaker Tapestry exhibition at Kendal, or contact them for more details:
  Tel: 01539 722975
  Email: info@quaker-tapestry.co.uk
  Website: www.quaker-tapestry.co.uk

- find out if there's a book with pictures from the tapestry in your meeting house library, or you could order a book or postcards from the exhibition

Quaker Tapestry panels about faith in action include:

- A7 Conscientious objection

- B8 Quaker Peace Action Caravan

- D2 Simplicity

- D5 Innocent trades and D6 Merchants

- E4 Criminal justice and E5–E6 Elizabeth Fry

- E10 Unemployment and poverty

- F3 The slave trade

- F6–F7 Relief work

- F16–F17 Peace work

Deepening

Deepening 1

Your own experience of living out your beliefs

You might like to spend some time on your own or with your Becoming Friends companion reflecting on your experience of living out your beliefs.

Think of a time when you put your values into action.

- What did you do? Why was it important to you?

- Was it easy or difficult?

- Why did you do it? Did you want to do it?

- Did other people ask you about what you did? How did you explain it?

- How does this experience fit with any of the Quaker testimonies?

Deepening 2

Reflecting with *Advices & queries*

You could look at *Advices & queries* 31–42 (in section 1.02 of *Quaker faith & practice*), taking time to read them slowly and meditatively. If you prefer to listen to *Advices & queries*, there are mp3 audio files available in this unit of the online Becoming Friends course.

- Is there one that particularly speaks to you at the moment? It may be one that you feel passionately about, or perhaps one that challenges you in some way.

- You could write or print out that advice and put it somewhere that you will see it over the next few days or weeks, so that you can allow it to speak deeply to you.

- You could also reflect on this with your Becoming Friends companion when you next meet.

Deepening 3

A Testimony to the grace of God in your life

Advices & queries 27 (in section 1.02 of *Quaker faith & practice*) invites us to 'Live adventurously' and to 'Let your life speak.' If you imagine the Testimony that would be written to celebrate the grace of God in your life, what would you want or hope it would say about how you put your faith into action?

- You might like to write out this Testimony about your own life in a journal or record it creatively in some other way.

- Does it have anything to teach you about how you may be led to live?

- You could also share some of your reflections with your Becoming Friends companion when you next meet.

Deepening 4

A fourfold blessing

The 'Fourfold blessing' comes from the Franciscan tradition. You might like to read it and let it speak to you at a deep level. It can be a focus for prayer or spiritual practice over a period of time, inviting these blessings into your life as part of living out your faith.

You'll find an adaptation of the blessing on page 173.

If you would like to take some time to reflect deeply on your own response to these blessings, you could:

- respond by drawing, painting, or using another creative method

- respond in music, song or movement

- respond in writing

- go online and blog about your response

- discuss your response on a Quaker discussion forum:
  - the Britain Yearly Meeting forum at: www.quakerweb.org.uk/forum
  - www.friendlink.org.uk (aimed mainly at young Quakers)
  - the Faith in Action unit forum

- share some of your reflections with your Becoming Friends companion when you next meet.

Deepening 5

How have other people's lives spoken to you?

You could talk to your Becoming Friends companion, or you may prefer to write in a journal or book of spiritual discipline, about people whose lives inspire you, either now or in the past.

- In what ways do/did they live out their faith or principles?
- What are the everyday or extraordinary things that they do/did which inspire you?
- Are there ways that you could act on this inspiration?

Further exploration

If you would like to explore further how Quakers put our faith into action, here are some suggestions for reading, listening or viewing.

Advices & queries 31–42 in *Quaker faith & practice* 1.02

Beyond the spirit of the age, Jonathan Dale, Quaker Books, 1996 (Swarthmore Lecture).

Circles UK website: www.circles-uk.org.uk

Engaging with the Quaker testimonies: a toolkit, Quaker Peace & Social Witness Testimonies Committee, Quaker Books, 2007.

'Finding the prophetic voice for our time', Marion McNaughton and Lizz Roe, *Woodbrooke Journal*, Autumn 2007, No 21

Forgiving justice: a Quaker vision for criminal justice, Tim Newell, Quaker Books, 2000 (Swarthmore Lecture).

Good lives study pack, Pam Lunn and Lizz Roe, Woodbrooke Quaker Study Centre, 2009

An introduction to Watford Quakers (DVD), 'The Quaker Testimonies', Just Film, 2007. Also available at: www.watfordquakers.org.uk/videos.html (or at: www.youtube.com as 'The Quaker Testimonies').

Living Witness project website: www.livingwitness.org.uk

New light: 12 Quaker voices, edited by Jennifer Kavanagh, O Books, 2008. Individual themes such as *Twelve Quakers and Peace, Twelve Quakers and Simplicity* also available in the *Twelve Quakers and...* series, Quaker Quest 2004–2007.

No extraordinary power: prayer, stillness and activism, Helen Steven, Quaker Books, 2005 (Swarthmore Lecture)

Peace Exchange website: www.peaceexchange.org.uk

Pictorial guide to the Quaker Tapestry, Quaker Tapestry at Kendal, 1998.

Quaker faith & practice, chapter 18, 'Faithful Lives'.

Quaker faith & practice, chapter 20, 'Living Faithfully Today'.

Quaker faith & practice, chapter 23, 'Social Responsibility'.

Quaker faith & practice, chapter 24, 'Our Peace Testimony'.

Quaker faith & practice, chapter 25, 'Unity of Creation'.

Quaker Peace & Social Witness pages on the Britain Yearly Meeting website: www.quaker.org.uk/peace-social-witness

Quaker Tapestry website: www.quaker-tapestry.co.uk

Searching the depths: essays on being a Quaker today, edited by Harvey Gillman and Alastair Heron, Quaker Books, 1996

Spirited living: waging conflict, building peace, Simon Fisher, Quaker Books, 2004 (Swarthmore Lecture).

Testimony and tradition, John Punshon, Quaker Home Service, 1990 (Swarthmore Lecture).

The Retreat website: www.theretreatyork.org.uk

Turning the Tide project website: www.turning-the-tide.org

Woodbrooke's website or brochure for details of courses about faith in action or testimony: www.woodbrooke.org.uk

Many of these titles are available from the Quaker Centre bookshop:

Friends House
173 Euston Road
London NW1 2BJ

Tel: 020 7663 1030
Fax: 020 7663 1001

Website: www.quaker.org.uk/bookshop
Email: quakercentre@quaker.org.uk

Many of them will also be in your local meeting house library. You could ask your Becoming Friends companion to help you track down titles that interest you.

Closing activity

As you finish your exploration of how Quakers try to put our faith into action, you are invited to reflect on what you have gained through this unit, how your understanding of both yourself and Quakerism has changed, and what areas you would like to explore further.

This closing reflection can be a very good opportunity for sharing with your Becoming Friends companion, or you may prefer to write in a journal or book of spiritual discipline (there's guidance for journalling in Appendix 2 – Guidance on page 282), or to reflect using creative methods such as drawing, collage, model-making or working with materials such as textiles or wood.

- You might like to use one or more of the following questions as a focus for your reflection:

- What have you gained from your work on this unit, whether as a result of positive or more challenging experiences?

- In what ways has your understanding changed as a result of your work on this unit?

- Are there areas that you would like to explore further – either as part of your own spiritual journey or relating to Quakerism?

- Has anything arisen that you would find it helpful to reflect on with your Becoming Friends companion?

Extract for Distinctives 2:
Acting under a 'concern'

Extract from Marion McNaughton's presentation to QPSW Conference 2009

Discernment

How is it that we as Quakers collectively, and all of us individually, come to know what it is that we are called to do to in response to all that is wrong in the world? Where do we start? We hope we can perhaps play a small part, with the gifts we have and the resources we can call on, though most of us will always feel our efforts are inadequate.

There are many factors involved in determining and carrying out a piece of Quaker work, whether it is central or local, small or large, individual or corporate. We will hear the origins and the growth of some of our central work tomorrow. But in all of them, we say, the work must be rightly discerned.

Discernment is a word that is often used casually in everyday speech, a matter of choosing or selecting what seems to be appropriate. But to Quakers discernment is a spiritual discipline, because it is about the spirit, or the divine, or God, – whatever we choose to call it – being there, and being active, all of the time, in every aspect of our lives, and guiding us. And about our learning to notice this, to pay attention and respond to it. Someone has said, it is about 'God being up to something' in our lives. Discerned work is God's work.

If we turn to *Advices & queries* and listen to advice number 7, it sounds very simple, but if we stop and let it in, it is breathtaking:

> Be aware of the spirit of God at work in the ordinary activities and experience of your daily life.

That's it.

> Be aware of the spirit of God at work in the ordinary activities and experience of your daily life.

It is inescapable. And it is addressed to all of us, not just a few special, 'spiritual' people. And notice that these are the ordinary activities and experiences of our daily life – this is not about thunderclaps or lightning flashes, or a voice speaking out of the clouds. It is about God, at work, all of the time. God at work in the mundane, in the ordinary, in the everyday. Sometimes hidden, sometimes manifesting for a second, and then disappearing again. In my life, and in yours. It helps me to understand this by looking at the tangles of wool and yarn that seem to appear regularly at the bottom of my sewing basket. Here is one.

Discernment acknowledges that the divine and the worldly always come to us intertwined. We have to concentrate to know which is which. The dictionary tells us that discernment means to separate, to distinguish and to determine, what is of God, from what is not of God. So our task, in the ordinary activities and experiences of our daily life, is to take on the tangle of our lives and do three things. To notice and separate the different elements. To learn to distinguish one from the other. And to determine when one comes from a divine source, from God. You will see that there is a slender gold thread in this tangle. It appears and it disappears, but even when you can't see it, you know it is always there, at the heart, running right through the whole. And when you catch sight of it, it is unmistakeable.

This glimpse of the divine is what we wait for in meeting for worship, what we listen for, what we search for in our lives. And when we find it, we stop and pay attention to it, though we may not know exactly what we are meant to do with it. All the threads are important in their way, all are valuable, but one will carry a spiritual charge. It stands out, it seems to prompt us, it may disturb us, and sometimes require something of us that we know we must carry out, even if we don't quite know how. We call this situation 'being under Concern'. All QPSW work, all Quaker work, is work carried out under Concern.

So clearly this habit of seeking and developing awareness is something we must practise, because the more we practise it, the better we will become at it. We must practise it individually in our daily lives, because only then can we practise it together when we try to discern corporately what we are called to do in the world as Quakers. We cannot live our daily lives shut down and unaware of God, and then suddenly come together in a business meeting or a committee, hit the Discern button and come up with the right answer. The right answer grows from our patient, persistent sifting, individually and corporately. All of the work you will hear about this weekend is work carried out under Concern, and it has grown from this inspiration and this discipline, has been discerned, tested, and lived with – faithfully and patiently.

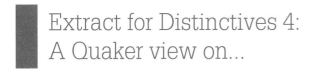

Extract for Distinctives 4:
A Quaker view on...

The following is the text of a leaflet published by Quaker Peace & Social Witness.

A Quaker view on...
   peace, conflict & violence
      crime & punishment
         the environment
            human rights
               racial & religious prejudice

Members of the Religious Society of Friends (Quakers) try to put their faith into practice. Our inner experience leads us to a commitment to equality, peace, simplicity and truth, which we try to live out in our lives. This is often referred to as Quaker testimony and underpins a lot of Quaker thinking and work.

There are no declared creeds or statements that you have to believe to be a Quaker. Our understanding of faith is that true fulfilment comes from attempting to live life in the spirit of love, truth and peace, and by seeking and acknowledging that of God in everyone. The concept of 'that of God in everyone', by which each human being is considered both unique and precious, is a key tenet of Quaker belief. Interpreting what or who God is, and how God manifests in individuals, is for personal discernment.

This does not make Quakers unrealistic. We know and feel the often unjust and painful world we live in. But in our worship we are led to recognise and foster in our hearts a vision of a world of justice, peace and equality. We strive to let our lives speak to these and try to build that world in the ways we live and act.

Peace, conflict & violence

Quakers believe...
A commitment to peace lies at the heart of Quaker faith and practice. It is part of our striving to live faithfully and is one of our testimonies to the world. Quakers believe that conflict can be a positive force for change, if handled creatively, but it is the use of violence, or the threat of violence, as a means of dealing with conflict, that is problematic.

Quakers think of peace as an approach to living in the world and working for social change, rather than simply an ideological opposition to war and to violence. The use of violence to bring change may create temporary good, but also increases the chance of violence becoming a permanent way of resolving conflict.

Peace is not simply the absence of direct violence, such as murder or domestic violence. Structural violence and cultural violence must also be dealt with for true peace to be present.

Structural violence is present when poverty and hunger are prevalent alongside great wealth. United Nations statistics on the Millennium Development Goals for 2007 show that the seven richest people in the world have a total wealth greater than the combined GDP (gross domestic product) of the world's 41 poorest countries. Cultural violence is present in a society when a dominant culture asserts its position and symbols to the detriment of others, e.g. attacking or otherwise disrespecting the symbols of their identity, language, dress or forms of worship.

For Quakers, such situations represent an unjust and violent world system.

We consider suffering, as a result of both direct and structural violence, to be an avoidable tragedy. When governments and citizens devote significant resources to tackling the root causes of conflict and injustice, the use of violence as a force for change can be greatly reduced and possibly even eliminated.

Faith into action

We strive to practice peace in our own lives, both as individuals and as a community. A key element for Quakers is that we seek to live what we believe. Our work on peace is rooted in the Quaker testimony to peace and to equality.

Corporately, Quakers in Britain have always opposed the use of violence in any form, for any end. Instead, we work to build the conditions of peace that 'take away the occasion of all wars'. Therefore, a central part of the work of Quakers is to respond to human need in the belief that if the problems of poverty and injustice are not attended to, there will not be peace.

In our relationship with others, be they friends, family or strangers, we aim to recognise the dignity of the other alongside our own. This means working to manage conflict with others without seeking their destruction or subjugation.

We also consider the impact of our actions and life choices on the world, for example considering both how we make and how we spend and invest money.

Past

Quakers are probably best known for their stand against war as conscientious objectors. In times of war, Quakers have refused to take up arms and instead tried to help the victims on all sides of the conflict. During past wars, Quakers have participated in war relief work, with many Quakers joining the Friends Ambulance Unit. Quakers have also been involved in humanitarian work in parts of the world where there is violent conflict. In recognition of this work, Quakers were awarded the Nobel Peace Prize in 1947.

Present

Quakers work together as a community, at local, national and international level. Locally we work to introduce peace education, conflict resolution skills and peer-mediation to schools. We organise peace vigils and Nonviolent Direct Action, as well as promoting and supporting the understanding and use of active nonviolence. Information on these can be found at: www.quaker.org.uk/peaceexchange and www.turning-the-tide.org

Quakers support and provide training for groups that are working creatively to build a more peaceful world by challenging injustice and overcoming oppression. Quaker meeting houses are used as community resources, hosting public events to raise awareness of current issues that challenge a peaceful society.

Friends have been involved internationally in highly delicate and sensitive negotiations and mediation, and have worked to support local peacemaking initiatives across the world. Quakers were also involved in developing the Alternatives to Violence Project training, created to assist prisoners in handling personal anger.

Many Quakers join in nonviolent protests against weapons, particularly nuclear weapons. Quakers work for disarmament and against the arms trade, sharing the belief that the more weapons there are in a society, the more likelihood there is of war. Many Quakers believe that war is also made more likely if the military have a strong influence on governmental policies.

Human rights

Quakers believe...

Quakers recognise the equal worth and unique nature of every person. A Quaker statement in 1991 said, 'Our concern for human rights arises from our understanding of how God works in the world and our understanding of God's will for humankind. We believe that all human life has a sacred bond with God and that all people have a holy duty to live the will of God. To develop and grow into the persons God would have us be requires a social environment which provides security and protection for life and personal liberty.'

Faith into action

For many Quakers, a core principle is to try and live what we believe. Our work on human rights is rooted in the Quaker testimony to equality and to peace. These values underpin much of Quaker work.

Past

Quakers were instrumental in setting up Amnesty International. Using his contacts, experience and position, Quaker Eric Baker campaigned for the humane treatment of political prisoners. He wrote an article for *The Observer* entitled 'The Forgotten Prisoner' in 1961. This article called for 'the amnesty of all political prisoners' and began a campaign that resulted in the founding of Amnesty International in 1962.

Many Friends continue to be involved with Amnesty International, both as members and as volunteers.

By meeting with MPs, Quakers worked for the introduction of a Private Members' Bill to raise the age of recruitment into the armed forces to 18 years old. This bill was then used to press the UK government to ratify the optional protocol on the rights of the child in relation to armed conflict.

Present

The work of Quaker Peace & Social Witness (QPSW), the department which works on behalf of Friends in Britain to translate faith into action, and Quaker United Nations Office (QUNO), based in Geneva and New York, is focused at a variety of levels – from grassroots to global – on supporting the promotion and protection of human rights.

Human rights protection has been a core aspect of the work of QUNO since its inception in the 1920s. Current work focuses on: women in prison and children of imprisoned mothers; child soldiers; refugees and conscientious objectors.

QPSW programmes in Palestine and Israel, and in the post-Yugoslav countries, work on monitoring, reporting and opposing violations of human rights and international law. Ecumenical accompaniers, trained and supported by QPSW, travel to Israel–Palestine to provide a peaceful and supportive presence to both Israeli peace groups and Palestinian communities. They offer protection through nonviolent presence, advocacy and human rights monitoring.

Our Statement on Torture states that 'British Quakers are deeply concerned at the continued existence of torture and at recent attempts to justify it, in the context of the 'war on terror', by countries that would previously have condemned it.' Quaker Concern for the Abolition of Torture works to raise awareness and campaigns to end the use of torture.

In Britain, Quakers raise issues relating to the treatment of refugees and asylum seekers with their MPs. This includes highlighting how changes to legislation, and the rhetoric used in Parliament when debating these changes, impact upon refugees' day-to-day lives. We believe that we have a duty to challenge some of the bills that are brought before Parliament and pursue dialogue with MPs. Quakers have a long tradition of working in this way, which we call 'speaking truth to power'.

Crime & punishment

Quakers believe...

Our Quaker belief that there is that of God in everyone prompts us to see criminals as human beings with dignity and rights and to care for their welfare regardless of their crime. We believe no one is outside of God's love and that both justice and forgiveness are needed in dealing effectively with crime. In a world of increasing violence, we still believe in the Christian principle of overcoming evil with good.

This perspective has led Quakers to be at the forefront of penal reform, emphasising the need for rehabilitation rather than retribution in the criminal justice system. We believe that by working towards rehabilitation it is possible to heal not only those directly affected by the crime/offence but also to have a positive impact on the community.

Quakers oppose capital punishment. Our Statement on the Death Penalty states that 'private vengeance or judicial execution serves no purpose but to perpetuate... the trauma. Killing... as a judicial act, brutalises a society that kills.'

Faith into action

Putting their faith into practice, many Quakers work to support people in prison and their families, and are involved in working for change in the criminal justice system.

Too often, the needs of the victim tend to be ignored and the offender is punished without reference to the victim. Equally, no redress is made to right the wrong committed.

Quakers feel that 'punishment is useful only when it helps people to realise the hurt they are doing to [the] sense of worth in themselves and others.'

Past

Quaker George Fox was imprisoned under the Quaker Act of 1662, which made holding and attending Quaker meetings illegal. Following this experience, Fox identified the 'corrupting influence of prison life', whereby prisoners learn about a life of crime from other prisoners.

Another Quaker, Elizabeth Fry, is well known for her work on prison reform during the early 19th century, especially with imprisoned women and children, as depicted on the back of a five-pound note. As well as setting up a school for the children of prisoners, Fry also campaigned against capital punishment and against the deportation of prisoners to Australia.

Present

Quaker prison ministers work as part of multifaith chaplaincy teams to offer spiritual support and friendship to prisoners.

The Quaker Crime, Community & Justice Group is involved in supporting and working for restorative justice in the criminal justice system. Restorative justice is based on dialogue and negotiation, rather than the adversarial process of the criminal justice system. It respects the basic human needs of the victim, the offender and the community, and is based on the principle that victims desire recognition of the harm done. Restorative justice requires the offender to take responsibility for their crime and to make amends to the victim and the community.

Quakers also work to introduce the principles of restorative justice to schools, in the form of peer-mediation, conflict resolution and restorative conferencing. This work is aimed at prevention as well as resolution. The language used doesn't refer to victim and offender, but rather acknowledges that conflict can be more complicated and that no one is completely blameless or wholly responsible for the harm caused.

Racial & religious prejudice

Quakers believe...

Endeavouring to see that of God in everyone translates into a testimony to equality. We believe that our common humanity transcends our differences and leads us to work for a society where difference is respected and celebrated. We do not believe it is reasonable to expect assimilation or to ignore difference by claiming to treat everyone the same, as this denies the value of variety.

Quakers understand that prejudice can be caused by ignorance and fear. We work to teach tolerance and understanding so that all forms of prejudice are recognised and challenged.

We believe that a community which values the good in everyone and respects the diversity of faiths is essential for a peaceful and just society, where everyone can live without hostility. We assert that achieving such a society requires a long-term commitment by everyone, through the building of good relationships.

Faith into action

The Society of Friends was founded in Britain, by George Fox, during the turbulent mid 17th century. Quakers were seen as subversive and faced discrimination, ridicule and hostility and were imprisoned and persecuted for their beliefs. They published a peace testimony, knowing that there can be no peace without justice and equality for all.

Our experiences have reinforced our belief in the importance of religious freedom, the freedom to worship without state interference and the freedom to form and express one's own beliefs. We consider hastily crafted legislation and short-term measures devised to prevent extremism to be not only unhelpful but also counterproductive. Such legislation frequently risks alienating and radicalising those we need to reach out to.

Past

The problems of racism and religious discrimination are not new. Quakers have been involved with demands for reforms and justice over the past 280 years. For Quakers, the subject was first discussed with regard to slavery in 1727. London Yearly Meeting (Quakers in Britain) stated:

> It is the sense of this meeting, that the importing of negroes from their native country and relations by Friends, is not a commendable nor allowed practice, and is therefore censured by this meeting.

In the years that followed, Quakers were instrumental in ending the slave trade in Britain.

Quakers also recognised that 'the roots of racial prejudice lie deep within us, and in seeking a solution to the evil results of racial tensions we need to search our own hearts.' (Yearly Meeting, 1952).

In 1988 Meeting for Sufferings, a nationwide Quaker committee, made a Statement of Intent on Racism. In this they stated:

> ...there is incontrovertible evidence that people who belong to ethnic minority groups... are subject to a variety of disadvantages. In addition to discrimination... our fellow citizens are often subjected to abuse, harassment and violence. The Religious Society of Friends has a duty to play its part in ending these abuses.

In 1992 they set up a working group to explore racism in the Quaker Society in Britain – Britain Yearly Meeting. Searching our own hearts, a video and study guide, was produced in 1997 for use by meetings to provoke discussion and deepen awareness among Friends.

Some Quakers regularly played a part in local initiatives such as a series of multifaith public vigils and the nonviolent escorting of people going to vote in an East London local government by-election.

Present

Quakers continue working to create and maintain a society which lives at peace, promotes harmony, values difference and nurtures each individual.

We are aware that global migration brings with it major challenges, which are not likely to ease in the near future. Many who arrive in Britain face uncertainty, isolation, separation from family, loss of familiar ways of living and, frequently, poverty.

Quakers wish to embrace the diversity that immigration brings and see it as a gift, not a problem. We wish to support the receiving communities, often themselves under strain, and to encourage local Quakers to welcome and nurture those who arrive here, to meet that of God in them and to enable them to live fulfilling lives.

In March 2008, Northern Friends Peace Board held a conference on 'Building Peace – Tackling Racism'. Although academic in focus, a study guide with DVD is planned, looking at more practical skills such as responding to casual racism at work and the need to tackle racism nonviolently. To find out more, visit the website: http://nfpb.gn.apc.org

The environment

Quakers believe...

> We do not own the world, and its riches are not ours to dispose of at will. Show a loving consideration for all creatures and seek to maintain the beauty and variety of the world. Work to ensure that our increasing power over nature is used responsibly, with reverence for life.
>
> *Advices & queries* 42

Compassion and a sense of that of God in the other point to a path of nonviolence towards other people, other species and the earth. We seek to understand and reduce the real and potential harm caused by our lives and actions. This means moving to a way of life that does not cause ecological damage or depend on violence to secure resources.

Faith into action

Simplicity is a component of the Quaker testimonies, and is connected to sufficiency: knowing how much is enough. Quakers try to live simply, by resisting the urge to buy what we do not need and by avoiding the clatter of fashion and consumerism, and by focusing on what matters. This means keeping ourselves informed of the effect our lifestyle has on the environment and the global economy, as well as reminding ourselves that we do not need very much in material terms.

Past

Quaker witness to sustainability and the environment has deep roots. During the 17th century, Friends wrote of their concern for the human relationship with the earth and all its inhabitants. In the 18th century, John Woolman wore undyed clothes, partly because of his concern for the environmental damage caused by the dyeing process.

He expressed his concern for the soil and animal husbandry of the time, noting that:

> ...landlords... by too much tilling, so robbed the earth of its natural fatness that the produce thereof hath grown light.

John Woolman was also conscious of the duty that one generation had to the next, in how they cared for the natural resources of the earth. He noted in early writings that:

The produce of the earth is a gift from our gracious creator to the inhabitants and to impoverish the earth now to support outward greatness appears to be an injury to the succeeding age.

Since the 1920s, British Friends have produced many minutes and epistles of their annual meeting, highlighting the urgent need for action to halt ecological decline and declaring a sense of unity with all creation.

This is a rapidly developing area of Quaker testimony and one which prompts us to question assumptions we have always taken for granted; the needs of the earth can sometimes seem at odds with our own needs.

Present

Many Quakers are making individual decisions regarding the impact of their own lifestyles on the environment. Several Quaker meetings have run 'EcoTeams' sessions, looking at issues such as household waste, recycling, energy and water use, and travel. They found that participating Quakers had waste production levels of approximately one quarter of the UK average.

The Living Witness Project aims to support the development of Quaker corporate witness to sustainable living, and explore ways of taking it to the wider community in Britain and elsewhere, via a growing and vibrant network of Quaker meetings. The project explores corporate witness through study groups and practical activities. They produce resources for individuals and meetings. More information can be found on their website: www.livingwitness.org.uk

QPSW has done some exploratory work on the concept of human security: examining the links between environmental degradation, economic injustice and violent conflict. We believe that human security differs from the prevailing global security model in that it puts safeguarding people, rather than territory, at the centre of security concerns.

QPSW also carries out research on the ethical policies and practices of multinational corporations, on behalf of their partner organisation, the Ecumenical Council for Corporate Responsibility. An example of this is the recently published report Water Sustainability: Meeting the Challenge, a comparative analysis of water consumption in the food processing and beverage industries. Information on this and other such projects can be found on the website: www.eccr.org.uk

Want to know more?

Quakers are formally known as the Religious Society of Friends and hence often refer to each other as 'Friends'. The public more commonly refer to them as Quakers.

The information in this booklet refers specifically to the beliefs of Quakers in Britain and the work done by and on behalf of them. Quakers around the world vary in how they worship and in their theology, though the testimonies are lived out in the lives of Quakers everywhere.

To find out more about the centrally managed work of Quakers in Britain, check out our website: www.quaker.org.uk

For information on our work for peace and justice check out: www.quaker.org.uk/qpsw

For information on Quakers as a religious and spiritual movement have a look at: www.quaker.org.uk/different

This booklet has been written specifically for use by secondary schools and pupils, but will be of interest to anyone wanting to know more about how Quakers translate faith into practice.

To contact us:

Jaci Smith
Peace Education Advisor
Friends House
173 Euston Road
London
NW1 2BJ

Email: pea@quaker.org.uk
Telephone: 020 7663 1000

January 2009

Quaker Peace & Social Witness

Faith into action on behalf of the Religious Society of Friends in Britain

Economic Justice

QPSW's Economic Justice work seeks to promote a fairer and more equitable international economic system that meets the needs of all. We work to influence the policies of governments, companies and international economic institutions and to encourage greater popular understanding of these issues.

Multinational corporations have a huge impact on the lifestyles, livelihoods and environment of people all over the world. Quaker Peace & Social Witness (QPSW) challenges the practices of multinational corporations to ensure this impact is positive.

A community in the Philippines says 'No' to mining that threatens their food security

Credit: WGMP

With its partner, the Ecumenical Council for Corporate Responsibility (ECCR), QPSW carries out research on the ethical policies and practices of a number of corporations in which the churches have investments. ECCR encourages its members to use this information to enter into dialogue with multinational companies and exert pressure on them to improve their practices in areas of concern.

ECCR's latest report '*Vulnerable migrant workers: the responsibility of business*' considers the vulnerable position of many migrant workers employed in the UK and Ireland and offers a comparative analysis of the extent to which nine food production, manufacture and retail (supermarket) companies address this vulnerability.

Ethical Trade

Under the auspices of the Ethical Trading Initiative (ETI), QPSW works with British high street retailers and trade unions to improve the working conditions of the workers, who manufacture the goods that we buy. The highly competitive and dynamic nature of modern retailing means that many retailers now have complex, multi-layered supply chains.

The tripartite nature of the ETI brings together different perspectives and experiences and NGO participation in the initiative is an important way to hold companies to account; to ensure that they are fulfilling their commitments and to challenge them to go further.

www.quaker.org.uk/economics

Our Witness

The belief that justice in our economic system is a necessary condition for peace is informed by Quaker testimonies to simplicity, truth and equality. Quakers try to avoid unnecessary consumption and advocate living simply in the belief that economic opportunity and advancement should benefit the whole community.

Some Quakers act from within the established economic system and others work for radical change of the system itself.

"Economics is presented as though it has unchanging laws, but it is a human creation.

As Quakers we must believe that we can make a difference. Where do we start? We can encourage each other not just to doubt the conventional but to know where differences have been made."

Tony Weekes, Ferguson Fellow at Woodbrooke Quaker Study Centre

Supporting action for economic justice

QPSW supports Friends advocating greater international economic justice.

Through our membership of the Trade Justice Movement and the Jubilee Debt Campaign we provide resources and information to help Friends to get involved in campaigning for trade justice and debt relief.

As a Fairtrade Churches Stakeholder we encourage Friends and meetings to support Fairtrade and take action in Fairtrade Fortnight.

Credit: QPSW

We are a part of Stand Up and Take Action Against Poverty – an annual global event in mid-October in which millions of people take action to demonstrate their support for the fight against poverty – and can provide support and resources for Friends to take part.

The Economic Issues programme is also currently considering ways in which to support Friends, who are, or are interested in, supporting migrant workers in their local communities.

Keeping informed

QPSW is committed to keeping Quakers informed of important international economic issues and supporting those campaigning for economic justice.

We have a range of educational resources to help Quakers and others gain a better understanding of issues such as trade and debt.

These include a regular newsletter *Better World Economics* and an introductory briefing pack on economic issues and institutions and campaigning materials such as postcards and posters.

We can provide speakers for Meetings who wish to learn more about the Economic Issues programme.

A large print version of this resource is available from qpsw@quaker.org.uk or call 020 7663 1158

Quaker Peace & Social Witness works with, and on behalf of, the Religious Society of Friends in Britain to translate our faith into action. As Quakers we are impelled by our faith to make our lives an active witness for peace and justice. Our historic testimonies to equality, justice, peace, simplicity and truth challenge us to alleviate suffering and seek positive social change.

This work is overseen by QPSW's Economic Issues Group, which sets policy and determines priorities.

Get involved

Visit www.quaker.org.uk/qpsw to see the full range of our resources and materials for campaigning.

Ask to receive our introductory guide to international economic issues and institutions

Subscribe to the *Better World Economics* newsletter.

Read *Responding to Climate Change* – a briefing to help Friends learn more about, reflect and take action on climate change.

Ask about the latest economic justice campaigning opportunities.

Support this work with a donation.

Ask about a speaker for your Meeting.

Contact

Suzanne Ismail
QPSW
Friends House
173 Euston Road
London NW1 2BJ

020 7663 1055

suzannei@quaker.org.uk

June 2009

Registered charity: 1127633

Fourfold blessing

May God bless me with discomfort –
at easy answers, half-truths, and superficial relationships,
so that I may live from deep within my heart.

May God bless me with anger –
at injustice, oppression and the exploitation of people,
so that I may work for justice, freedom and peace.

May God bless me with tears to shed
for those who suffer from rejection, starvation and war,
so that I may reach out to comfort them and turn their pain to joy.

May God bless me with enough foolishness
to believe that I can make a difference in this world,
so that I can do what others claim cannot be done.

adapted from a traditional Franciscan blessing

The Sacred in the Everyday

Exploring the Quaker understanding that all times, places and people can be sacred and how this affects our everyday lives.

This unit invites you to find out more about the Quaker approach to sacredness and living 'in the light'. Quakers believe that all of life is sacred and that we can be in touch with the Divine in any time or place without the need for external sacraments. This leads Friends to see our faith as an integral part of everyday life and not just something we do on Sundays.

The Sacred in the Everyday unit aims

This unit aims to help you:

- explore the Quaker understanding of the sacramental nature of life

- find out how Quakers try to live in the light of this understanding

- reflect on your own experience of sacredness in everyday life

Overview

Early Friends had a clear understanding that this moment, now, is 'God's time' and that the whole of life is sacramental. This means actively looking for the sacred in every person, place and time, and living 'in the power of God', as George Fox put it.

This approach led to the development of a Quaker testimony about sacraments: since we are living 'heaven on earth' now, we do not need outward forms and symbols of our connectedness with God, but can experience this oneness at any time, without the special intervention of a sacramental ritual or priest. Rather than abolishing sacraments, Quakers claim that all is sacrament. As one early 20th century Friend said,

> It is a bold and colossal claim ... that the whole of life is sacramental, that there are innumerable 'means of grace' by which God is revealed and communicated...
>
> *Quaker faith & practice* 27.43

Can we live up to this claim by honouring the sacred dimension of all that we experience?

Seeing all times as sacred also led to a testimony among Friends of refusing to celebrate special 'times and seasons' such as Christmas, since every day could be experienced as Christmas (*Quaker faith & practice* 27.42). Many modern British Quakers, however, are less strict about this; it is not unusual to see Christmas trees and Easter eggs in Quaker homes, and many Friends experience a deep connection with the sacred in nature and the turning of the seasons. The fundamental idea of finding the sacred in all the ordinary experiences of life, however, and of being one with God in the present moment, is still central to the Quaker faith.

This insight of Quakerism is not a notion but a way. We are called to live out our faith in the challenges and joys of our everyday lives, in our daily decisions and relationships. It means that we have to pay attention to the apparently unimportant details as well as the big things; it means being the change we want to see in the world. So our lives 'speak' on our behalf about what really matters (*Advices & queries* 27 in *Quaker faith & practice* 1.02), whether it is in our decisions about what to buy, where to shop, how to spend and save our money or what job we do and how we conduct our relationships.

In order to embody this approach to the best of our ability, we must use careful discernment about the choices in our lives. Discernment has been described as 'seeking a graced awareness of how we are to respond to God's invitation in a concrete situation,'* and Quakers try to make this an ongoing discipline. For some Friends this will form part of a regular spiritual practice, or informal conversations with friends and family, but there are also specific Quaker methods which have been developed over the years to help with discernment about life's bigger decisions: these include meetings for clearness and threshing meetings (see Distinctives 3).

In our demanding 21st-century lives, it is as important as ever to take time to connect with the sacredness of life, to experience our oneness with all that is, and to hear the invitation from God to live faithful lives. Taking time for 'inward stillness' (*Advices & queries* 3 in *Quaker faith & practice* 1.02) or developing our own spiritual discipline, prayer or meditation practice is an essential part of living with an awareness of 'the spirit of God at work in the ordinary activities and experience of...daily life.' (*Advices & queries* 7 in *Quaker faith & practice* 1.02).

---

*   Kathleen Fischer, *Women at the Well: feminist perspectives on spiritual direction*, SPCK Publishing 1989, page 123. Reproduced by permission of SPCK publishing.

Quaker distinctives

Distinctives 1

The sacramental nature of life

The following sections of *Quaker faith & practice* give an overview of the Quaker understanding that all of life is sacred:

- inward life of the spirit: *Qf&p* 27.37
- centrality of ordinary experience: *Qf&p* 27.38
- the whole of life as sacramental: *Qf&p* 27.39
- 'a bold claim': *Qf&p* 27.43

You could also read the following extracts, which explore the Quaker approach to specific sacraments such as baptism and communion:

- baptism: *Qf&p* 27.40
- eucharist: *Qf&p* 27.41 and 26.15
- a sacramental meal: *Qf&p* 10.08

Distinctives 2

How does being a Quaker affect everyday life?

The following extracts from *Quaker faith & practice* talk about the effect that our Quaker faith can have on our everyday lives and behaviour:

- it's about the whole of our humanity: *Qf&p* 20.20
- impact of our choices on people and the earth: *Qf&p* 25.11
- coping with everyday conflict: *Qf&p* 20.69
- the much loved story of William Penn's sword: *Qf&p* 19.47
- young Friends on our use of money: *Qf&p* 20.57
- tobacco and alcohol: *Qf&p* 20.40

For more about living faithfully according to our testimonies, see the Faith in Action unit.

Distinctives 3

Choices and discernment

Quakers try to make choices that reflect our understanding of the sacredness of life. To do this we must exercise discernment, both individually and as a community.

'Live adventurously'. You could read *Advices & queries* 17 (in *Quaker faith & practice* 1.02) which guides Quakers in everyday discernment.

Quaker faith & practice also gives guidance about specific Quaker discernment and support methods:

- Meetings for clearness: *Qf&p* 12.22–12.25

- Threshing meetings: *Qf&p* 12.26

- Support groups: *Qf&p* 12.27

- Guidance if you have a particular concern: *Qf&p* 13.08 (and for more about 'concerns', see the Faith in Action unit)

Distinctives 4

The confident Quaker voice

Speaking of our faith in everyday situations can be an important part of witnessing to the sacred aspect of life. This could be at work, with friends, or through 'outreach' activities such as Quaker Quest meetings or Quaker Week activities. You could:

- explore the websites of Quaker Quest: www.quakerquest.org or Quaker Week: www.quakerweek.org.uk

- read extracts about 'Coming Out as a Quaker' at work (you'll find these extracts on page 190)

- read Thomas Ellwood's account from 1659 of telling his friends he was a Quaker in *Qf&p* 19.16

Distinctives 5

Everyday spiritual practice

Quakers have found that making time each day for stillness or spiritual practice helps us become more deeply aware of the sacramental nature of life. The following extracts from *Quaker faith & practice* speak of this understanding:

- An exercise of the spirit: *Qf&p* 20.08

- love can break through: *Qf&p* 20.09

- love silence: *Qf&p* 20.11

- I had given up: *Qf&p* 20.12

For more on everyday spiritual practice, see the Deepening activities in this unit.

Discovery

Discovery 1

Discussion about Quaker approaches to everyday choices

You could consider the introductory questions below, then go to the Sacred in the Everyday unit forum and post your own thoughts on the issues raised. You might like to comment on other posts on this forum too.

Alternatively, you could discuss the forum's introductory questions with your Becoming Friends companion, or others in your meeting.

Introductory questions:

- What aspects of your everyday life might Quakerism affect, for example shopping choices, use of money and resources, relationships, holidays and travel?

- How do you live as a Quaker?

Discovery 2

Exploring Quaker discernment methods

To find out more about Quaker discernment methods, you might like to ask your Becoming Friends companion to arrange for you to talk to a Friend in your local or area meeting who has experience of any of these:

- a Quaker support group

- a meeting for clearness

- a threshing meeting

- the Experiment with Light practice

- informal help with discernment

You could ask the Friend what was involved and whether they found it helpful in making a choice in their life.

Discovery 3

How have local Friends spoken with a confident Quaker voice?

You could ask your Becoming Friends companion or an overseer in your meeting to discuss with you the approach to outreach in your local or area meeting.

- How have Friends communicated about themselves locally? Have they held special outreach activities such as Quaker Quest or Quaker Week?

- If so, what were the challenges or joys? If not, what are the reasons?

Or you could ask your Becoming Friends companion to talk to you about a time in their own life when they have talked about their faith or taken a stand as a result of it.

- What was this experience like? Did your companion feel 'led' to speak or take this action?

Discovery 4

How are you different since coming to Quaker meeting?

This question might be the focus for a small group session, to explore the effect of their Quaker faith on the lives of local Friends. You could ask your Becoming Friends companion or an elder in your meeting to help you set up this group, or you may simply prefer to discuss the question with your Becoming Friends companion.

You or your companion can share the question with the group as a starting point for reflection (it might be helpful to write or print out copies of the question):

- How are you different since coming to Quaker meeting/becoming a Quaker?

After people have had a brief opportunity for personal reflection on the question, spend some time in worship-sharing mode as a group, sharing with one another any responses, insights, experiences or challenges relating to the questions.

Guidance for worship sharing is found in Appendix 2 – Guidance on pages 283–284.

Discovery 5

How do you experience the Spirit in the everyday?

You could ask your Becoming Friends companion (or another Friend in your meeting) to discuss with you their experience of the Spirit in the everyday.

Are there aspects of this experience that they find challenging, or welcome?

You could also discuss this question by making a post on a Quaker discussion forum:

- the Britain Yearly Meeting forum at: www.quakerweb.org.uk/forum

- www.friendlink.org.uk (aimed mainly at young Quakers)

- the Sacred in the Everyday unit forum

Deepening

Deepening 1

Drawing on practices from other spiritual traditions

You might like to spend time reflecting on *Advices & queries* 3 (in section 1.02 of *Quaker faith & practice*), which focuses on stillness and spiritual practice.

Many Friends find their spiritual life enriched by drawing on practices from other spiritual traditions.

- You might like to try one of the spiritual practices in Appendix 1 – Spiritual Practices (page 265).

- You could explore other possibilities – talk to Friends about what they have found helpful.

Deepening 2

Looking for the sacred by reviewing the day

It can be helpful to develop a deliberate habit of reviewing the day or week just gone to find points of growth, and times when we have been particularly aware of the sacred or the work of the Spirit in our life.

The 'review of the day' is a practice which gives us a structure for doing this: see Appendix 1 – Spiritual Practices (page 269).

You could also reflect on this experience with your Becoming Friends companion when you next meet.

Deepening 3

Responding creatively to the sacredness of life

We often experience the sacredness of life through our senses. You can read a reflection on this in *Quaker faith & practice* 21.24.

If you would like to take some time to reflect deeply on your own response to the sacredness of life, you could:

- respond by drawing, painting, or using another creative method

- respond in music, song or movement

- respond in writing

- go online and blog about your response

- discuss your response on a Quaker discussion forum:
  - the Britain Yearly Meeting forum at: www.quakerweb.org.uk/forum
  - www.friendlink.org.uk (aimed mainly at young Quakers)
  - the Sacred in the Everyday unit forum

- share some of your reflections with your Becoming Friends companion when you next meet.

Deepening 4

Mindfulness as a way to awareness of the sacred

Mindfulness practices have formed part of monastic traditions in East and West, and many Quakers find them very helpful in developing a deeper awareness of the sacramental nature of life. There are extracts about mindfulness by writers from both traditions on pages 191–193.

- You could read these and reflect on how you could become more mindful in your everyday life.

- You can also find guidance on mindfulness practices such as 'walking' or 'working' meditations online at:
  - www.plumvillage.org/practice.html
  - www.youtube.com - try searching for 'Walking meditation with Thich Naht Hanh' or 'We Live Love Mindfully', also from Thich Naht Hanh's Plum Village community

- You could try eating a meal or doing a household chore mindfully.

You may wish to reflect on how you have got on with this exercise at a future meeting with your Becoming Friends companion.

Deepening 5

Reflecting with Your Becoming Friends companion

You might like to spend time with your Becoming Friends companion reflecting on your response to any of the following questions:

- How am I living differently since first walking into a Quaker meeting?

- Has my interest in Quakerism brought me into any interesting conversations, experiences or conflict with people?

- How do I live my life? How do I know the right course to take?

Alternatively, you might like to make a post in response to any of these questions on the Sacred in the Everyday unit forum.

Further exploration

If you would like to explore the subject of the sacred in the everyday further, here are some suggestions for reading, listening or viewing.

Advices & queries 1–7 and 21–30 (in *Quaker faith & practice* 1.02).

A faith to call our own: Quaker tradition in the light of contemporary movements of the Spirit, Alex Wildwood, Quaker Home Service, 1999 (Swarthmore Lecture).

A light that is shining: an introduction to the Quakers, Harvey Gillman, Quaker Books, 2003.

Light to live by, Rex Ambler, Quaker Books, 2002 (about 'Experiment with Light')

Listening spirituality 1: personal spiritual practices among Friends, Patricia Loring, Openings Press, 1997.

New light: 12 Quaker voices, edited by Jennifer Kavanagh, O Books, 2008. Individual themes such as *Twelve Quakers and Worship*, *Twelve Quakers and Simplicity* also available in the *Twelve Quakers and...* series, Quaker Quest 2004–2007.

Quaker identity and the heart of our faith, Quaker Life Study Materials, Quaker Life, 2008. Includes 'Nurturing the spiritual life' by Deborah Rowlands (page 64). Available online at www.quaker.org.uk/sites/default/files/Faith-and-practice-proceeding.pdf or in hard copy by contacting Quaker Life on 020 7663 1140 or email: ql@quaker.org.uk

Women at the well: feminist perspectives on spiritual direction, Kathleen Fischer, SPCK Publishing, 1989.

Woodbrooke's website or brochure for details of courses about discernment, spiritual practice and living faithful lives: www.woodbrooke.org.uk

Many of these titles are available from the Quaker Centre bookshop:

Friends House
173 Euston Road
London NW1 2BJ

Tel: 020 7663 1030
Fax: 020 7663 1001

Website: www.quaker.org.uk/bookshop
Email: quakercentre@quaker.org.uk

Many of them will also be in your local meeting house library. You could ask your Becoming Friends companion to help you track down titles that interest you.

Closing activity

As you finish your exploration of the Quaker understanding of the sacred in the everyday, you are invited to reflect on what you have gained through this unit, how your understanding of both yourself and Quakerism has changed, and what areas you would like to explore further.

This closing reflection can be a very good opportunity for sharing with your Becoming Friends companion, or you may prefer to write in a journal or book of spiritual discipline (there's guidance for journalling in Appendix 2 – Guidance on page 282), or to reflect using creative methods such as drawing, collage, model-making or working with materials such as textiles or wood.

You may like to use one or more of the following questions as a focus for your reflection:

- What have you gained from your work on this unit, whether as a result of positive or more challenging experiences?

- In what ways has your understanding changed as a result of your work on this unit?

- Are there areas that you would like to explore further – either as part of your own spiritual journey or relating to Quakerism?

- Has anything arisen that you would find it helpful to reflect on with your Becoming Friends companion?

Extract for Distinctives 4:
The confident Quaker voice

Coming out as a Quaker

Friend 1

I work in a Day Care setting and it seemed really important to me to come out straight away to my colleagues because we work so closely together.

No-one really knew much about Quakers but they did ask, at first as a kind of joke and later more seriously, about what it meant. I don't go on about it but if anyone asks me what I am doing on a particular weekend and it happens to be Quaker activity then I always tell them. They are used to it now.

We also have a Jehovah's Witness among the staff and one or two who are interested in Buddhism and being open about my faith life means that conversations about these things are possible.

I feel happy about being able to say 'I am a Quaker' and so I say it whenever the occasion arises.

Friend 2

'Coming out' has been an important activity for those of us who don't fit into the general assumption that everyone is, or would like to be, heterosexual. For me it has been about naming and accepting a truth about who I am, and then facing up to telling people that I just don't fit a particular image. It goes against the grain of the prevailing culture in society. It's about correcting people's false assumptions and expectations about me; perhaps most painfully, when they are trying to be kind and welcoming.

When I started attending Quaker Meeting seriously, I realised that I would have to start coming out all over again, but that this time I had to come out to my rational, sceptical friends as a Quaker. In many ways, this second process has been just as hard as coming out as a lesbian. Being Quaker goes against the grain in so many ways today, just as it has always done. It goes against the grain of the anti-religious, rational-scientific approach to life. It goes against the grain of religion based on rules, creeds and dogma. It goes against the grain of a life based on appearances and a primary focus on personal pleasure-seeking. There's a well-loved story of a 17th-century Quaker who started wearing plain clothes and refusing to take part in the elaborate and meaningless social rituals of his friends: eventually the truth dawned on them that he had become a Quaker. The testimonies we hold to may not be quite so visible for our generation, and they challenge us to speak up and 'come out' against false assumptions. In what ways will you be 'coming out'?

Extract for Deepening 4:
Mindfulness as a way to awareness of the sacred

Extracts on mindfulness

Walking

I leave the bedroom...I begin walking
through my house. I will traverse it
many times today like a creature
covering her turf. It is a journey
that zigzags and returns upon itself...
a circumambulation...a re-remembering of 'place.'
I know this is the way many ancients prayed –
circling a holy site to deepen their devotion.
I wonder if animals offer their speechless prayers to You
by scudding over their well-known ground?
My foot rises. Before it falls
there is a tiny moment when
neither of my feet are really carrying weight –
a suspension, a moment of physical trust.
Something in me knows
that the ground will still be there.
Let me return to this innate knowledge –
this ancient confidence.
The floor in this house is wood...wide, old boards.
When I walk I am walking on the wood and in the woods.
I am walking on the life of these trees.
They have been cut and planed...offered up
for this sheltering. Let me remember to offer myself
to be shelter for something in Your world.
My foot falls. The ground rises to meet it.
A holy, ordinary moment is repeating itself.
All the time I am meeting and being met like this.
Your whole creation is ground.
Help me to remember that in this mutuality
we can become home for each other.
You are asking us slowly to become
Your holy site.

Gunilla Norris

*   Excerpts from *Being Home: Discovering the Spiritual in the Everyday*, by Gunilla Norris, Copyright © 1991, 2001
by Gunilla Norris. Paulist Press, Inc., New York/Mahwah, NJ. Reprinted by permission of Paulist Press, Inc.
www.paulistpress.com

Tangerine Meditation

If I offer you a freshly picked tangerine to enjoy, I think the degree to which you enjoy it will depend on your mindfulness. If you are free of worries and anxiety, you will enjoy it more. If you are possessed by anger and fear, the tangerine may not be very real to you.

One day, I offered a number of children a basket filled with tangerines. The basket was passed around, and each child took one tangerine and put it in his or her palm. We each looked at our tangerine, and the children were invited to meditate on its origins. They saw not only their tangerine, but also its mother, the tangerine tree. With some guidance, they began to visualize the blossoms in the sunshine and in the rain. Then they saw petals falling down and the tiny green fruit appear. The sunshine and the rain continued, and the tiny tangerine grew. Now someone has picked it, and the tangerine is here. After seeing this, each child was invited to peel the tangerine slowly, noticing the mist and the fragrance of the tangerine, and then bring it up to his or her mouth and have a mindful bite, in full awareness of the texture and taste of the fruit and the juice coming out. We ate slowly like that.

Each time you look at a tangerine, you can see deeply into it. You can see everything in the universe in one tangerine. When you peel it and smell it, it's wonderful. You can take your time eating a tangerine and be very happy.

Washing Dishes

To my mind, the idea that doing dishes is unpleasant can occur only when you aren't doing them. Once you are standing in front of the sink with your sleeves rolled up and your hands in the warm water, it is really quite pleasant. I enjoy taking my time with each dish, being fully aware of the dish, the water, and each movement of my hands. I know that if I hurry in order to eat dessert sooner, the time of washing dishes will be unpleasant and not worth living. That would be a pity, for each minute, each second of life is a miracle. The dishes themselves and the fact that I am here washing them are miracles!

If I am incapable of washing dishes joyfully, if I want to finish them quickly so I can go and have dessert, I will be equally incapable of enjoying my dessert. With the fork in my hand, I will be thinking about what to do next, and the texture and the flavor of the dessert, together with the pleasure of eating it, will be lost. I will always be dragged into the future, never able to live in the present moment.

Each thought, each action in the sunlight of awareness becomes sacred. In this light, no boundary exists between the sacred and the profane. I must confess it takes me a bit longer to do the dishes, but I live fully in every moment, and I am happy. Washing the dishes is at the same time a means and an end – that is, not only do we do the dishes in order to have clean dishes, we also do the dishes just to do the dishes, to live fully in each moment while washing them.

Thich Nhat Hanh

---

*   from *Peace is Every Step: the Path of Mindfulness in Everyday Life* by Thich Nhat Hanh, published by Rider. Reprinted by permission of The Random House Group Ltd.

Taking Out the Trash

The trash bin is overflowing under the sink.
It's time to feed the big outdoor garbage can
again. How quickly it happens...how astonishing
that every week my bins are full to the brim
with the wastes of my daily existence.
Here I am dumping everything
from carrot peelings to junk mail.
What a mess I make!
I try to remember that You planned waste
as an essential part of life. It, too, is holy.
I want to keep in mind
the pine tree by the front door
and how it keeps dropping its numberless needles
- a tall and humble prayer.
I want to shed my waste with quiet reverence
like the pine. I want somehow to have a
conscience, a responsibility, for what it means
personally, socially, and ecologically to have
this much trash EVERY WEEK.
Help me to stop this hurry
to get my psychological and actual trash
out of sight and out of mind
and learn instead.
This task is a kind of surrender...
surrender to the knowledge that by being alive
and human I do make a human mess
as a pine tree makes its kind of mess.
Let me surrender any fake and pristine sense
of not affecting my fellow beings
and my environment with my waste.
Let me own my part of the landfill...
the one outside of town with the bulldozer
and the psychological one we all share.
Keep me mindful of what I take
into my home, the items bought to substitute
for real living – the food and drink I consume
instead of examining my feelings.
Help me slowly to surrender all excess.

Gunilla Norris

---

*   Excerpts from *Being Home: Discovering the Spiritual in the Everyday*, by Gunilla Norris, Copyright © 1991, 2001
     by Gunilla Norris. Paulist Press, Inc., New York/Mahwah, NJ. Reprinted by permission of Paulist Press, Inc.
     www.paulistpress.com

Silence and Waiting

Exploring the Quaker experience of worship, silent waiting and spoken ministry.

This unit invites you to explore the Quaker experience of worship, silent waiting and spoken ministry. Our shared worship is the foundation of our experience of life as a spiritual community. We may well worship or hold silence alone but we believe that in worshipping together we are opening ourselves to a more powerful experience. We are a mixed gathering, people with disparate backgrounds, and we are at many different places on our inward journey; however, all Friends would experience worship as a core element in their spiritual practice.

Silence and Waiting unit aims

This unit aims to help you:

- become more familiar with the Quaker practice of worship and silent waiting

- find out how other Friends experience worship and ministry

- reflect on your own understanding of and relationship to silence and worship

Overview

The fundamental shared experience of the Quaker way is the silent meeting for worship. We seek a communal gathered stillness, where we can be open to inspiration, to God's presence, and to finding peace of mind and a renewed sense of purpose for living. Quaker worship is spontaneous and flexible in its freedom from credal structure and liturgy. It is unique as an exercise in silent corporate contemplation that draws individual worshippers into a depth of unity, while they remain fully themselves.

People arrive at a meeting as separate individuals with their own particular joys and anxieties, and the group begins to 'gather'. Those present settle quietly and begin 'waiting on God' together, becoming open to one another at a deep level. This may happen quickly, or it may take most of the hour.

The silence is different from that experienced in solitary meditation. The listening and waiting in a Friends meeting is a communal experience of shared seeking of the Divine.

Silence is valued by Quakers because it allows us for a while to be aware of the inner and deeper meaning of our individual and shared lives and creates a space in which we can begin to sense the Divine within us. We are able to begin to accept ourselves as we are and to find some release from fear, anxiety, emotional confusion and selfishness. The silence is more than an absence of sound: one can be aware on one level of external sounds but these sounds are not distractions. They are absorbed, often unconsciously, as people try to be open to that of God within them.

> Worship is the response of the human spirit to the presence of the divine and eternal, to the God who first seeks us. The sense of wonder and awe of the finite before the infinite leads naturally to thanksgiving and adoration.
>
> *Quaker faith & practice* 2.01

For some Friends this quotation fully expresses their understanding of worship while for others its emphasis upon a 'God who first seeks us' may be challenging. For many Friends worship is a strong guiding force in their lives as it enables them to experience a sense of connectedness with the Divine. For others a profound sense of the healing and unifying power of silence is central to their understanding of what we are doing when we meet together to silently wait. For most Quakers, this diversity of experience is to be celebrated.

Early Friends spoke of the leadings of the Divine Light that 'shows us our darkness and brings us to new life' (*Advices & queries* 1 in *Quaker faith & practice* 1.02). This power of the Light to change our lives is enormous, and a vital part of the Quaker experience of silent worship. Both for early Friends and many contemporary

Friends the importance of worship as a time for discerning and understanding how we respond to the choices and dilemmas of life is central:

> Wait to feel the light of life .... where the light begins to lead, do thou there begin to follow.
>
> Isaac Pennington, *Works* vol 11

Our silent waiting has a liberating quality. It is an active experience in which we become more present. Our silent waiting may open us to leadings of the Spirit.

Out of the silence may arise words, if Friends feel led to offer spoken ministry, but some meetings for worship remain completely silent: spoken words in meeting aim to express aloud what is already present in the silence.

> Such words as these have at least as much power as silence to gather into stillness.
>
> Caroline E. Stephen, *Quaker faith & practice* 2.39

Anyone may feel the call to speak, adult or child, Friend or first time visitor. There is a wide variety of sources of spoken ministry and the acceptance of them is an important part of Quaker worship. Since the Society is part of the Christian tradition, people may speak of the life and teaching of Jesus. They may use words from other sources or refer to events in daily life. Because ministry may arise from personal experience and insights there will be different approaches.

A fundamental part of the Quaker discipline of silent waiting and listening is to try to 'receive the vocal ministry of others in a tender and creative spirit,' reaching for the 'meaning deep within it' (*Advices & queries* 12 in *Quaker faith & practice* 1.02), rather than listening with our normal critical ear. Sometimes these words of ministry may speak directly to our heart, at others they may not seem relevant to us, but those words may be a vital source of comfort, challenge or inspiration to others.

The hope is that by the close of the meeting, all will feel united through our experience of silent waiting together, and be aware that we have come close to the Divine, whatever our understanding of it.

Quaker distinctives

Distinctives 1

The nature of Quaker worship

Chapter 2 of *Quaker faith & practice* speaks about Quaker worship. You might like to read the following selection of extracts:

- a giving and receiving: *Qf&p* 2.11
- response to a vision of greatness: *Qf&p* 2.07
- communing with the divine: *Qf&p* 2.08
- inspired by God: *Qf&p* 2.09
- all one life: *Qf&p* 2.36
- corporate waiting and listening: *Qf&p* 2.37

You could also read the guidance of *Advices & queries* about meeting for worship. If you prefer to listen to *Advices & queries*, there are mp3 audio files available in this unit of the online Becoming Friends course. The sections are as follows:

- *A&q* 1–7: the inner life
- *A&q* 8-13: meeting for worship

Distinctives 2

Why silence?

The following sections of *Quaker faith & practice* reflect on what it is that Quakers value about silence:

- silence – active and redemptive: *Qf&p* 2.12
- nourishment and refreshment: *Qf&p* 2.13
- prayerful expectancy: *Qf&p* 2.14
- an intensified pause: *Qf&p* 2.16
- silence sets you free: *Qf&p* 2.17

You might like to take one extract at a time and really allow space and time to reflect deeply on it.

Distinctives 3

Friends' experiences of meeting for worship

Friends might speak of the movement or development of the silence that happens in a meeting for worship; the quality of silence can be felt to change and deepen throughout the worship. Our waiting becomes more active and we become more present as the silence deepens.

You might like to

- read extracts about Quakers' experiences of meeting for worship, which are on pages 211–215

- or listen to the audio clips about experiences of meeting for worship on the Becoming Friends online course

Distinctives 4

The 'gathered' meeting

You could watch the video 'An introduction to Quakers' made by Friends at Watford Quaker Meeting, which includes discussion about Friends' experiences of meeting for worship and the idea of a 'gathered' meeting. You can access the video in a number of different ways:

- online at
  - www.watfordquakers.org.uk/videos.html
  - www.quakerweek.org.uk/intro/quaker-worship
  - www.youtube.com as 'Introduction to Quakers'

- on the DVD *An introduction to Watford Quakers*, available from the Quaker Centre bookshop (see Further exploration for contact details).

You can also read about the 'gathered' meeting in *Quaker faith & practice* 2.38, 2.39 and 2.47.

You might like to discuss with your Becoming Friends companion the idea of a 'gathered' or 'covered' meeting and their experience of it.

Distinctives 5

Spoken ministry in meeting for worship

Sections 2.55–2.73 in *Quaker faith & practice* reflect on spoken ministry in meeting for worship. Here is a selection of extracts you might read:

- guidance about true ministry being led by the Spirit: *Qf&p* 2.60

- George Fox on spoken ministry: *Qf&p* 2.73

- ministry is what is on one's soul: *Qf&p* 2.66

- the experience of finding oneself moved to minister: *Qf&p* 2.58

- hearing ministry we dislike: *Qf&p* 2.68

You could take one extract at a time and really allow space and time for it to speak to you.

Discovery

Discovery 1

Experiencing different meetings for worship

It can be interesting to experience meeting for worship in meetings of different kinds and sizes, or in different locations. You may find that your experience of both silence and spoken ministry in meeting for worship varies considerably in these contexts.

If your local meeting has a number of meetings for worship throughout the week, try attending one that you have not been to before.

Try attending a meeting for worship at a different meeting house, either near you or when you are away from home. You could:

- ask your Becoming Friends companion, or an elder or overseer

- look in the Book of Meetings (available in most meeting houses)

- or search for a meeting online at: www.quaker.org.uk/fam

You might try a meeting for worship outdoors. Early Friends often met outside and were aware of how a deep connection with the earth can enable our inner silence to grow. There are present-day outdoor meetings for worship, for example at Speakers' Corner in London (monthly) and Faslane naval base in Scotland (occasional). Some local meetings hold a meeting for worship outside or in their town centre during Quaker Week.

You could reflect with your Becoming Friends companion on your experience of different meetings for worship.

Discovery 2

Discussion about our experiences of meeting for worship

You might like to ask one or two Friends in your meeting about their experience of meeting for worship and how it is different from keeping silence on your own. You could ask them about ways in which they feel we are connected in the silence. For example, some Friends will uphold each other in love, some might imagine the lines of connection between us, others might see us as 'covered' by the loving presence of God.

You could do this during the coffee time after meeting for worship, or you might like to ask your Becoming Friends companion to help you set up an informal meeting with other Friends.

Alternatively, you could consider these introductory questions:

- What is your experience of meeting for worship?

- How is this experience different from keeping silence on your own?

then go to the Silence and Waiting unit forum and post your own thoughts on the issues raised. You might like to comment on other posts on this forum too.

Discovery 3

Sharing our experiences of silence and waiting

What is your own experience of the quality and depth of silence and attentive waiting changing and developing throughout meeting for worship? You could ask your Becoming Friends companion or other Friends about their experience of silence and waiting in meeting for worship. The following questions provide starting points for discussion:

- Are you aware of any shifts in the quality or depth of silence or waiting during meeting for worship?

- What seems to influence those changes?

- What do you understand by 'waiting' in meeting for worship?

- What might we be waiting for?

You could also join in a discussion about experiences of silence and waiting on a Quaker discussion forum:

- the Britain Yearly Meeting forum at: www.quakerweb.org.uk/forum

- www.friendlink.org.uk (aimed mainly at young Quakers)

- the Silence and Waiting unit forum

Discovery 4

How do Quakers become still in meeting for worship?

The process of settling into a focused silence is called 'centring down' by Quakers. Some Friends enter the silence with an awareness of their breathing, while others mentally focus their intentions, or pray for each of the Friends gathered with them. Many Friends will be informed by an understanding of meditation from various religious traditions but also hold to the distinctiveness of our corporate waiting worship.

You could:

- discuss with your Becoming Friends companion the ways they 'centre down' or enter the silence

- ask other Friends in your meeting the same question over coffee, or ask your Becoming Friends companion to help you set up an informal opportunity for group discussion

Experiment with different approaches to settling into and maintaining your own inner silence. Notice what works well for you.

One possibility is to centre yourself using a simple breathing practice. You'll find a guide to this practice on page 275.

Discovery 5

Spoken and sung ministry

Each worshipping individual brings their presence to meeting whether spoken or unspoken and it affects the meeting as a whole. Try to notice what you are bringing to the quality of the worship each week.

You could ask your Becoming Friends companion or another experienced Friend about:

- their experience of feeling led to minister in meeting for worship – how do they know when it is right to stand up and speak?

- their experience of hearing spoken ministry in meeting for worship – have there been occasions when spoken ministry has really spoken to them personally, or been difficult to come to terms with?

As we listen attentively to any ministry that arises in meeting, we can renew our awareness that we listen not only to the words but where the words come from. Ministry can stay with us throughout our week.

You could experiment with writing down what you saw to be the key element of the ministry for you on your spiritual/faith journey.

Deepening

Deepening 1

Reflections on silence in the whole of our lives

Our world is very noisy and it can be hard to make a place for silence in our lives.

- Notice the ways in which you may avoid silence through the use of the radio, television, computer or other distractions.

- How much space for silence is there in your relationships?

- Could you find ways of building moments of silence into your day?

- Do you experience silence differently in the city, in natural or wild places, with people, on your own?

You could explore this further by:

- responding in writing

- drawing or using another creative method

- going online and blogging

- discussing these issues on a Quaker discussion forum:
  - the Britain Yearly Meeting forum at: www.quakerweb.org.uk/forum
  - www.friendlink.org.uk (aimed mainly at young Quakers)
  - the Silence and Waiting unit forum

- sharing some of your reflections with your Becoming Friends companion when you next meet

Deepening 2

Speaking in meeting for worship

Have you ever felt led to speak in meeting for worship? You might like to reflect on any times when you have considered the possibility of being led to give spoken ministry. What would enable you to speak? What would hold you back?

There is modern Quaker guidance about speaking in meeting for worship, which you'll find on page 216. Do you find this guidance helpful?

You could share some of your reflections with your Becoming Friends companion when you next meet.

Deepening 3

Silence and worship online

There are many websites which offer experiences of silence, prayer or worship online. You might try the following sites:

- an online Quaker meeting for worship at: quakerworship.org/default.asp

- an online labyrinth 'walk', with different contemplative activities along the way at: www.rejesus.co.uk/site/module/labyrinth

- a prayer site based on short bible readings at: http://sacredspace.ie

- a daily prayer download at: www.pray-as-you-go.org

- a Buddhist pebble meditation at: www.youtube.com – search for 'Pebble for your pocket meditation'

- Taize chants and prayers to listen to or download at: www.taize.fr/en_article681.html (to download mp3s, right click on the name of the track, then 'save target as' or similar and choose where to save on your computer/mp3 player)

- guidelines for centering prayer at: www.youtube.com – search for 'Thomas Keating Centering Prayer guidelines intro'

You could reflect on this experience of online silence and worship by:

- discussing it on a Quaker discussion forum:
  - the Britain Yearly Meeting forum at: www.quakerweb.org.uk/forum
  - www.friendlink.org.uk (aimed mainly at young Quakers)
  - the Silence and Waiting unit forum

- responding through writing or creative activity

- sharing some of your reflections with your Becoming Friends companion when you next meet

Deepening 4

Knowing your worshipping community

If the presence of each of us changes the quality of the silence we experience, it is important to acknowledge each other's presence. Depending on the size of your meeting, you may or may not know everyone by name.

- If possible, notice or name who is present and who is absent at meeting next time you go.

- You might 'send light to' or pray for those who are not with you in worship.

- You could reflect on the other Quaker meetings that are near and imagine them also sitting in expectant waiting. Extend your thoughts even wider and think about the meetings all over Britain, Europe and the world, imagining how we are connected by our silent expectant waiting.

You might like to reflect on this experience with your Becoming Friends companion when you next meet

Deepening 5

Practising the discipline of silent waiting and listening

Quakers have a distinct practice of listening – waiting in silent attentiveness. Experiment with how you listen to others in your life, noticing when you are really listening to someone and when your mind is wandering. All listening can be part of our listening to the Spirit.

You might like to spend some time alone reflecting on your experiences of listening, using the questions in 'Listening in a new way', which you'll find on page 217.

You could share these reflections with your Becoming Friends companion, who might also do the exercise; or you could write, journal or make a creative response.

There is an exercise in listening prayer in Appendix 1 – Spiritual Practices on page 268. You could practise this with your Becoming Friends companion or another Friend, listening to each other with focused, prayerful attention.

Further exploration

If you would like to explore the subject of silence and waiting further here are some other resources

Advices & queries 1–7 and 8–13 (in *Quaker faith & practice* 1.02).

The amazing fact of Quaker worship, George Gorman, Quaker Books, 1973 (Swarthmore Lecture).

A book of silence, Sara Maitland, Granta Books, 2008.

Coming home: an introduction to the Quakers, Gerald Priestland, Quaker Books, 2003.

Focusing: how to open up your deeper feelings and intuition, Eugene Gendlin, Rider, 2003.

God is silence, Pierre Lacout, Quaker Books, 1970.

Ground and spring: foundations of Quaker discipleship, Beth Allen, Quaker Books, 2007 (Swarthmore Lecture).

An introduction to Watford Quakers (DVD), part 1 'An Introduction to Quakerism', Just Film, 2007. Available at: www.watfordquakers.org.uk/videos.html or www.quakerweek.org.uk/intro (or on www.youtube.com as 'Introduction to Quakers').

Light to live by, Rex Ambler, Quaker Books, 2002 (about 'Experiment with Light').

A light that is shining: an introduction to the Quakers, Harvey Gillman, Quaker Books, 2003.

Listening spirituality 1: personal spiritual practices among Friends, Patricia Loring, Openings Press, 1997

New light: 12 Quaker voices, edited by Jennifer Kavanagh, O Books, 2008. Individual themes such as *Twelve Quakers and Worship*, *Twelve Quakers and Simplicity* also available in the *Twelve Quakers and...* series, Quaker Quest 2004–2007.

Quaker faith & practice chapter 2, 'Approaches to God – worship and prayer'.

Quaker identity and the heart of our faith, Quaker Life Study Materials, Quaker Life, 2008. Includes Beth Allen on 'An exploration of the nature of Quaker worship'. Available online at www.quaker.org.uk/sites/default/files/Faith-and-practice-proceeding.pdf or in hard copy by contacting Quaker Life on 020 7663 1140 or email: ql@quaker.org.uk.

The quaking meeting: transforming our selves, our meetings and the more-than-human world, Helen Gould, Australia Yearly Meeting, 2009 (James Backhouse Lecture).

Radio 3 programme about silence with Rowan Williams (Sunday 22 February 2009). Download or listen at: www.christianmeditation.org.uk/public_html/web/news_media.php .

Searching the depths: essays on being a Quaker today, edited by Harvey Gillman and Alastair Heron, Quaker Home Service, 1996. 'The meeting for worship' chapter by Elizabeth Barnett.

Many of these titles are available from the Quaker Centre bookshop:

Friends House
173 Euston Road
London NW1 2BJ

Tel: 020 7663 1030
Fax: 020 7663 1001

Website: www.quaker.org.uk/bookshop
Email: quakercentre@quaker.org.uk

Many of them will also be in your local meeting house library. You could ask your Becoming Friends companion to help you track down titles that interest you.

Closing activity

As you finish your exploration of silence and waiting, you are invited to reflect on what you have gained through this unit, how your understanding of both yourself and Quakerism has changed, and what areas you would like to explore further.

This closing reflection can be a very good opportunity for sharing with your Becoming Friends companion, or you may prefer to write in a journal or book of spiritual discipline (there's guidance for journalling in Appendix 2 – Guidance on page 282), or to reflect using creative methods such as drawing, collage, model-making or working with materials such as textiles or wood.

You might like to use one or more of the following questions as a focus for your reflection:

- What have you gained from your work on this unit, whether as a result of positive or more challenging experiences?

- In what ways has your understanding changed as a result of your work on this unit?

- Are there areas that you would like to explore further – either as part of your own spiritual journey or relating to Quakerism?

- Has anything arisen that you would find it helpful to reflect on with your Becoming Friends companion?

Extracts for Distinctives 3
Friends' experiences of meeting for worship

1

Quaker Meeting

Someone said
our bodies are like reeds;
we must let the breath
of the divine blow through us
become like piccolos and flutes;
make a living music.

Today
I feel the sharpness
of morning air,
listen to the sky soughing,
notice how leaves
on the tree tremble.

> Denise Bennett, *Quaker Monthly*,
> October 2008, p272

2

On one never-to-be-forgotten Sunday morning, I found myself one of a small
company of silent worshippers who were content to sit down together without
words, that each one might feel after and draw near to the Divine Presence,
unhindered at least, if not helped, by any human utterance. Utterance I knew
was free, should the words be given; and, before the meeting was over, a sentence
or two were uttered in great simplicity by an old and apparently untaught man,
rising in his place amongst the rest of us. I did not pay much attention to the
words he spoke, and I have no recollection of their purport. My whole soul was
filled with the unutterable peace of the undisturbed opportunity for communion
with God, with the sense that at last I had found a place where I might, without
the faintest suspicion of insincerity, join with others in simply seeking His
presence. To sit down in silence could at the least pledge me to nothing; it might
open to me (as it did that morning) the very gate of heaven. And, since that day,
now more than seventeen years ago, Friends' meetings have indeed been to me
the greatest of outward helps to a fuller and fuller entrance into the spirit from
which they have sprung; the place of the most soul-subduing, faith-restoring,
strengthening, and peaceful communion, in feeding upon the bread of life, that I
have ever known.

> Caroline E. Stephen, 1890: *Quaker faith & practice* 2.02

3

Quaker Meeting

At half past ten the talking stops;
slowly we settle down.
Hard seats, few are cushioned,
an hour is a long time.
Only our breathing
and the ticking of the friendly clock
disturb the silence.
Sitting in a circle, the others close,
I am aware of their presence
as they are of mine.
Reaching inward to their utmost being,
seeking the Spirit, seeking
the Inner Light.
Or wondering what to get for dinner.
I look at the polished table, the scent of old wood.
Someone has brought a cyclamen
in a pot.
In its bright reflections
A flame burns, but still I'm no closer
to the thing I seek.

Yet all these everyday objects,
hard seat, the clock, the breathing,
wood scent, flower, pot.
Even the uncertain passage of time
and thoughts about dinner.
None of these nor even the words themselves
reach out, or make demands,
corral or take possession;
they do not ape our driven
grasping human condition.

No, they simply are themselves,
unseeking unsought.
Perhaps I, like them,
forgoing all urgency
must wait in silence
as the inner light seeks me out.
Its invasion illuminating
my free capitulation.

> Amyon Corbould-Taylor and David Stuart,
> *Quaker Monthly*, August 2008, page 209

4

I usually try to start by sitting comfortably so I will not be distracted by bodily fidgeting. I try to relax and breathe deeply.

After a few minutes I check who is there and briefly pray for each of them. Then consider regulars who are not there, and pray for each of them.

Then I try to clear my mind and wait for what surfaces – sometimes insights come to me that I had not realised by 'worldly worrying'. Sometimes new ideas surface, that had been crowded out by daily concerns. Sometimes other people minister, sometimes their ministry addresses my meditations, sometimes it is completely different. Sometimes I fall asleep. There is the excitement of the unexpected, the unstructured nature of worship, knowing we can all equally approach God, or whatever we call our approach to the 'divine intent', that we have many varied beliefs, but respect each other, and can share our insights and help and guide each other on life's journey.

a Quaker, 2008

5

Some Friends are able to recall with clarity the first occasion on which they attended a Quaker meeting. While I cannot remember when or where I did so, I do have a vivid recollection of the meeting which I began to attend regularly.

It was held in a rather hideous building: the meeting room was dingy. We sat on rickety chairs that creaked at the slightest movement. The whole place gave little hope that those who worshipped there might catch a glimpse of the vision of God. It was in stark contrast to the splendour of the Anglican churches to which I had been accustomed, where through dignified ritual the beauty of holiness was vividly portrayed.

However, it was in this unlikely setting that I came to know what I can only describe as the amazing fact of Quaker worship. It was in that uncomfortable room that I discovered the way to the interior side of my life, at the deep centre of which I knew that I was not alone, but was held by a love that passes all understanding. This love was mediated to me, in the first place, by those with whom I worshipped. For my journey was not solitary, but one undertaken with my friends as we moved towards each other and together travelled inwards. Yet I knew that the love that held me could not be limited to the mutual love and care we had for each other. It was a signal of transcendence that pointed beyond itself to the source of all life and love.

George Gorman, 1973: *Quaker faith & practice* 2.03

6

At meeting for worship relax and let your baby be with you; my small daughter called it 'the best cuddle of the week' when I couldn't rush off and do something busy. It's not easy for the parents to believe that their child's gurglings actually help the meeting rather than interrupt it. Nonetheless, that is true, and you shouldn't give way to the temptation to take a happily babbling child out of the meeting (though howling is something different!).

Anne Hosking, 1986: *Quaker faith & practice* 2.50

7

When I sit down in meeting I recall whatever may have struck me freshly during the past week. This is in part, initially at least, a voluntary and outward act. It means that the will is given up to service; and it is quite possible to stop everything by taking an opposite attitude. So thoughts suggest themselves – a text that has smitten one during the week – new light on a phrase – a verse of poetry – some incident, private or public. These pass before the door whence shines the heavenly light. Are they transfigured? Sometimes, yes; sometimes, no. If nothing flames, silence is my portion.

John William Graham, 1920: *Quaker faith & practice* 2.52

8

As I silence myself I become more sensitive to the sounds around me, and I do not block them out. The songs of the birds, the rustle of the wind, children in the playground, the roar of an airplane overhead are all taken into my worship. I regulate my breathing as taught me by my Zen friends, and through this exercise I feel the flow of life within me from my toes right through my whole body. I think of myself like the tree planted by the 'rivers of water' in Psalm 1, sucking up God's gift of life and being restored. Sometimes I come to meeting for worship tired and weary, and I hear the words of Jesus, 'Come unto me, all that labour and are weary, and I will give you rest'. And having laid down my burden, I feel refreshed both physically and spiritually. This leads me on to whole-hearted adoration and thanksgiving for all God's blessings. My own name, Tayeko, means 'child of many blessings' and God has surely poured them upon me. My heart overflows with a desire to give him something in return. I have nothing to give but my own being, and I offer him my thoughts, words and actions of each day, and whisper 'Please take me as I am'.

Tayeko Yamanouchi, 1979: *Quaker faith & practice* 2.54

9

consolation
God talk
depths and shallow splashing
moments of flame
presence
difficulty and preaching
boredom
the pause, letting go, before action
our longing for Oneness,
even God,
at the core

a Quaker, 2008

Deepening 2:
Speaking in meeting for worship

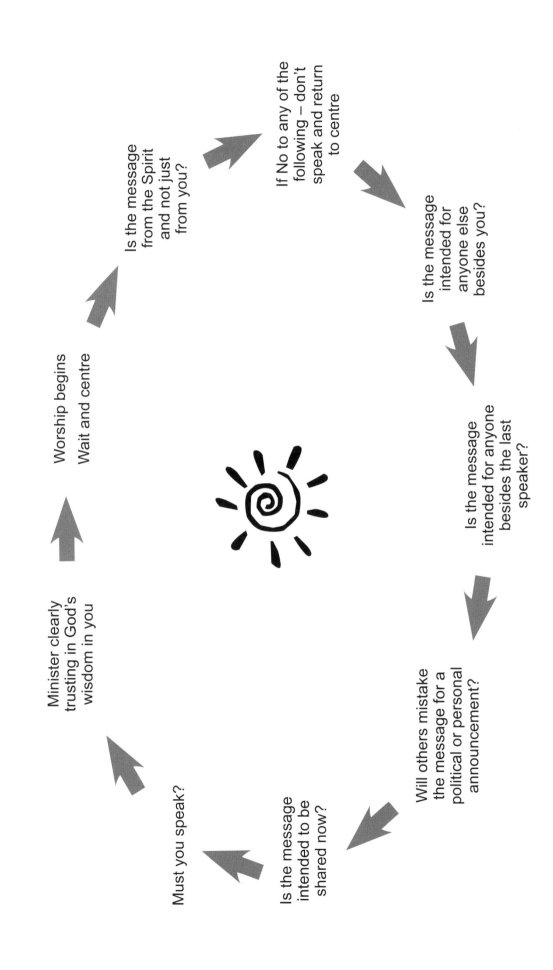

Worship begins
Wait and centre

Minister clearly
trusting in God's
wisdom in you

Must you speak?

Is the message
intended to be
shared now?

Will others mistake
the message for a
political or personal
announcement?

Is the message
intended for anyone
besides the last
speaker?

Is the message
intended for
anyone else
besides you?

If No to any of the
following – don't
speak and return
to centre

Is the message
from the Spirit
and not just
from you?

██ Extract for Deepening 5:
    Practising the discipline of silent waiting and listening

Listening in a new way

- Who is the last person you really listened to?
- Who was the last person who really listened to you?
- List the people who never listen to you
- List the people you never listen to
- What was the content of the last news report you heard?
- What did you discuss with your partner/friend yesterday?
- What did you discuss at work/school yesterday?
- What was the last piece of music you heard that stays with you?
- How often do you think you have missed information?
- How often do you interrupt?
- How often do you assume you know what is coming up in conversation?
- How often do you need to hear simple instructions before understanding them?
- When did you last hear words that changed you?
- When did you last hear a voice that affected you?
- Who listened to you when you were younger?

Speaking of God

Exploring Quaker experiences of God, and how we try to hear where words about faith come from.

This unit invites you to find out more about the variety of ways Quakers conceive of and experience God, and to explore the language we use to describe religious experience. Quakers try to learn from other people's experiences of the Light, reaching beyond the particular words used, to hear what has nourished the lives of others.

Speaking of God unit aims

This unit aims to help you:

- explore ways in which Quakers experience God

- understand how Quakers try to reach for the deeper meaning within the words we use to describe these experiences

- consider and reflect on your own experience of the Divine and how you speak of it

Overview

There is great variety among Quakers in the ways we conceive of and experience God, and the different kinds of language we use to describe religious experience. Some Quakers have a conception of God which is similar to that of orthodox Christians, and would use similar language. Others are happy to use God-centred language, but would conceive of God in very different terms to the traditional Christian trinity. Some describe themselves as agnostics, or humanists, or non-theists, and describe their experiences in ways that avoid the use of the word God entirely. Quaker faith is built on experience and Quakers would generally hold that it is the spiritual experience which is central to their faith, and not the use of a particular form of words (whether that be 'God' or anything else).

The 18th-century Quaker John Woolman wrote:

> There is a principle which is pure, placed in the human mind, which in different places and ages hath different names; it is, however, pure and proceeds from God. It is deep and inward, confined to no forms of religion nor excluded from any where the heart stands in perfect sincerity. In whomsoever this takes root and grows, of what nation soever, they become brethren.
>
> *Quaker faith & practice* 26.61

This concept of the universality of the experience of God, though it may manifest itself or be expressed in very different ways in each of our lives, is still a central principle of Quakerism.

Quakers are encouraged: 'treasure your experience of God, however it comes to you' (*Advices & queries* 2 in *Quaker faith & practice* 1.02); and 'take time to learn about other people's experiences of the Light' (*Advices & queries* 5 in *Quaker faith & practice* 1.02). Sometimes this sharing of faith experiences can be challenging for us, due to the limitations of the language we must use to describe them – as noted by Harvey Gillman, a present-day British Friend:

> The choice of the words soul, God, spiritual, sacred, holy, authentic, religious, devout, divine, deep, even reverence, awe and others like worship and devotion, depends very much on who is using them, when, to whom, in what context, and for what reason.
>
> Harvey Gillman, *Consider the blackbird: reflections on spirituality and language*, page 31

So Quakers try to reach beyond the particular words used to describe experiences of God or 'Light', to 'sense where they come from and what has nourished the lives of others' (*Advices & queries* 17 in *Quaker faith & practice* 1.02).

In keeping with this understanding about the limitations of language, Quakers do not write creeds or statements of belief for members to sign up to; Quakers generally consider that such fixed statements of belief can never fully represent all Truth, and may limit both current perceptions of Truth and the continuing search for further understanding. While Friends try to learn from the insights of the past, we do not want those past insights to limit present and future understanding.

The variety of approaches to belief and religious experience among Quakers also extends to our approaches to the Bible: for some Quakers, it is a book of wisdom inspired by God; for others, it is of equal significance to holy writings from other religious traditions; while some Friends find its contents difficult, or irrelevant to their lives. For most Quakers, however, George Fox's words about scripture in 1652 still speak strongly to us:

> You will say, Christ saith this, and the apostles say this; but what canst thou say? Art thou a child of Light and hast walked in the Light, and what thou speakest is it inwardly from God?

> *Quaker faith & practice* 19.07

Quaker distinctives

Distinctives 1

How do Quakers experience God?

The wide variety of ways Quakers conceive of and experience God is reflected in *Twelve Quakers and God*, produced by Quaker Quest. You'll find extracts from this on pages 235–237.

If you would like to read the full text of *Twelve Quakers and God*, see Further exploration for details.

You might also like to read any of chapter 26 'Reflections' in *Quaker faith & practice*, which covers experience of God, in particular *Qf&p* 26.01–26.15.

Distinctives 2

Who is Jesus for Quakers?

The following extracts from *Quaker faith & practice* talk about the meaning of Jesus in the lives of individual Quakers.

- Christ as friend: *Qf&p* 26.47

- Jesus as symbol of God: *Qf&p* 26.50

- the mystery of God as human being: *Qf&p* 26.53

- a window through to God: *Qf&p* 26.54

- Jesus is the question: *Qf&p* 26.55

- Jesus in our suffering: *Qf&p* 26.59

You could also read *Twelve Quakers and Jesus* or *What Jesus means to me*, which are short collections of very varied Quaker writings about Jesus. See Further exploration for details.

Distinctives 3

What do Quakers believe about God?

The video 'What do Quakers believe about God?', made by Friends at Watford Quaker Meeting, includes some reflections on how different Friends experience and conceive of God. You can access the video in a number of different ways:

- online at
  - > www.watfordquakers.org.uk/videos.html
  - > www.youtube.com as 'What do Quakers believe about God?'

- on the DVD *An introduction to Watford Quakers* available from the Quaker Centre bookshop (see Further exploration for contact details).

Distinctives 4

Quakers, the Bible and creeds

The video 'Quakers and the Bible', made by Friends at Watford Quaker Meeting, includes reflections from different Friends on the significance of the Bible for them. You can access the video in a number of different ways:

- online at
  - > www.watfordquakers.org.uk/videos.html
  - > www.youtube.com as 'Quakers and the Bible'

- on the DVD *An introduction to Watford Quakers* available from the Quaker Centre bookshop (see Further exploration for contact details).

The following extracts from *Quaker faith & practice* discuss Quaker approaches to the Bible and Creeds:

- our understanding of the Bible: *Qf&p* 27.34

- take the Bible as a whole: *Qf&p* 27.31

- dangers of formulated statements of belief: *Qf&p* 27.23

- 'Credo' as 'I commit myself to...': *Qf&p* 27.25

- living truth not fettered by words: *Qf&p* 27.26

Distinctives 5

The universal Light

Quakers have found the metaphor of 'Light' important in speaking of our religious experience. Sections 26.42–26.78 of *Quaker faith & practice* cover the 'light that shines for all', and the following extracts in particular explore the Quaker understanding of the universal nature of the Light:

- the light for which the world longs: *Qf&p* 26.62

- the Light of Christ: *Qf&p* 26.65

- Divine principle of Light: *Qf&p* 26.78

- the Light is One: *Qf&p* 26.68

Distinctives 6

Can you be a Quaker if you don't believe in God?

A humanist Quaker explains how he sees his beliefs as entirely compatible with Quakerism in an extract from *Quaker identity and the heart of our faith*. You'll find this extract on pages 238–239.

If you would like to read the full text of *Quaker identity and the heart of our faith*, see Further exploration for details.

Discovery

Discovery 1

Discussion about Quaker approaches to Jesus

Introductory questions:

- Who do you believe Jesus was?

- Who is Jesus for you?

You might consider these introductory questions, then go to the Speaking of God unit forum, and post your own thoughts in response. You might like to comment on other posts on this forum too.

Alternatively, you could discuss the questions with your Becoming Friends companion, or others in your meeting.

You could do this during the coffee time after meeting for worship, or you might like to ask your Becoming Friends companion to help you set up an informal meeting with other Friends.

Discovery 2

Translating and letting go

Section 26.76 of *Quaker faith & practice* reflects on the difficulty of expressing our deepest spiritual truths in words. You could discuss this section with your Becoming Friends companion.

It might be interesting to ask your Becoming Friends companion or another Friend in your meeting to reflect with you on words or ideas that you have each found tricky or liberating on your spiritual journey.

You could do this by both writing down three words or ideas that:

- currently sustain you on your spiritual journey

- were more important to you in the past than they are today

- you feel attracted to or intrigued by, even if you do not use them

- 'press a button' for you or cause a negative reaction

- you use when you speak of that reality which is unnameable

- you do not use when you speak of that reality which is unnameable.

Then reflect on what you have written together.

Discovery 3

Favourite Bible or other sacred writing extracts

You might like to ask your Becoming Friends companion (or another Friend in your meeting) to share with you three favourite extracts each from the Bible or other sacred writing.

- You could take turns to read your extracts with a period of silence between each one, then spend some time sharing with one another how these extracts speak to you and whether any words are especially meaningful.

- You could also do this activity with a group of Friends from your meeting.

- Or you might like to join the online discussion about favourite sacred writings by making a post on the Speaking of God unit forum.

Discovery 4

'Speaking of God' in my local meeting or online

You could ask your Becoming Friends companion or an elder in your meeting to help you set up a small group session to explore local Friends' experiences and thoughts about God (or you may prefer to simply discuss this with your Becoming Friends companion).

- Before the group session, you or your companion could ask Friends to write a paragraph or two about their own experience of or beliefs about God (like those used in Distinctives 1 in this unit).

- In the session, Friends would read their paragraphs out, then spend some time in worship sharing mode, sharing with one another any responses, insights, experiences or challenges relating to what has been said.

Guidance for worship sharing is found in Appendix 2 – Guidance on pages 283–284.

Alternatively, you could read some young Quakers' thoughts on God at: www.newstatesman.com/200612180102 or
www.fgcquaker.org/quakers-and-god
and post a response on those sites, or start a new thread on the Speaking of God unit forum.

Discovery 5

'Experiment with Light' groups

'Experiment with Light' is a Quaker practice whereby Friends 'wait in the Light' for guidance and insight about our lives. You can read about it in *Light to live by* by Rex Ambler. See Further exploration for details.

Your Becoming Friends companion could help you find out whether anyone in your local or area meeting has been to an 'Experiment with Light' group or course. If so, you could ask them about the practice and their experience of it. If there is a group or course currently running locally, you might try it out yourself.

Or you could arrange to go on a course about 'Experiment with Light'. See if there are courses coming up at:

- Charney Manor
  Tel: 01235 868206
  Website: www.charneymanor.demon.co.uk

- Swarthmoor Hall
  Tel: 01229 583 204
  Website: www.swarthmoorhall.co.uk

- Woodbrooke Quaker Study Centre
  Tel: 0121 472 5171
  Website: www.woodbrooke.org.uk

Deepening

Deepening 1

Responding to an awareness of God

Our response to an awareness of God is the focus of the following extracts:

- Advice from early Quaker Isaac Pennington in *Quaker faith & practice* 26.70.

- A piece by 20th-century American Quaker mystic Thomas Kelly, which you'll find on page 240.

How does either of these speak to you?

Deepening 2

Writing your own statement of belief

While Quakers do not have creeds, it can be interesting and revealing to write your own statement of belief or religious commitment as part of a spiritual practice.

You might like to read an extract from a modern statement of belief and try writing some phrases for your own statement. This need only be very short but can still be a significant focus for understanding your own religious position.

You'll find an extract from a statement of belief on page 241.

You could also reflect on this experience with your Becoming Friends companion when you next meet.

Deepening 3

A letter about your journey so far

Many Quakers have experienced other faith traditions during their lives, or have made significant changes along their spiritual journey. This can leave us with things to celebrate, or difficulties that we wish to leave behind.

Try writing a letter – it could be addressed to God, to yourself, or to a person who is significant for you, expressing in your own words what it is that you:

- wish to leave behind or want healing about

- wish to celebrate or be grateful for

- hunger or hope for now

- want to bring with you from your journey so far

You might wish to reflect on how you have got on with this exercise at a future meeting with your Becoming Friends companion.

Deepening 4

Responding to words and images of Jesus

Who is Jesus for you? You could read and reflect on an extract from Luke's gospel, where Jesus asks his followers 'And you, who do you say that I am?' (Luke 9:18-20). What would your answer be?

You could use words about or images of Jesus to help you reflect on this question, asking yourself 'What does this word or image mean to me?'

- There are Jesus word cards on pages 242–244

- If you prefer using images, you could use the Jesus postcards included with the *Hearts & minds prepared* pack (there should be a copy in your local or area meeting) or search online at http://images.google.co.uk for 'Jesus Christ' or alternative depictions of Jesus such as 'African Jesus'

You may like to take some time to reflect deeply on your own response to this activity. You could:

- respond by drawing, painting, or using another creative method

- respond in music, song or movement

- respond in writing

- go online and blog about your response

- discuss your response on a Quaker discussion forum:
    - the Britain Yearly Meeting forum at: www.quakerweb.org.uk/forum
    - www.friendlink.org.uk (aimed mainly at young Quakers)
    - the Speaking of God unit forum

- share some of your reflections with your Becoming Friends companion when you next meet.

Deepening 5

Sacred reading practice

It can be helpful to develop a practice of slow, meditative reading of sacred texts. Traditionally this practice was called 'Lectio Divina' and practised by monks with the Bible. Many modern Quakers find this practice helpful and use it with all kinds of sacred writings as part of their regular spiritual practice.

You might like to try it out for yourself using the Bible or whatever writings are sacred for you.

- You'll find the sacred reading practice in Appendix 1 on page 270

- There is also a short collection of extracts that you can use for sacred reading included on pages 271–274

Further exploration

If you would like to explore the subject of Speaking of God further, here are some suggestions for reading, listening or viewing.

Advices & queries 1–7 and 17 (in *Quaker faith & practice* 1.02).

The Bible: for looking up any passage from the Bible in a variety of translations, you can use www.biblegateway.com

Charney Manor's website for details of courses, including 'Experiment with Light': www.charneymanor.demon.co.uk

Consider the blackbird: reflections on spirituality and language, Harvey Gillman, Quaker Books, 2007.

Creeds and the search for unity, Rex Ambler, Quaker Books, 2004.

The end of words, Rex Ambler, Quaker Books, 2004.

'Experiment with Light' resources online: www.charlieblackfield.com/light

A faith to call our own: Quaker tradition in the light of contemporary movements of the Spirit, Alex Wildwood, Quaker Home Service, 1999 (Swarthmore Lecture).

An introduction to Watford Quakers (DVD), 'What do Quakers believe about God' and 'Quakers and the Bible' sections, Just Film, 2007. Available at: www.watfordquakers.org.uk/videos.html (or on www.youtube.com as: 'What do Quakers believe about God?' and 'Quakers and the Bible').

Light to live by, Rex Ambler, Quaker Books, 2002 (about 'Experiment with Light').

Listening spirituality 1: personal spiritual practices among Friends, Patricia Loring, Openings Press, 1997.

New light: 12 Quaker voices, edited by Jennifer Kavanagh, O Books, 2008. Individual themes such as *Twelve Quakers and God*, *Twelve Quakers and Jesus* also available in the *Twelve Quakers and...* series, Quaker Quest 2004–2007.

Quaker identity and the heart of our faith, Quaker Life Study Materials, Quaker Life, 2008. Includes 'David Boulton's personal stance in the discussion of Quaker identity'. Available online at: www.quaker.org.uk/sites/default/files/Faith-and-practice-proceeding.pdf or in hard copy by contacting Quaker Life on 020 7663 1140 or email: ql@quaker.org.uk

Rooted in Christianity, open to new light: Quaker spiritual diversity, Timothy Ashworth and Alex Wildwood, Pronoun Press & Woodbrooke, 2009.

Searching the depths: essays on being a Quaker today, edited by Harvey Gillman and Alastair Heron, Quaker Books, 1996. Especially chapter 2 'To an unknown God' by Andrew Greaves.

Swarthmoor Hall website, for details of courses, including 'Experiment with Light': www.swarthmoorhall.co.uk

A testament of devotion, Thomas R. Kelly, Harper & Row, 1939.

'What Jesus means to me', various authors, *Friends Quarterly*, July 2003. This is included in the *Hearts and minds prepared* pack.

Woodbrooke's website or brochure for details of courses about God, Jesus, Quaker belief, spiritual practice: www.woodbrooke.org.uk

Many of these titles are available from the Quaker Centre bookshop:

Friends House
173 Euston Road
London NW1 2BJ

Tel: 020 7663 1030
Fax: 020 7663 1001

Website: www.quaker.org.uk/bookshop
Email: quakercentre@quaker.org.uk

Many of them will also be in your local meeting house library. You could ask your Becoming Friends companion to help you track down titles that interest you.

Closing activity

As you finish your exploration of how Quakers experience and speak of God, you are invited to reflect on what you have gained through this unit, how your understanding of both yourself and Quakerism has changed, and what areas you would like to explore further.

This closing reflection can be a very good opportunity for sharing with your Becoming Friends companion, or you may prefer to write in a journal or book of spiritual discipline (there's guidance for journalling in Appendix 2 – Guidance on page 282), or to reflect using creative methods such as drawing, collage, model-making or working with materials such as textiles or wood.

You may like to use one or more of the following questions as a focus for your reflection:

- What have you gained from your work on this unit, whether as a result of positive or more challenging experiences?

- In what ways has your understanding changed as a result of your work on this unit?

- Are there areas that you would like to explore further – either as part of your own spiritual journey or relating to Quakerism?

- Has anything arisen that you would find it helpful to reflect on with your Becoming Friends companion?

Extracts for Distinctives 1:
How do Quakers experience God?

From *Twelve Quakers and God*

1

I was brought up in a home where traditional Christian teaching prevailed. Of course I asked questions, and as life went on I found fewer and fewer satisfactory answers. Like so many others I found myself unable to accept much of what seemed important in the practice of my church. In retrospect I think that for me the external practice hid the truth. Eventually, after some really hard searching, I was confronted with the truth. With the word God.

2

I need God in the same way that I need food, drink and sleep. I am absolutely sure that needing God is an integral part of the human condition, and that some people find it harder than others to accept it. They, in their turn, of course, know that I am deluding myself. I believe in God. David Steindl-Rast has said that God is a name for a reality which cannot be named, and that is the closest definition I have ever encountered for the indefinable. For me, God is a reality. I believe in God because I experience it.

3

I can feel the force of God's light at unexpected moments: as I walk down the street, as a stranger smiles in a crowd, as I look at the sky. I feel the power of God in the vastness of the universe, in the minuteness of a grain of sand. I experience my life both as brief as the day-lily's and yet as part of the aeons of history. God is manifest in this relativity of time.

4

I feel God as a power to be drawn on and from which to receive strength. Sometimes in my life, when all else has failed, I have prayed for this strength and felt at peace.

5

Another metaphor for God is a ball of many mirrored facets. We all see a part of it, and what we see reflects back to us a unique perspective, which is a true reflection yet only part of the whole. In this way, I can accept that others will have a different view of God, different words for God, different experiences of God, and yet all these are but glimpses of fragments of the same thing, which is greater than anything we can comprehend.

6

God is a guiding force in my life. Until recently I could not feel God as love, but I have come to an understanding recently that the love is in the relationship, the connectedness which I experience consciously through others and, vividly, unexpectedly, through acts of synchronicity. Glimpses of connections that I had not previously understood: connections that show me the way, affirm my steps on the path, nurture me, not with the cuddly limited love of my imaginings, but with the mature love and acceptance of my real self.

7

I encounter, rather than believe in, God. But I have chosen, and it is a choice, to bet my life (literally) on the power, the love, the challenge, that I call God. For me it has always been a stark choice. You take it seriously (or try to) twenty-four hours a day or not at all. Like pregnancy, there are no half measures – I can no more be 'a little bit religious' than ' a little bit pregnant'!

8

This experience of the Divine comes to me unexpectedly in flashes, sudden openings, when the penny drops, or things click into place. This is a glimpse of the other, 'rumours of angels', a tangential glancing blow of the holy. No Damascus visions or burning bushes, but humble occasions which I recognise, often long afterwards, as times of inner enlargement when my own spirit has magnified or manifested something greater.

9

In my life experience the Divine has been a reality. The God of love, compassion and tender upholding is one that I have known. But my God is not just personal; S/he is also power or energy, the Divine Source. This Divine Power is part of all creative energy, which cannot be defined or confined, just glimpsed in creation and creative forms. It is a mystical Other, in which and with which I am engaged. Jesus was someone who more clearly knew this Divine Spirit than most, and lived his life in joyful response to it.

10

Sometimes I think I am verging on being atheist, because I think it is quite possible that the inspiring and leading God I believe in could be a product of my mind (and the minds of other people). The human brain is such a marvellous thing, full of mystery, that I don't think it is a problem to find one more mystery in it. But God may equally be outside us all – I really don't know. I don't spend much time worrying about theology – it is the inspiration and the impetus to change the world for the better that really matter.

11

I use many names for the Divine, sometimes lingering with one sacred name, but wary of becoming territorial, my god shrinking to mere possession. Early

Quakers used Light, giving life and clarity, showing me the next steps, and Light is probably the word I use most of all.

12

The ever-present Energy is there to be drawn on by anyone who opens himself or herself to it. It calls us in the direction of love and compassion, understanding and forgiveness, and whatever else supports the unity of life, from social inclusion on local and global scales to care of the natural environment. Opening yourself up is challenging, a direction which is in tension with the opposite drive to control your life, protect and enhance your position and become less vulnerable.

from *Twelve Quakers and God*, Quaker Quest, 2004

Extract for Distinctives 6:
Can you be a Quaker if you don't believe in God?

Quaker identity and the heart of our faith: extract by David Boulton

I have never, since I ceased to be a child in the mid 1950s, been persuaded of the reality of supernatural forces or dimensions, even when they are smuggled in under such euphemisms as 'transcendence', 'the numinous', 'the divine', or 'the mystical'. I can no more entertain the notion of gods and devils, angels and demons, disembodied ghoulies and ghosties, or holy and unholy spirits, than I can believe in the magic of Harry Potter or the mystic powers of Gandalf the Grey. I think William Blake hit the nail on the head when he concluded, in The Marriage of Heaven and Hell, that 'all deities reside in the human breast' – the human imagination.

I am satisfied – utterly, deeply satisfied – with one life in this one wonderful, natural world.

I fully understand that belief in a transcendent realm and a transcendent god as the guarantors of meaning and purpose have inspired millions. They do not inspire me. Instead, they seem to me illusions we can well do without, and I find myself raging at the toxic effects of literal, uncritical belief in divine guidance, divine purpose, divine reward and punishment.

Does such unqualified scepticism disqualify me as a Quaker? I don't think so, and you don't seem to think so, since you welcomed me into the Society after a meeting for clearness and a lengthy process of discernment, following my application for membership in which, as a matter of scrupulous integrity, I was clear and open about my humanist convictions. What is it, then, about the Religious Society of Friends that can command the love and loyalty of a dyed-in-the-wool non-theist like me? That can absorb me in its history, inspire me with its radical reforming tradition, 'gather me as in a net'?

In a word, it is the glory of the Society's creedlessness. It's our obstinate, almost obsessive refusal to be tied down to a form of words defining what Quakers believe, or what we think we should believe. Yes, early Friends described themselves as Publishers of Truth, but they were wise enough not to try to reduce truth to a set of articles of faith. We are not so foolish as to believe that what we believe doesn't matter; but our founding fathers and mothers knew that to tie beliefs down in a form of words, a formulary endowed with divine sanction, would be to kick the living daylights out of the Quaker way, truth and life: and to impose a form of words on each other as a badge of Quaker orthodoxy and sound doctrine, an approved dogma, would be to repeat the tragic history of the confessional churches and institutional religion through the ages. Go down that road and we switch off the lights.

So we have no creed. Not even an irreducible minimum creed. Not even 'Credo in unum Deum'. 'I believe in God' is too crude, too inadequate, too loose. What about 'seeking the will of God'? What about 'answering that of God in every person'? What about being 'open to the Spirit'? Fine, but that's not a creed. Potent poetry, but not a creed.

Poetry? Yes. Religious language is surely best understood as metaphorical, not literal; expressive, not descriptive; nonrealist rather than realist. Poetry opens up what creeds close down. The Quaker humanist who does not believe that God exists may nevertheless love, honour and obey what the image of God symbolises or represents: to quote Blake again,

> ...Mercy, Pity, Peace, and Love
> Is God, our Father dear.
> And Mercy, Pity, Peace and Love
> Is man, His child and care.
>
> For Mercy has a human heart,
> Pity a human face,
> And Love, the human form divine,
> And Peace, the human dress.

And he concludes:

> Where Mercy, Love and Pity dwell,
> There God is dwelling too.

So God becomes for us the imagined symbol of the human values that we recognise as making an ultimate claim upon us. We can respond with all our heart and all our mind and all our strength to the promptings of love and truth in our hearts without first having to sign up to belief in a transcendental prompter. Love and truth are themselves the prompts.

from *Quaker identity and the heart of our faith*,
Quaker Life, 2008

Extract for Deepening 1:
Responding to an awareness of God

Extract by Thomas Kelly

Open your eyes to the flaming vision
of the wonder of such a life.
Begin where you are. Now.
If you slip and stumble,
don't spend too much time in anguished regrets
and self-accusations but begin again.
Don't grit your teeth and clench your fists and say,
'I will! I will!' Relax.
Take hands off. Submit yourself to God....
Let life be willed through you.

> from *A Testament of devotion* by Thomas Kelly,
> Harper & Row, 1939

Extract for Deepening 2:
Writing your own statement of belief

A personal statement of belief

I believe
in God
the Oneness of whom we are all part
the Mother and Father of us all
Creative Energy of Love from whom we all spring
the Ground of our Being

I believe
in the embodiment of love in our world
in people of every kind

I believe
in the Spirit of Lovingkindness
at work in our hearts
bringing peace, compassion and love
transforming and challenging us to growth

I believe
in the eternity of now
the mystery of our connectedness
through and beyond time and space

a Quaker, 2008

saviour	cosmic Christ
Lamb of God	friend
teacher	Beloved
Son of God	radical preacher
prophet	man of his time

King	universal Light
The Way, The Truth and The Life	One with God
enlightened being	embodiment of the divine
just a man	Jesus–Sophia (embodiment of divine wisdom)
carpenter	healer

a Jew	Lord
Messiah	mystery
God	wandering wise man
leader of an apocalyptic movement	The Word of God
Christ – the anointed one of God	

Closing Unit

Reflecting on the learning, saying goodbye and journeying on...

This closing unit will offer you opportunities to reflect on your learning during the Becoming Friends course and on the journey you have shared with your Becoming Friends companion. You will be invited to consider steps you wish to take to further your learning and spiritual development from here, and to take time to say goodbye to your companion.

Closing Unit aims

This unit aims to help you:

- Reflect on your learning during the Becoming Friends course

- Find out about Quaker ways of continuing our spiritual learning and development

- Consider steps you could take to further your spiritual journey with Friends

- Celebrate the work you and your Becoming Friends companion have done together

What if I now want to apply for membership?

While the Becoming Friends course has not been specifically aimed at bringing participants into membership of the Religious Society of Friends, you may have found that the process of taking part in the course has led you to consider applying to become a member. If that is the case, then please approach the overseers or elders in your local meeting and they will explain the membership procedure to you.

 What if I have realised Quakerism is not for me?

We hope that the Becoming Friends course has been of interest to you anyway and that you will be able to take something useful from it on your spiritual journey from here. If you want any help in finding out about other local faith communities, your Becoming Friends companion should be able to help you find contact details for them.

 Guidance for working through this closing unit

1. The introductory information (pages 246–247) and overview (pages 248–250) are good places to start.

2. The Reflective activity on pages 251–252 provides you with an opportunity to reflect on all your learning during the Becoming Friends course, so this exercise is highly recommended. Take as long as you wish to over it.

3. You can then choose one (or more if you like) of the seven Journeying on activities on pages 253–258 to find out more about Quaker approaches to spiritual learning and development, and consider doing your own follow up work after this course is finished.

4. You might like to arrange a meeting with your Becoming Friends companion towards the end of the unit so that you can reflect on your learning and your journey together, possibly following the format for the closing session with your Becoming Friends companion given on pages 259–260.

5. There's no time limit for working through this unit – you can take as long or as short a time as you like.

Overview

> Spiritual learning continues throughout life, and often in unexpected ways... Are you open to new light, from whatever source it may come?
>
> Advices and queries 7 (in *Quaker faith & practice* 1.02)

For Quakers, seeking to be open to new light and learning is a central part of our ongoing spiritual development, both as individuals and as a community.

Each of us has a unique spiritual journey to make, a unique way of learning and being open to the Spirit; by sharing what we have found along the way, we enable this diversity to enrich us, so that

> the Society of Friends might be thought of as a prism through which the Divine Light passes, to become visible in a spectrum of many colours; many more in their richness, than words alone can express.
>
> *Quaker faith & practice* 18.20

Being open to spiritual learning can be exciting and interesting but also challenging and not always easy. So we try to find ways to support one another in our seeking, and finding, of new light: some of these ways include study groups in local meetings, special interest groups, courses, publications in text and audio-visual formats, online learning communities, and regional or national gatherings. Although you are now coming to the end of the Becoming Friends course, you are invited to explore some of these possibilities for continuing your spiritual learning and development with Friends.

Local and area meetings often arrange study group sessions for local Quakers: these may be planned to suit local learning needs or may make use of national Quaker learning packs. Recent learning packs *include Hearts and minds prepared, Good lives, Quaker identity and the heart of our faith*, a Testimonies 'toolkit' *Engaging with the Quaker testimonies, Responding to climate change* and *Creating community, creating connections* (see Further exploration for more details).

Within Britain Yearly Meeting, there are many special interest groups which enable Quakers to follow their interests or concerns with other like-minded Friends. These 'listed informal groups' range from faith based groups, such as the Christian Quaker Renewal Fellowship and the Quaker Universalist Group, to interest groups such as the Friends Historical Society and Quaker Theatre Group, and faith in action groups such as Quaker Action on Alcohol and Drugs or Quaker Disability Equality Group (see Journeying on activity 1).

Courses are offered by Quaker centres on a wide range of subjects based around exploring Quakerism and the themes of interest to Quakers, such as peace and reconciliation, Quaker history and spiritual journeys. Quaker centres include

Woodbrooke Quaker Study Centre, Swarthmoor Hall, Charney Manor and Claridge House. Courses are offered in different formats including retreats, seminars and conferences, and may be short courses or longer programmes of study; many courses are offered at the centres while others are delivered off-site in local meetings and regional venues around Britain (see Journeying on activity 2).

Quakers aim to support children and young people in their spiritual journeys in ways that enable them to make their own choices and decisions. Meetings may have separate children's meetings or times of all age worship, and there are specific resources, events and gatherings for children and young people within Britain Yearly Meeting. The Quaker Life department at Friends House supports work with children and young people and produces a resource called *Journeys in the Spirit* to help meetings with this work (see Journeying on activity 3). For more about events and gatherings for children and young people see Journeying on activity 6.

Quaker publications can be found in local meeting house libraries and also the Quaker libraries at Friends House and Woodbrooke Quaker Study Centre – their catalogues can be browsed in person or online at: www.quaker.org.uk/library and www.woodbrooke.org.uk/library. The Quaker Centre Bookshop also stocks a wide range of publications of interest to Friends (see Further exploration for contact details).

The Swarthmore Lecture was established in1907 'to interpret further to the members of the Society of Friends their Message and Mission... and ... to bring before the public the spirit, the aims and the fundamental principles of the Friends.' The lecture is given annually at Yearly Meeting, the annual gathering to which all Friends are invited, and is accompanied by an audio recording of the lecture and a book which deals in more detail with the subject of the lecture (see Journeying on activity 4).

Periodicals and journals published by Friends provide opportunities to share news and discuss issues of importance to Friends; these publications include *The Friend*, *The Friends Quarterly*, *Quaker Voices* and *Quaker News* (see Journeying on activity 5).

Being a learning community involves meeting up and spending time together – Quakers enjoy going along to gatherings on local, regional and national levels ranging from Quaker camping trips to conferences about peace work. Details of local and regional events will be given in local Quaker newsletters and websites, while the main national Quaker gatherings are listed in Journeying on activity 6. Another way of being in touch with one another is through Quaker online discussion forums such as the Britain Yearly Meeting forum at: www.quakerweb.org.uk/forum or the young Quaker forum Friendlink at: www.friendlink.org.uk . Many of the special interest groups referred to in Journeying on activity 1 also have email groups for sharing news and ideas.

And, importantly, you may feel that the most significant way for you to continue your journey with Friends is to deepen your own spiritual practice or prayer life.

Journeying on activity 7 offers reminders of some of the disciplines offered during the Becoming Friends course and ways of seeking support along the way.

In the words of a British Friend, Quakers

> offer a spiritual journey: a journey that is undertaken with others in our meeting and which is reflected in their journeys ... We don't have all the answers: what we have is some very good questions.
>
> Geoffrey Durham, 'The Heart of Quakerism'
(see Further exploration page 261)

Whichever ways you choose to move forward in your journey, Friends hope that 'love may grow in you and guide you.' (*Advices & queries* 2 in *Quaker faith & practice* 1.02)

Reflective Activity

During the Becoming Friends course you have explored the Quaker Way and your relationship to it by working on a range of subjects that you have selected from the eight topic units shown in the diagram below. Through each subject area, we hope that you have been able to find out more about the **distinctive** Quaker faith and **discover** some of the riches of the Quaker community and tradition, while **deepening** your own spiritual life.

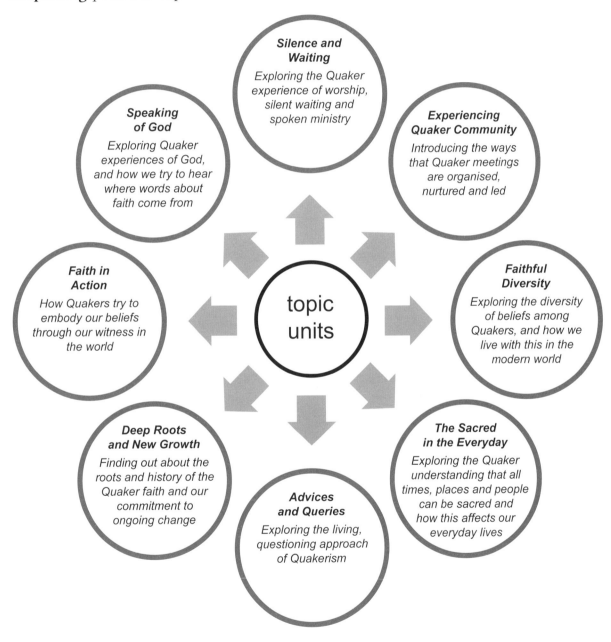

Silence and Waiting
Exploring the Quaker experience of worship, silent waiting and spoken ministry

Speaking of God
Exploring Quaker experiences of God, and how we try to hear where words about faith come from

Experiencing Quaker Community
Introducing the ways that Quaker meetings are organised, nurtured and led

Faith in Action
How Quakers try to embody our beliefs through our witness in the world

topic units

Faithful Diversity
Exploring the diversity of beliefs among Quakers, and how we live with this in the modern world

Deep Roots and New Growth
Finding out about the roots and history of the Quaker faith and our commitment to ongoing change

Advices and Queries
Exploring the living, questioning approach of Quakerism

The Sacred in the Everyday
Exploring the Quaker understanding that all times, places and people can be sacred and how this affects our everyday lives

At the beginning of the course, we suggested that you might find it helpful to practise becoming more aware of your learning experiences through means such as reflection, writing, blogging, drawing or creating something, conversations, group sharing (face to face and online).

As you finish your work on the Becoming Friends course, we invite you to reflect on what you have learned during the whole course, how your understanding has changed and what areas you would like to explore further. This is a good moment to look back at any writing, drawing or other records you have of your reflections and learning throughout the course and see what they have to teach you at this stage.

You could use one or more of the following questions as a **focus for your reflection**:

- What has been especially valuable or important in the learning you have done?

- What has been new or surprising for you? What new light, insight, perspective or questions have come to you?

- In what ways do the Quaker approaches you have learned about reflect your own experience and thoughts?

- In what ways has the learning challenged you? What questions has it raised for you?

- Are there areas of Quakerism or your own spiritual journey that you would like to explore further now?

- Has anything arisen from your learning that you would find it helpful to focus on in reflection with your Becoming Friends companion?

You could also take some time to reflect on your own spiritual practice or prayer life. Do you feel led to continue or develop any practice that you have experienced during the Becoming Friends course?

As before, this closing reflection can be a very good opportunity for sharing with your Becoming Friends companion, or you may prefer to write in a journal or book of spiritual discipline (there's guidance for journalling in Appendix 2 – Guidance on page 282, to blog or share online, or to reflect using creative methods.

Journeying on activities

You might like to choose one or more of the following seven activities.

Journeying on activity 1

Find out about a listed informal group

Within Britain Yearly Meeting, there are many informal groups which enable Quakers to follow their interests or concerns with other like-minded Friends.

You can find out about them by:

- looking at the list of groups on the Britain Yearly Meeting website at: www.quaker.org.uk/other-quaker-sites and follow the links to explore some groups' websites

- looking in the annual Book of Meetings, where the groups are listed, with contact details, towards the back of the book; it is in most meeting houses, but if you can't find a copy, contact Quaker Life at Friends House, 173 Euston Road, London NW1 2BJ tel: 020 7663 1140 email: ql@quaker.org.uk for details of groups

Is there a group which interests you? You could get in touch and ask for more information, subscribe to a newsletter or email group, or arrange to attend an event.

Journeying on activity 2

Go on a Quaker course

There are courses available at various Quaker centres and locally in meetings, covering a wide range of subjects. Why not find out about a course and book yourself on it!

You could ask your Becoming Friends companion, or an elder or overseer at your meeting what courses or study group sessions are coming up locally in the near future.

Or check out the websites or ring and ask for the programmes for the following Quaker centres to find out if there are courses coming up that might interest you:

- Woodbrooke Quaker Study Centre 0121 472 5171 www.woodbrooke.org.uk

- Swarthmoor Hall 01229 583204
  www.swarthmoorhall.co.uk

- Charney Manor 01235 868206
  www.charneymanor.org.uk

- Claridge House 0845 3457281
  www.claridgehousequaker.org.uk

- Glenthorne Quaker Centre 015394 35389
  www.glenthorne.org

Some Quaker centres have bursary funds to assist with the cost of courses, as do many local and area meetings. For example, look in the Woodbrooke brochure or go to www.woodbrooke.org.uk/pages/financial-help.html for information about financial help with Woodbrooke courses. Don't hesitate to apply for help with costs if you need to – that's what bursaries are there for. You can ask an elder or overseer in your meeting for help sorting out bursary assistance.

Journeying on activity 3

Check out resources for children and young people

You might like to get hold of copies of *Journeys in the Spirit,* the resource for Friends working with children and young people in meetings. What do you think about the information and activities offered? Are there any you would like to try out yourself?

- You could go to www.quaker.org.uk/resources to access samples of *Journeys in the Spirit* online – you can also subscribe to *Journeys in the Spirit* on this webpage.

- Or contact Quaker Life on 020 7663 1013 or email ql@quaker.org.uk and ask for a copy of *Journeys in the Spirit* to be sent to you.

Does your meeting use the *Journeys in the Spirit* resource? How it has been received? Speak to one of the overseers or elders to find out. Are you interested in getting involved with work with children and young people in your meeting?

You could also check out the young Quaker website www.yqspace.org.uk or the online forum www.friendlink.org.uk which is aimed mainly at young Quakers.

Journeying on activity 4

Read a Swarthmore Lecture

You could read one or more of the Swarthmore Lectures, for an insight into Quaker thinking on issues of importance to Friends through the years. More recent lectures are also available in audio formats.

- A full list of Swarthmore lectures is available on Wikipedia at: en.wikipedia.org/wiki/Swarthmore_Lecture
  or you'll find a list of recent lectures on pages 263–264

- You could have a look at the collection of Swarthmore Lectures in your local meeting house library and borrow any that interest you

- Or contact the Quaker Centre bookshop (contact details in Further exploration) to buy a copy

- You could attend Yearly Meeting to hear the next Swarthmore Lecture live. For information about Yearly Meeting, contact Friends House on 020 7663 1094 or go to www.quaker.org.uk/britain-yearly-meeting

Journeying on activity 5

Read and engage with Quaker publications

You might like to read a recent edition of *The Friend*, *Friends Quarterly*, *Quaker Voices* or *Quaker News* and find out what's going on among British Friends. Are there any articles, letters or adverts that especially speak to you? Will you do anything to follow up that interest?

Copies of these publications are available to borrow in most meeting house libraries.

You can access them online or make contact to order them as follows:

- *The Friend* www.thefriend.org
  Tel: 020 7663 1178
  Email: subs@thefriend.org

- *The Friends Quarterly* www.thefriend.org
  Tel: 020 7663 1178
  Email: subs@thefriend.org

- *Quaker Voices* www.quaker.org.uk/qv
  Tel: 020 8446 5772
  Email: qv@quaker.org.uk

- *Quaker News* www.quaker.org.uk/qn
  Tel: 020 7663 1119
  Email: qnews@quaker.org.uk

Journeying on activity 6

Explore Quaker gatherings

You could find out about Quaker gatherings and consider whether you are interested in attending one. Speak to your Becoming Friends companion, or an elder or overseer at your meeting, to find out about local Quaker gatherings and any of the national Quaker gatherings listed below, or contact direct:

- Junior Yearly Meeting (for young Quakers aged 15 to 18)
  www.quaker.org.uk/junior-yearly-meeting
  Tel: 020 7663 1013
  Email: ql@quaker.org.uk

- Yearly Meeting
  www.quaker.org.uk/ym
  Tel: 020 7663 1040
  Email: rco@quaker.org.uk

- Summer Gathering
  www.summergathering.org.uk
  Tel: 020 7663 1040
  Email: rco@quaker.org.uk

- Yorkshire Friends Holiday School (for young Quakers aged 13 to 18)
  www.yfhs.org.uk/index.htm
  Email: secretary@yfhs.org.uk

- other summer schools for Young Quakers – see Book of Meetings for information or contact Quaker Life children and young people's team
  Tel: 020 7663 1013
  Email: ql@quaker.org.uk

- Quaker Peace & Social Witness Conference
  www.quaker.org.uk/conferences-and-events
  Tel: 020 7663 1000
  Email: qpsw@quaker.org.uk

- Young Friends General Meeting (for young Quakers aged 18 to 30)
  www.yfgm.quaker.org.uk
  Tel: 0121 472 1998
  Email: yfgm@quaker.org.uk

You can also check out forthcoming Quaker events at: www.quaker.org.uk/events

Is there an event that particularly interests you? You could ask your elders or overseers if you could be considered for nomination as a rep for your local or area meeting at that gathering when it is next held.

Journeying on activity 7

Deepen your own spiritual practice

You may like to continue with or try out one of the spiritual disciplines that have been offered during the Becoming Friends course such as prayer, meditation or journalling. Some possibilities are given below, with a reminder of where they were first mentioned:

- Listening practice: Experiencing Quaker Community – Deepening 4, page 268

- Fourfold blessing: Faith in Action – Deepening 4, page 173

- Review of the day: The Sacred in the Everyday – Deepening 2, page 269

- Mindfulness practice: The Sacred in the Everyday – Deepening 4, page 186

- Simple breathing practice: Silence and Waiting – Discovery 4, page 275

- Silence and worship online: Silence and Waiting – Deepening 3, page 206

- Sacred reading: Speaking of God – Deepening 5, page 270

There are also courses on spiritual practice and prayer and retreats available at Quaker centres and locally in meetings.

You could ask your Becoming Friends companion, or an elder or overseer at your meeting, what spiritual practice courses or retreats are available locally. Alternatively, check out the websites or ring and ask for the programmes for the following Quaker centres to find out if there are relevant courses or retreats coming up (there may be bursaries available – see Journeying on activity 2), or simply arrange to spend some quiet time there.

- Woodbrooke Quaker Study Centre
  www.woodbrooke.org.uk
  Tel: 0121 472 5171
  Email: enquiries@woodbrooke.org.uk

- Swarthmoor Hall
  www.swarthmoorhall.co.uk
  Tel: 01229 583204
  Email: info@swarthmoorhall.co.uk

- Charney Manor
  www.charneymanor.org.uk
  Tel: 01235 868206
  Email: charneymanor@quaker.org.uk

- Claridge House (Friends Fellowship of Healing Centre)
  www.claridgehousequaker.org.uk
  Tel: 0845 3457281
  Email: welcome@claridgehousequaker.org.uk

- Glenthorne Quaker Centre
  www.glenthorne.org
  Tel: 015394 35389
  Email: info@glenthorne.org

You could also contact:

- The Quaker Retreat Group
  www.qrg.threetowers.org.uk
  Tel: 01943 863213
  Email QuakerRetreats@waitrose.com

- Quaker Voluntary Action (working retreats programme)
  www.qva.org.uk
  Tel: 01484 687139
  Email mail@qva.org.uk

Finishing the work of Becoming Friends with your companion

Having worked together during the Becoming Friends course, it is important that you and your Becoming Friends companion take time to reflect on your journey together and to say 'goodbye', at least where the Becoming Friends course is concerned –you may very well continue to see plenty of each other in other ways! A suggested outline for a final meeting is given below for you and your companion to adapt as suits you.

Suggested elements for a final meeting with your Becoming Friends companion

1. Worship
Taking time in silence together at the beginning will help to ground your conversation in worship, so that even your last meeting together is a Quaker 'meeting for learning'.

2. Review and evaluation
Consider any of the reflections you wish to share from the Reflective activity, as well as generally reviewing your journey together.

3. Journeying on activity/taking things further
Share with your companion about the 'Journeying on' activity that you chose. What might you want to take further? What might you want to do or know more about? Consider resources in your local meeting, area meeting, Woodbrooke, Quaker Life or other learning opportunities.

4. Any needs and how to meet them
Is there anything that you need in the way of further information, support or guidance, whether about Quakers or your own needs? Your companion may be able to point you in the right direction to find sources of help, such as local elders and overseers, or specific groups or organisations outside of the Religious Society of Friends.

5. Ongoing spiritual friendship?
Your relationship with your Becoming Friends companion is now ending, but if you are interested in finding other opportunities for spiritual friendship, talk to your companion about spiritual friendship arrangements or groups in your meeting or local area.

6. Appreciations and thanks

Take time to mark your appreciation for the gift of each other's time and friendship during the course.

7. Cake and celebration!

Perhaps you would like to share a little something to celebrate the end of the course?

8. Letting go and saying goodbye

It is good to take the chance to say goodbyes (as far as your work together on Becoming Friends is concerned) and acknowledge the end of this particular time you have spent together.

9. Closing worship

Finish your session together with a few minutes of worship. It is important after all the conversation and practicalities are finished with that you take a moment to return to the spiritual ground for your work together.

Further exploration

If you would like to explore some resources that go into more depth about aspects of Quakerism, here are some suggestions for reading, listening or viewing.

Creating community, creating connections, Lizz Roe and Zelie Gross, Quaker Books, 2009. Yearly Meeting Gathering 2009 study materials. Available online at: www.ymg.org.uk/workpack-for-meetings or in hard copy by contacting Friends House on 020 7663 1161 or email: rco@quaker.org.uk

Engaging with the Quaker testimonies: a toolkit, Quaker Peace & Social Witness Testimonies Committee, Quaker Books, 2007.

Good lives study pack, Pam Lunn and Lizz Roe, Woodbrooke Quaker Study Centre, 2009.

'The heart of Quakerism', Geoffrey Durham: talk to London Quakers, 2009. Text or MP3 download available from: http://www.londonquakers.org.uk/news/lqagm09feature

Hearts and minds prepared study pack, Jennie Levin, Woodbrooke Quaker Study Centre, 2003. Available in many meetings, but no longer for sale as a full pack.

An introduction to Quakerism, Pink Dandelion, Oxford University Press, 2007.

The nature and mission of the Church: a response from the Religious Society of Friends (Quakers) in Britain to the World Council of Churches faith and order paper 198, 'The nature and mission of the Church: a stage on the way to a common statement', Document from Meeting for Sufferings, 7 Feb 2009. Download the minute and the full response from www.quaker.org.uk/nature-and-mission-church .

New light: 12 Quaker voices, edited by Jennifer Kavanagh, O Books, 2008. Individual themes also available in the *Twelve Quakers and...* series, Quaker Quest, 2004–2007.

Quaker faith & practice: the book of Christian discipline of the Yearly Meeting of the Religious Society of Friends (Quakers) in Britain, 4th edition, Britain Yearly Meeting, 2009 (first published 1995).

Quaker identity and the heart of our faith, Quaker Life Study Materials, Quaker Life, 2008. Available online at: www.quaker.org.uk/sites/default/files/Faith-and-practice-proceeding.pdf or in hard copy by contacting Quaker Life on 020 7663 1140 or email: ql@ quaker.org.uk .

Responding to climate change, Quaker Peace & Social Witness study materials. Available online at: www.quaker.org.uk/environment or in hard copy by contacting Quaker Peace & Social Witness on 0207 663 1000 or email: qpsw@ quaker.org.uk

Searching the depths: essays on being a Quaker today, edited by Harvey Gillman and Alastair Heron, Quaker Home Service, 1996.

A very short introduction to Quakerism, Ben Pink Dandelion. Podcasts of lectures, available to download from www.woodbrooke.org.uk/news.php/6/a-very-short-introduction-to-quakerism

Many of these titles are available from the Quaker Centre bookshop:

Friends House
173 Euston Road
London NW1 2BJ

Tel: 020 7663 1030
Fax: 020 7663 1001

Website: www.quaker.org.uk/bookshop
Email: quakercentre@quaker.org.uk

Many of them will also be in your local meeting house library. You could ask your Becoming Friends companion to help you track down titles that interest you.

For Journeying on activity 4:
Swarthmore lectures list

1960	Kenneth C. Barnes	Creative imagination
1961	Richard K. Ullmann	Tolerance and the intolerable
1962	J. Duncan Wood	Building the institutions of peace
1963	L. Hugh Doncaster	God in every man
1964	Richenda C. Scott	Tradition and experience
1965	John Macmurray	Search for reality in religion
1966	William E. Barton	The moral challenge of Communism: some ethical aspects of Marxist/Leninist society
1967	Kathleen M. Slack	Constancy and change in the Society of Friends
1968	William Homan Thorpe	Quakers and humanists
1969	Maurice A. Creasey	Bearings, or, Friends and the new reformation
1970	Kenneth E. Boulding	Prospering of truth
1971	Charles Frederick Carter	On having a sense of all conditions
1972	Richard S. Peters	Reason, morality and religion
1973	George H. Gorman	Amazing fact of Quaker worship
1974	Wolf Mendl	Prophets and reconcilers: reflections on the Quaker peace testimony
1975	Ralph Hetherington	The sense of glory: a psychological study of peak-experiences
1976	W. Grigor McClelland	And a new earth: making tomorrow's society better than today's
1977	Damaris Parker-Rhodes	Truth: a path not a possession
1978	John Ormerod Greenwood	Signs of life: art and religious experience
1979	John Reader	Of schools and schoolmasters. some thoughts on the Quaker contribution to education
1980	Janet Scott	What canst thou say? Towards a Quaker theology
1981	Adam Curle	True justice: Quaker peace makers and peace making
1982	Gerald Priestland	Reasonable uncertainty: a Quaker approach to doctrine
1983	Michael Rutter	A measure of our values: goals and dilemmas in the upbringing of children
1984	Laurence Lerner	The Two Cinnas: Quakerism, revolution and poetry, a dialogue

1985	Christopher Holdsworth	Steps in a large room: a Quaker explores the monastic tradition
1986	Quaker Women's Group	Bringing the invisible into the Light: some Quaker feminists speak of their experience
1987	John Lampen	Mending hurts
1988	Harvey Gillman	A minority of one
1989	S. Jocelyn Burnell	Broken for life
1990	John Punshon	Testimony and tradition: some aspects of Quaker spirituality
1991	Geoffrey Hubbard	Patterns and examples. Quaker attitudes and European opportunities
1992	Brenda Clifft Heales & Chris Cook	Images and silence: future of Quaker ministry
1993	Sydney D. Bailey	Peace is a process
1994	Margaret Heathfield	Being together: our corporate life in the Religious Society of Friends
1995	Anne Thomas	Only fellow-voyagers. creation stories as guides for the journey
1996	Jonathan Dale	Beyond the spirit of the age
1997	Christine Trevett	Previous convictions and end of the millennium Quakerism
1998	Young Friends General Meeting	Who do we think we are? Young Friends' commitment and belonging
1999	Alex Wildwood	A faith to call our own: Quaker tradition in the light of contemporary movements of the Spirit
2000	Tim Newell	Forgiving justice: a Quaker vision for criminal justice
2001	Tony Stoller	Wrestling with the Angel
2002	Jackie Leach Scully	Playing in the Presence: genetics, ethics and spirituality
2003	Eleanor Nesbitt	Interfaith pilgrims: living truths and truthful living
2004	Simon Fisher	Spirited living: waging conflict, building peace
2005	Helen Steven	No extraordinary power: prayer, stillness and activism
2006	Roger and Susan Sawtell	Reflections from a long marriage
2007	Beth Allen	Ground and spring: foundations of Quaker discipleship
2008	Christine A. M. Davis	Minding the future
2009	Peter Eccles	The presence in the midst: reflections on discernment

Appendix 1

Spiritual Practices

A blessing (lovingkindness) practice

In the Christian tradition blessing practices involve asking that God's love enfold or protect someone, while in Eastern traditions 'lovingkindness' towards the self and others is practised to bring a deep realisation of oneness with all beings.

1. Begin by taking a moment to still yourself and become open to the presence of God/Spirit.

2. Bring a person to mind whom you wish to bless, or evoke lovingkindness for. This can be someone you love, someone you hardly know (for instance, someone you met in a shop this morning) or someone you find difficult. You can also practice blessing yourself – sometimes this can be the most important place to start.

3. Now spend some time in silence simply upholding that person, 'holding them in the Light' (to use the Quaker expression).

4. You may then like to use some very simple phrases to focus your upholding of that person; these can be repeated silently or under your breath throughout your period of prayer. Phrases could include one or two like the following:

   may you be well
   may you be free from suffering
   may you be happy
   may you be at peace

   bless you in your sleeping
   bless you in your waking
   bless you in your work
   bless you in your play
   bless you in your good moods
   bless you in your bad moods

   bless you when you....

   It can be very healing to use a blessing practice towards someone with whom we have argued or have a difficult relationship, or again towards ourselves, choosing relevant phrases such as 'bless you when you stay out all night'

5. Bring the blessing practice to a close by spending a short time in silence, allowing the Light of God's love to shine on you and anyone whom you have been upholding.

A contemplative prayer practice

Contemplative prayer involves any practice through which we seek to be aware of the presence of God/Love and to remain silently and attentively in that presence, completely open to God. Prayerfully repeating a single word or short phrase is one form of contemplative prayer, designed to help us swim out beyond the ego and realise our oneness with the Divine. As we pray, our will keeps consenting to God by returning to the sacred word. This simple but demanding discipline helps reduce the obstacles to an expanded awareness of a fuller level of reality.

1. Begin by finding a quiet place where you can sit in a well supported position.

2. Close your eyes lightly.

3. Sit relaxed but alert. Take time to become quiet and centred. You may find that gently focusing on your breath helps.

4. Silently, within your own heart, begin to say a single word or short phrase. You may consider one of the following or choose your own:

   Peace
   One
   Beloved
   Amma/Abba (Mother/Father)
   Love
   Jesus
   Maranatha (Come, Lord)

5. If a word does not come immediately, allow yourself to wait on a word and trust that it will come. This may take several prayer sessions, but this waiting in itself is a practice of surrender. You can use your breath as a focus until a word comes.

6. Listen to your prayer word or phrase as you say it gently but continuously. Allow the repetition to be an anchor for your intention to be open to God's presence.

7. Do not try to think or imagine anything – spiritual or otherwise. When thoughts or other distractions come, do not try to suppress them but just keep returning gently to your word or breath.

Listening prayer practice

Listening lies at the heart of the Quaker way. This listening prayer practice is simple but challenges us to listen deeply both to ourselves and to another. There is no discussion, only listening. Listening deeply and prayerfully to one another can draw both speaker and listener to a deeper understanding of the sacred thread running through their lives.

1. Find a partner to do the listening prayer practice with you and a quiet place where you will not be interrupted.

2. Each of you will have 5 minutes to speak while the other person listens without interrupting. Your speaking and listening time will be surrounded by time when both of you will be silent together.

3. Agree which of you will speak first and then agree a focus question, such as 'In what ways have you experienced God in your life during the last week? or 'What has been going on in your prayer life this month?'

4. Begin the practice with 5 minutes of shared silence to enable you both to become still and centred.

5. The first person then has 5 minutes to speak without interruption (and afterwards there should be no commentary on what is said). The first listener keeps time and signals the beginning and end of the 5 minutes.

6. There is then a 5 minute silence for centring before the second person speaks.

7. The second person speaks for 5 minutes.

8. Finish with another 5 minutes of shared, prayerful silence.

A review of the day

Reflecting on the events of each day can help us see the work of the Spirit in our lives – the sacred in the everyday. Like beachcombing, this practice can help us notice all kinds of things which we may have passed over in the busyness of the day. As you prayerfully explore the mystery of yourself in the midst of your daily actions, you can grow more familiar with your own spirit and become more aware of the promptings of Love and Truth within you.

1. Begin by taking a moment to still yourself and become open to the presence of God/Spirit.

2. Accept and be thankful for any gifts that the day has brought, however small – a smile or kindness, work done, a glimpse of beauty, even the resilience that has enabled you to get to the end of the day in one piece!

3. Let the Light of the Spirit shine on the events of your day, and on your own actions, attitudes and motives, helping you to be open to growth.

4. Now go over the events of the day briefly in your mind, from the moment you woke up until the present moment.

   With each event, observe not just what happened but also your thoughts, feelings and responses. Don't judge yourself or the event – just observe.

5. Are there any things in the experience of your day today, however small or seemingly insignificant, that you notice, that particularly catch your attention?

   Be still and allow yourself to be with whatever surfaces in connection with each experience.

6. Open yourself to any new ways of seeing or understanding that may arise.

   Are there ways you responded to or cooperated with the promptings of Love and Truth in your heart? Are there ways you resisted them?

   Are there ways in which you feel God is calling you to a change of heart? Or to a new response to pain or joy in your life?

7. Let yourself really see deeply, allowing the Light to shine on the experiences of your day, speaking to your heart, challenging, encouraging and teaching you.

8. Open your heart to the grace to respond to what has come up.

Sacred reading practice (lectio divina)

Sacred reading has been part of the Christian prayer tradition for centuries and is an important spiritual practice for many modern people. It is different from our normal, analytical reading of information and involves a slow meditative reading of a short text – reading not so much with the mind as with the heart.

1. Begin by choosing a short extract from a sacred text: this could be the Bible, poetry, other sacred writings or anything that speaks deeply to you.

   Even this choosing can be done in a way that allows the text to 'choose' you, rather than you making an intellectual selection; for example, you could choose at random from a collection of extracts or use a lectionary or book of daily readings.

2. Read the text slowly and meditatively two or three times. Allow the words to soak in.

3. Is there a word or phrase that jumps out at you?

   Allow yourself to become aware of any words that cause a particular response, whether because they speak deeply and positively to you or perhaps cause resistance in you.

4. Now read the passage again, lingering over this word or phrase. Pay attention to what resonates in you, to your own response to the words. Stay with the word or phrase and repeat or reread them as often as you wish.

   It can be helpful to spend 10 or 15 minutes simply meditating on the word or phrase by repeating it (aloud or silently) in this way.

5. Allow the words to speak to you at a deep level. What is the Spirit teaching you through this word or phrase and your response to it?

6. If you feel drawn to make any kind of response to this deep reflection, give expression to it: this could be in prayer, writing, drawing, or simply speaking to God about it.

7. Then spend some time in silent waiting on God – not necessarily expecting an answer to any questions, but simply resting in contemplation of the Divine presence in your heart.

8. As you move back into the ordinary activities of your day, do you feel called to live out any understanding you have reached as a result of this practice of sacred reading?

Extracts for use in sacred reading practice (lectio divina)

Jesus, tired out by his journey, was sitting by the well. It was about noon. A Samaritan woman came to draw water, and Jesus said to her, 'Give me a drink' ... The Samaritan woman said to him, 'How is it that you, a Jew, ask a drink of me, a woman of Samaria?' ... Jesus replied: 'If you knew the gift of God, and who it is that is saying to you, 'Give me a drink,' you would have asked him, and he would have given you living water.'

John 4:6–10

What we are looking for
Is what is looking.
     St. Francis of Assisi

There the angel of the Lord appeared to him in the shape of a flame of fire, coming from the middle of a bush. Moses looked; there was the bush blazing but it was not being burnt up. 'I must go and look at this strange sight,' Moses said, 'and see why the bush is not burnt.' Now the Lord saw him go forward to look, and God called to him from the middle of the bush, 'Moses, Moses!' he said. 'Here I am,' he answered. 'Come no nearer,' he said. 'Take off your shoes. The ground where you stand is holy ground.'

Exodus 3:2–6

Closer is He than breathing
And nearer than hands and feet.
     Alfred, Lord Tennyson

God is in the water of the lake; he is
also in the cracked bed of the lake
when the lake has dried up.

God is in the abundant harvest; he is
also in the famine that occurs when
the harvest fails.

God is in the lightning; he is also in
the darkness when the lightning has
faded.

Mansur al-Hallaj
(poem attributed to Mansur, translator unknown)

In the beginning was the Word,
And the Word was with God,
And the Word was God.
All things came into being through him,
And without him not one thing came into being.
What has come into being in him was life,
And the life
Was the light
Of all people.
The light shines in the darkness,
And the darkness
Did not overcome it.

John 1:1–5

There is a season for everything, a time for every occupation under
heaven:

A time for giving birth,
A time for dying;
A time for planting,
A time for uprooting what has been planted.
A time for killing,
A time for healing;
A time for knocking down,
A time for building.
A time for tears,
A time for laughter;
A time for mourning,
A time for dancing.

A time for throwing stones away,
A time for gathering them up;
A time for embracing,
A time to refrain from embracing.
A time for searching,
A time for losing;
A time for keeping,
A time for throwing away.
A time for tearing,
A time for sewing;
A time for keeping silent,
A time for speaking.
A time for loving,
A time for hating; a time for war,
A time for peace.

Ecclesiastes 3:1–8

You never enjoy the world aright, until the Sea itself flows in your veins, until you are clothed with the heavens, and crowned with the stars: and perceive yourself as the sole heir of the whole world, and more than that, because people are in it who are every one sole heirs as well as you. Until you can sing and rejoice and delight in God, as misers do in gold, and Kings in sceptres, you never enjoy the world....

Thomas Traherne

I am the taste of water.
I am the light of the Sun and the Moon.
I am the original fragrance of the Earth.
I am the heat in fire.
I am the life of all that lives.

Bhagavad Gita

O LORD,
you have searched me and you know me.
You know when I sit and when I rise;
You perceive my thoughts from afar.
You discern my going out and my lying down;
You are familiar with all my ways.
Before a word is on my tongue
You know it completely, O Lord.

You hem me in – behind and before;
You have laid your hand upon me.
Such knowledge is too wonderful for me,
Too lofty for me to attain.
Where can I go from your Spirit?
Where can I flee from your presence?

If I go up to the heavens, you are there;
If I make my bed in the depths, you are there.
If I rise on the wings of dawn,
If I settle on the far side of the sea,
Even there your hand will guide me,
Your right hand will hold me fast.

If I say, 'Surely the darkness will hide me
And the light become night around me,'
Even the darkness will not be dark to you;
The night will shine like the day
For darkness is as light to you.

For you created my inmost being;
You knit me together in my mother's womb.
I praise you because I am fearfully and wonderfully made;
Your works are wonderful,
I know that full well.

My frame was not hidden from you
When I was made in the secret place.
When I was woven together in the depths of the earth,
Your eyes saw my unformed body.

All the days ordained for me
Were written in your book
Before one of them came to be.

How precious to me are your thoughts, O God!
How vast is the sum of them!
Were I to count them,
They would outnumber the grains of sand.
When I awake,
I am still with you.

Psalm 139:1–18

A simple breathing practice

Practising mindful awareness of our breath can be a helpful way to become centred at the beginning of meeting for worship and can offer, in its simplicity, a profound experience of connecting with the sacred in the present moment.

1. Begin by taking a moment to check your posture. You can, of course, do breathing practice in any position, but it can be very helpful to sit in a well-supported upright position: whatever position you choose, the important thing is to find one that enables you to be both relaxed and alert.

2. You may find it helpful to close your eyes gently.

3. Take a moment to release any tightness from your muscles – you can do this by imagining tension simply flowing away on each outbreath for several breaths. Don't forget areas that are often quite tense, such as shoulders, back and face.

4. Now bring your focus to your breathing. Simply let your attention rest on your breath, allowing it to flow naturally. Follow your breath with your full attention as it flows in and out of your body.

5. As you watch, notice how each breath is different: sometimes shallow, sometimes deep; smooth or ragged; fast or slow; cool or warm; silent or with a sound.

6. You may like to focus your awareness in one place as you watch your breath: the rise and fall of your chest or abdomen, or the feeling of air passing at the back of your throat or through your nose.

7. Continue to watch your breath with mindful attention for the rest of the time you have set aside.

8. Each time distractions arise, just bring your attention back to your breath, gently and without judgement. There's no success or failure. Just breathing. Simply being present to what is.

Appendix 2

Guidance

Becoming Friends: guidance for meetings

Local or area meetings working with the Becoming Friends process will all have different needs, but we hope that meetings will consider adopting guidelines for its implementation, to ensure the best possible support for newcomers. We offer the following suggested guidelines as a resource and help for meetings (but this is not in any way meant to be an imposed structure – meetings can adapt these guidelines to their own needs).

While it is not essential to have Becoming Friends companions available in a meeting in order to offer the learning materials to newcomers, experience has shown that newcomers are likely to get more from the process if they do have a companion. There will be some online companion support available for those without a local Becoming Friends companion or who prefer to work this way.

When there are no Becoming Friends companions in a meeting, it is all the more important that the meeting engages actively with the Becoming Friends process, for example by being prepared to take part in individual or group conversations with the newcomer as part of learning activities exploring Quaker experience.

1. Recruitment

Becoming Friends companions for newcomers need to be people who are familiar with the Quaker way and reasonably established in the life of the meeting.

It is recommended that Becoming Friends companions are recruited through a combination of:

- interested individuals making an offer, expressing interest or being encouraged by elders and overseers (this will, at least initially, be in response to publicity and information from the Becoming Friends project)

- discernment by elders and overseers

- a training/preparation process.

Recruitment of Becoming Friends companions need not be done through the traditional nominations route, so as not to add to the burden on the local nominations committee or create a barrier to engagement with the Becoming Friends process.

The training/preparation will be an essential last stage of the discernment process, both for the person offering to serve as a Becoming Friends companion and for the meeting.

2. Training/preparation of Becoming Friends companions

Friends offering service as Becoming Friends companions to newcomers need to prepare for the role. Just as *Advices & queries* urges us to come to meeting for worship with 'hearts and minds prepared', so it is with this service.

Courses to prepare Becoming Friends companions will be offered through events at Woodbrooke and Swarthmoor Hall, regional events and courses delivered locally with the support of experienced Becoming Friends companions or a Becoming Friends companion course handbook.

It is recommended that new Becoming Friends companions are not prepared for this role by simply undertaking it alongside an experienced Becoming Friends companion. This does not allow for the necessary challenges of self examination, discernment and reflection that will be part of the preparation process before engaging with a potentially vulnerable newcomer.

Meetings will be asked to provide a letter of support for Friends coming on the Becoming Friends companion courses, to ensure that local discernment has been made, and that the meeting is supporting those taking on this responsibility.

It will be helpful if meetings record when someone has attended a Becoming Friends companion course. This will serve as a local record and can also be provided when a companion applies to access the companions' area of the Becoming Friends online resources.

3. The process in local or area meetings

Local coordination

The Becoming Friends process for supporting newcomers will be coordinated at local or area meeting level, as fits individual meetings' circumstances. In either case, it is essential that an experienced local Friend or Friends be appointed to oversee the Becoming Friends support in that meeting. This could be done by elders and/or overseers, or a local Becoming Friends coordinator may be appointed specifically for this purpose. The meeting needs not only to arrange Becoming Friends companions for newcomers, but also any follow up and support to ensure the system works in their area.

Timing of the offer to newcomers

The appropriate point at which newcomers are offered the support of the Becoming Friends learning materials and a Becoming Friends companion will be for elders, overseers or experienced Friends in the local meeting to discern. This offer can be made at a relatively early stage, since there is no expectation that the new attender should be thinking about membership before being offered this learning opportunity and support. Indeed, it is not intended to be linked specifically to a newcomer's decision about joining the Society. It may be that the right time to make the offer will be when a newcomer has attended a number of Quaker Quest or other outreach sessions, or when they are beginning to establish a pattern of regular attendance at meeting. Equally, it can just as well be offered when someone is thinking about membership, or has recently joined.

Choice of Becoming Friends companion

The local and area meeting will ideally have a small pool of trained/prepared Becoming Friends companions for newcomers. The newcomer will be offered a choice of companion from that pool (after checks have been made about their current availability). If a newcomer expresses a strong wish for a specific Friend who is not in the existing pool of Becoming Friends companions, that person may be offered training and preparation, if they are willing to undertake the role.

How many Becoming Friends companions per newcomer?

In most cases, one person will act as Becoming Friends companion to each newcomer, although some meetings may prefer to aim for offering two Becoming Friends companions each time.

If one Becoming Friends companion is usually offered to newcomers, there may be exceptional situations where it is appropriate for another person to be present as an additional support or safeguard. There may also be occasions when the gender of the Becoming Friends companion is an issue for the newcomer, and it is necessary to offer an additional person to address this need. In these cases, the additional person need not be a trained Becoming Friends companion. These issues will be dealt with through the careful discernment of elders and overseers, or the local coordinator.

The Becoming Friends learning materials will often provide opportunities for newcomers to find out more about aspects of Quakerism by engaging in conversations with other local Friends on given subjects, thereby encouraging an awareness of a range of Quaker views and experiences in addition to those of their Becoming Friends companion.

How many newcomers can one person support? :

To avoid overburdening Friends undertaking service as Becoming Friends companions, the number of newcomers that an individual companion can support on a 1:1 basis at any one time will be a matter for discernment by the elders and overseers or the local Becoming Friends coordinator.

It is also possible that one Becoming Friends companion could work with several newcomers at once, in particular by working as a small group.

Timescales and endings

In each case, the Becoming Friends companion and newcomer will be encouraged to decide on a timescale for their work together, according to their own needs and availability. This can be very flexible, and may range from a few weeks to several months, but it is helpful at the outset to establish a date for reviewing the process, so that it is not an open ended commitment on either part. In a situation where the companion relationship does not work out, or a Becoming Friends companion becomes unavailable, elders and overseers or the local Becoming Friends coordinator will make arrangements for an alternative Becoming Friends companion to be offered to the newcomer.

Confidentiality and openness

Conversations between the newcomer and Becoming Friends companion are confidential. It will therefore not be appropriate for either newcomer or companion to be asked to give a detailed report on their work together (although it may sometimes lead to an application for membership, when the usual local membership procedures will apply). Of course, both newcomer and companion may agree to share elements of their experience of the Becoming Friends course without divulging personal information. This may encourage others to get involved with Becoming Friends, either as newcomers or companions.

Becoming Friends companions should not invite anyone else to meetings with the newcomer they are supporting, unless this is decided together with the newcomer. There may, however, be occasions when the newcomer may wish to invite someone else along, and this choice can be discussed with their companion.

Evaluation and feedback

There is a simple evaluation form at page 285 for newcomers and companions to copy and complete at the end of their work together, which will be given to elders and overseers or the local Becoming Friends coordinator for review. If meetings wish to give feedback to Woodbrooke and Quaker Life about the use of Becoming Friends in their area, the Becoming Friends project team welcomes such feedback on becoming.friends@woodbrooke.org.uk

Support for Becoming Friends companions

The Becoming Friends companions' network will provide resources and support for companions, including through online discussion forums. It can also be very helpful for Becoming Friends companions to receive support by:

- meeting with other Becoming Friends companions in the local or area meeting
- meeting with supporting elders and overseers or the local Becoming Friends coordinator.

Journalling guidance

Journalling is a way of using words and/or images to explore aspects of our lives. A journal is usually for our own eyes only, so there is no need to worry about how we express ourselves, or whether we are doing it 'properly'.

1. A journal can cover any or all of the following (and plenty more – the possibilities are endless):

   - a record and reflections on the events of the day, perhaps looking for the presence of God in that day

   - reflections in response to a particular question

   - exploring memories or incidents that have been important to us

   - conversation with / a letter to God, or a person who is significant for us

   - a record of creativity and activity (eg. gardening, craft work, painting)

   - a prayer journal eg. people you want to pray for, practices you have explored

   - a record of things you have been grateful for on a particular day

   - writing about 'griefs' and 'joys' during the day, or any period of time

   - a record of books or articles you have read that have struck you particularly, including any quotations that you want to remember

   - photos and drawings of people, places, animals, projects

   - responses to specific activities on a course such as 'Becoming Friends'

   - reflections on ministry in meeting for worship or sermons, articles etc

   - stories, poems, prayers

2. You may want to bear in mind these suggestions when working with a journal (and 'write' includes anything you might do in your journal, such as draw etc):

   - write spontaneously, without judging what you are writing

   - write whenever you feel like it, rather than setting a rule

   - write honestly

   - write about what really matters to you

   - value the different approaches and apparent contradictions that you bring to your writing – they may reveal much to you

Guidance for worship sharing

Worship sharing is a meeting for learning based on prayerful silence, where everyone has an opportunity to share in the spirit of worship. The discipline is similar to meeting for worship but more relaxed. It is a way of empowering those who find words less easily, as well as limiting the space for those who are natural speakers. The silence allows deeper reflection and sharing than group discussion, and enables openness to the Spirit of God which is often shut off by verbal debate.

There can be a particular theme, or none. Individuals speak as they feel led, from a heart-felt place but not awaiting the divine urge as in formal worship. The rest of the group listens with full attention, with open and receptive hearts but no verbal comment, trying to draw out the full message and understand what lies behind the words.

Each contribution is treated as confidential and is wrapped in silence before and after, so that the Spirit is free to move and be heard. No-one is obliged to speak unless they wish to. No-one speaks a second time until all who want to have spoken once. These rules may sound rather strict, but in fact they create a safe framework which is liberating. Laughter and light-heartedness are not excluded!

1. Set up the room with chairs in a circle. Be aware of the needs of anyone with hearing or visual impairments.

2. Do a brief round of introductions before focusing on the subject for the worship sharing session.

3. Remind people of the subject or focus question for the worship sharing.

4. It may be helpful to remind the group of this guidance:

   - Speak spontaneously from personal experience and listen with sensitivity. Be aware that everyone will need time to be heard. Often the deepest things can be said in the fewest words. Each person has equal potential for insight. It is important people don't use their turn to comment on or judge other contributions.

   - Only one person speaks at a time, followed by silent pauses of varying lengths, as the words are absorbed and reflected upon. People can speak in any order.

   - The content is confidential.

   - People speak for a second time only after everyone who wishes has spoken once.

   - People are free not to speak. Respect each other's privacy.

5. After the introduction, have a period of silence where each person moves into worship and opens themselves to the contribution they may feel called to make.

6. The group may agree before starting to place time limitations on each person so that everyone has a chance to speak. In this case, it is also worth agreeing how the facilitator or timekeeper will signal if a person is approaching the time limit.

Evaluation form for Becoming Friends course

Date:
Meeting:
Your role: Newcomer / Companion (please circle or highlight one)
Learning units you chose:
Was there anything you found particularly strong/helpful/positive in your learning experience?
Was there anything you found particularly weak/unhelpful/lacking?
Any other comments or suggestions?
Name (optional):

Please complete and return this form to your local Becoming Friends co-ordinator. An electronic version can be downloaded from www.woodbrooke.org.uk/becomingfriends